THE PHANTOM VIETNAM WAR

An F-4 Pilot's Combat over Laos

David R. "Buff" Honodel

Number 12 in the North Texas Military Biography
and Memoir Series

UNIVERSITY OF NORTH TEXAS PRESS

DENTON, TEXAS

10 9 8 7 6 5 4 3 2

Permissions:
University of North Texas Press
1155 Union Circle #311336
Denton, TX 76203-5017

The paper used in this book meets the minimum requirements of the American National Standard for Permanence of Paper for Printed Library Materials, z39.48.1984. Binding materials have been chosen for durability.

Library of Congress Cataloging-in-Publication Data

Honodel, David R., 1943–2018, author.
    The Phantom Vietnam War : an F-4 pilot's combat over Laos / by David R. "Buff" Honodel.
    pages cm. — Number 12 in the North Texas military biography and memoir series
    Includes bibliographical references and index.
    ISBN 978-1-57441-732-6 (cloth : alk. paper)
    ISBN 978-1-57441-952-8 (paper : alk. paper)
    ISBN 978-1-57441-743-2 (ebook)
1. Honodel, David R., 1943–2018. 2. Vietnam War, 1961–1975—Aerial operations, American. 3. Vietnam War, 1961–1975—Personal narratives, American. 4. Fighter pilots—United States—Biography. 5. Phantom II (Jet fighter plane)—History.
DS559.914.H66 A3 2018
959.704/348092—dc23
[B]
                    2018018482

The Phantom Vietnam War: An F-4 Pilot's Combat Over Laos is Number 12 in the North Texas Military Biography and Memoir Series

The electronic edition of this book was made possible by the support of the Vick Family Foundation. Typeset by vPrompt eServices.

Dedication

This book is dedicated to all who flew in the air war in Laos, both in support of our friends in the north and along the infamous Ho Chi Minh Trail. The air battle raged day and night. Many planes were lost. It is to all those flyers and especially to those who did not come back that this book is dedicated. A special dedication goes to my friends:

First Lieutenant Richard L. "Rick" Honey, Houston, TX. Born October 30, 1943. KIA November 6, 1969.

Captain Fielding W. "Wes" Featherston III, Wickliffe, OH. Born December 2, 1942. MIA December 30, 1969.

First Lieutenant Douglas D. "Fergie" Ferguson, Tacoma, WA. Born April 26, 1945. MIA December 30, 1969.

Captain Andrew "Andy" Ivan, Jr, South River, NJ. Born September 23, 1944. MIA September 10, 1971.

Under the wide and starry sky
Dig the grave and let me lie.
Glad did I live and gladly die,
And I laid me down with a will.

This be the verse you grave for me;
"Here he lies where he longed to be,
Home is the sailor, home from sea,
And the hunter home from the hill."

Requiem
By
Robert Louis Stevenson

Contents

Preface

TO MOST AMERICANS, INCLUDING me until mid-1969, the air war in Laos was a little-known backwater of the conflict in Vietnam—if it was known at all. The ground war in South Vietnam received the most attention, as it well should have. The air war over North Vietnam, operations Rolling Thunder and later Linebacker, also received considerable press. But the war in Laos got little attention except by those involved. Much of the battle was in the air, although there were brave Americans, both military and civilian, who served on the ground there.

The Laotian air war consisted of two principal areas: Barrel Roll in the isolated, primitive, northern part of the country, and Steel Tiger in the south along the borders with the panhandle of North Vietnam, the Demilitarized Zone, and the northern third of South Vietnam. Barrel Roll operations involved our support of the Hmong forces who fought both Communist Pathet Lao guerrillas and North Vietnamese regulars. Steel Tiger operations concentrated on attempting to stop the immense truck traffic on the Ho Chi Minh Trail. That traffic was the lifeline for the Viet Cong and North Vietnamese forces fighting in the south. The North Vietnamese eventually deployed more than seventy-thousand troops and hundreds of anti-aircraft weapons along the trail for its protection.

American air operations in support of non-communist forces in Laos began in 1960 before the major commitment to South Vietnam and continued for several weeks after the Paris Accords of January 23, 1973, ended American participation in the war in South Vietnam. Hundreds of American aircraft were destroyed in this secret war. With precious few exceptions, airmen shot down in Laos encountered two possible outcomes: get picked up quickly by our rescue forces or disappear forever. Hundreds disappeared.

Introduction

Before

IN THE LATE SPRING of 1962 I walked to a class on the campus of The Pennsylvania State University. It would be hard to picture a more beautiful, serene campus than that in State College, Pennsylvania. Far from any city, or even a significant town, it was nestled in the mountains at the foot of Mount Nittany. A car approached, which was unusual because in those days students were not permitted to drive on campus hence traffic was sparse. This vehicle was even more unusual, since it was a black limousine with small flags fluttering on both front fenders. As it neared, I saw a big man leaning far out of the window, as far as his waist, waving at students who walked nearby. Most of the students either ignored him or simply stared back. The man was Lyndon Baines Johnson, then the Vice-President of the United States. I suppose that this was my first encounter with the war in Vietnam.

Being a history buff, I was aware of Vietnam—not our early involvement, but the French experience there in the 1950s. After World War II, the French tried to re-establish their empire in what was called French Indochina, a region that encompassed Vietnam, Cambodia, and Laos. I remember my Dad talking in the early 1950s about the French defeat at a place called Dien Bien Phu. I had seen a black and white movie about the battle, how the brave French paratroopers had held out in bunkers

1

against masses of Vietnamese communists, then called the Viet Minh. The movie ended badly for the French, but movies back then didn't always have happy endings.

I wasn't well informed on all the politics of the area, other than that there had been some sort of "peace accord" in Geneva that covered Laos. But I had only a vague idea of where Laos was located. My knowledge of that region was meager, but it was likely better than that of most Americans. Sadly, as a sophomore I really wasn't even aware of the American military advisors' involvement in the Vietnam War.

Vietnam was a long way from central Pennsylvania, both in terms of distance and interest. At Penn State, as in most of the rest of the country, our attention was in the opposite direction. John Kennedy was the president, we had just gone through a fiasco called the "Bay of Pigs" invasion in Cuba, and relations with the Soviet Union were tense, at best. Ahead lay the Cuban Missile Crisis, the closest our nation had ever been to the nuclear holocaust we genuinely and rightfully feared. In just two years, Americans would watch movies such as *Fail Safe*, *Dr. Strangelove*, and *Seven Days in May*, that dramatized our fears. The so-called peace movement was in its infancy so "flower children" and "beatniks," while uncommon, were increasingly visible. I did not know any personally, but there were a few on campus. I had no idea what marijuana was, beer being the substance of choice for everyone I knew. I was a 19-year old small-town boy from the farm country of southern Pennsylvania.

We were the "duck and cover" generation. To us, CD meant civil defense, not compact disk. The threat of nuclear war was not some abstract topic discussed only in academia—it was a daily threat, one my generation had grown up with. Since we were children of the 1950s, we knew about Stalin, the Berlin Airlift, and the Iron Curtain. Most of us, though, knew little about Asia other than the war in Korea, and no one talked much about it.

We had the military draft back then, and all young men had to deal with it. While in college, we had the 2-S (student) deferment that protected us from call-up, but graduation would put most of us into 1-A status. Penn State required all male students to take two years of ROTC (Reserve Officers Training Corps), so like all my contemporaries, I walked out to Hammond Hall near Beaver Stadium once weekly for the required one-credit courses in Army ROTC. The courses were mostly classroom lectures taught by Army officers or senior sergeants. My favorite was military history. The other courses were generally boring, with topics such as organization of the Army, land navigation, and leadership. We had to wear green "Class A" Army uniforms, and drilled with the World War II M-1 rifle. Like most of my friends, I had problems with shining my uniform's brass, polishing my black G.I. shoes, and keeping my hair short enough to stay within the Army's limits. The long-hair look of the late 1960s was not here yet, but the "duck-tail" cut of the late 1950s had not disappeared. Fortunately, the "Princeton" haircut that was popular (short on the sides, longer on the top) satisfied the ROTC instructors.

After the required two years of basic ROTC, students could apply for advanced status. That meant doing an additional two years of courses and a summer camp, and culminated with a commission as a second lieutenant upon graduation. Advanced ROTC students received a monthly stipend which attracted a few of my friends. However, the peace movement spirit was catching on, so the military was not in favor on campus, even then. Many of the non-ROTC students made fun of those in the program. Being conscious of my social status, which was that of a country hick trying not to be a country hick, I opted not to do the advanced program. When my basic courses were finished, I put the military completely out of my mind. I'd deal with the draft "later." Who knew, maybe it would end. Being young, the day of reckoning seemed eons away.

As I have since learned, time slips by quickly. After graduation in 1964, I worked as an accounting trainee, temporarily protected by my still-effective student deferment. Kennedy was dead, LBJ had scared the bejesus out of the country and been elected in a landslide. Cuba was now a backwater; growing casualties from expanded combat forced our country's attention to the Far East. Vietnam was in political and military turmoil.

In early 1965, the draft board caught up on their paperwork, my status changed to 1-A, and I was called for a physical, along with a couple hundred other young guys. After the physical, about 30 of us were called by name and herded into a room. A military guy—Army, I think—scared the wits out of me. He said, "You college boys have gotten off free for years, but not anymore. You're 1-A now and you've passed your physicals. The law says we have to give you 21 days, and that's what you have. Expect your draft notices in three weeks."

Damn! I was shaken, to say the least. On the way home, I saw Dad's pickup truck at his favorite tavern, so I stopped. I needed a beer or two, and maybe even some advice. I got both.

Dad, a real news hound, brought me up to speed on events in Vietnam. The Army was engaged in active ground combat with battalions, not just advisors; the Air Force and Navy were bombing the North and losing planes in the process. Casualties were major news. Dad said that if I had to go in the military, it was better to go as an officer than as an enlisted man. His brother, who had been both in World War II and Korea, said life was better—and safer—as an officer.

The next day, after my hangover passed, I drove to the Army recruiter's office in Hagerstown, Maryland. The Army recruiter was great! As soon as I successfully completed the academic tests, he got my draft notice delayed while he processed my paperwork. He said I would soon be in Officer Candidate School. I just had to wait a week or two. I felt like I had won a stay of execution.

A few days later I stopped at the Army recruiter's office to check on the possibility of me getting a guaranteed assignment to Europe in exchange for my patriotic volunteering. Unfortunately, the office was closed for lunch and I didn't feel like waiting. During my walk back to my car, I passed the Air Force recruiting office near where I had parked. On the sidewalk stood a large street sign with a picture of a pilot, wearing a partial-pressure suit and holding his helmet, standing in front of the needle nose of the F-104 Starfighter. Underneath it said, "You, too, can be an Air Force Pilot."

What the hell! Being the 21-year-old smart-ass that I was, I went into the office. I told the sergeant on duty: "I want to be an Air Force pilot." He smiled, put his arm around my shoulder and said, "Son, sit down here and take these tests." He gave me the Officer Qualification test, followed by several aptitude tests. Almost as fast as I had them finished, he had them graded. I passed. He took a bunch of information about me, then told me to be at his office early the next morning to go to Washington, D.C., a mere 60 miles away, for a flight physical. I did, and I passed it. The recruiter told me to be at his Hagerstown office in two days to get sworn in.

I did, and I was. The next thing I knew, I was in San Antonio, at Lackland Air Force Base, as a new officer trainee, being screamed at by a short upperclassman because my bed wasn't made properly. My Mom said my draft notice arrived that day.

A half-century has passed, and many memories have faded. Yet there are some memories that, while not quite as sharp, persist. Top among them is combat. Not only are the memories still with me, so are the emotions.

This memoir represents my experience with the Vietnam war, or "the war" as I refer to it, from my first tour. I have heard that of the two and one-half million U.S. servicemen and women who served in it, there are two and one-half million different stories. That is probably true; each of us saw it differently from every other person who was there. We may have participated in the same battles, or the same formations, or even flown in the same aircraft, but we all saw things through our own eyes as I quickly learned when I got there. For all the emphasis on formations, squadrons, wings, or divisions, war—at least the war that I fought—was an amazingly lonely experience.

Chapter 1

The Summer of '69

MY WORLD CHANGED IN the summer of 1969.

No, it didn't change the way Bryan Adams's did in his 1980s hit song "The Summer of 69." That song was about a world where someone might have learned to play a guitar, fall in love, or any other normal thing. And it didn't change because of the riots and the protests so common in cities throughout our nation. And, no, it didn't change because of the political fallout from the assassinations of Martin Luther King and Bobby Kennedy the prior year.

The change in my life was not historic or distant; it was up close and personal.

After four long years of training and volunteering, I went to the Vietnam War.

***

One late-spring day of that year, an unduly cocky but quite naïve version of me piloted an F-4D Phantom II fighter high over northern Arizona. Being strapped onto the ejection seat in the front cockpit of that supersonic fighter meant my dream had become reality. True, the Air Force considered me as a trainee in the F-4, what was then the hottest fighter in the world. But I had other thoughts. I believed, no I KNEW, that I was a shit-hot fighter jock. Self-confidence was not something that I needed more of. I could do anything in that airplane. To paraphrase an old fighter song, "With my hand around its throttles, I'm in a separate class. I'm a fighter-bomber pilot, let the others kiss my ass." I believed that.

With my left thumb, I pushed down the radio transmit switch on the inboard side of the right throttle. "Albuquerque Center, Bags Two-Four, request."

I used my best professional fighter-pilot voice. It had taken a lot of practice in pilot training for a rural Pennsylvania boy to get the right combination of deep tone mixed with a slight back-in-the-hills of West Virginia twang. Some sage noted that all fighter pilots of that era sounded like Chuck Yeager, the super-sonic flight pioneer, air ace, and my former wing commander.

Cruising five miles above the earth meant visibility was spectacular, an almost limitless panorama especially over northern Arizona. Even in the eastern United States I would have been far above the ever-present haze. But in 1969 there was no haze in the west—except Los Angeles, of course. Just miles and miles of nothing but miles and miles. Distant mountains and deserts. No cities.

We had just passed Flagstaff and Mount Humphreys, the 12,000-foot peak north of the city. From my cockpit, the two-mile-high mountain appeared more like a bump in the vast earth, brown on top and dark-green below its tree line. The city appeared tiny, like a miniature setting from some model train display. To the north was the Grand Canyon, Monument Valley, and the expanse of Utah. The thin, cool air in the F-4's cockpit was a pleasant change from the heat in Tucson where I was based. It wasn't even summer yet and already the temperature had touched 100 degrees in southern Arizona.

Sitting in my fighter's cockpit with the world below me was heaven.

"Bags Two-Four, Albuquerque Center, go ahead," came a male voice in my headset.

"Albuquerque, Bags Two-Four would like to cancel IFR." IFR meant Instrument Flight Rules where the aircraft was subject to air traffic control authority. In the U.S., all aircraft above 18,000 feet must fly IFR. That rule irritated me when I flew Phantoms but was comforting when I rode on an airliner.

"Bags Two-Four, Albuquerque, descend to flight level one-eight-zero. Report reaching."

"Bags Two-Four is out of three-one-zero for one-eight-zero." Not using standard instrument flying procedures, I pulled the F-4's throttles back to the idle position and pushed the stick forward to descend. The Phantom rapidly dropped through the thin air. The vast, sparsely populated northern Arizona landscape, some desert-like, some forested, grew more distinct.

"Albuquerque, Bags Two-Four is leveling at flight level one-eight-zero," I radioed as I pulled back on the control stick to temporarily stop the descent.

"Bags Two Four, altimeter is three-zero-zero-three. IFR cancelled; maintain VFR. Squawk one-two-zero-zero. Cleared from Center frequency. Good day." Air Traffic Controllers were always professional and courteous.

"Roger, Albuquerque. Leaving your freq. So long." I switched the transponder code on my right console to twelve-hundred, the standard squawk for aircraft using visual flight rules. The Phantom continued its rapid descent. Even in the dry western air, I turned on the large defrosters that ringed the base of the front canopy. They made a noticeable roar of rushing air in the cramped cockpit.

"Herb, go squadron common frequency," I said into the intercom. "Have you ever seen the Grand Canyon?"

Herb was my navigator for the F-4 training program at David-Monthan Air Force Base outside Tucson, Arizona. We had been formally "crewed" for the six-month school, meaning we flew all our training missions together. We believed we would stay together as a crew since our end-assignments were to Udorn, Thailand, and the fighting in Vietnam. I had only known Herb since starting the school, but we had become good friends in the months since then. We were both bachelors, so we spent lots of time together when off duty. Herb lived in a rented house outside Tucson with several other bachelors, including my good friend Andy. They threw great parties each weekend. I became part of the group.

"Sure. I've been up there several times," he said.

"I don't mean while standing on the rim. Any tourist can do that."

We were well east of the Winslow TACAN, a navigation signal not far from the Canyon's most popular area on its south rim. I rolled the aircraft into a steep left bank so that we could look through the F-4's thick Plexiglas canopy. Below, like a huge crack in the flat earth, was the eastern part of the magnificent Canyon, a massive fissure that had been carved by the Colorado River over thousands of years. I found it hard to believe that the Canyon had once been flat like the land on its flanks.

"I mean have you ever flown through the Canyon, below the rim?"

There was a pause after I asked him that.

We were supposed to be flying an instrument training sortie, a single unsupervised airplane with no instructor. We were told to fly an instrument navigation route then make some approaches back at Davis-Monthan. But hell, I had lots of hours in the F-4 since I had been flying the bird for nearly three years. Admittedly, most of that time I had been in the back seat as a GIB, meaning "Guy in Back," a demeaning job for a pilot but a great one for a navigator. Between my back-seat time and my pilot training in the ancient T-33, I believed that I could fly instruments in my sleep. The last thing I needed to do was fly practice instrument approaches in Arizona on a clear day when I could see for a hundred miles or more.

"That's not legal, is it?" he said.

I guessed that Herb, still a second lieutenant, believed that rules were meant to be followed. Being a captain—with an attitude—I had other views.

"Who cares? I did it once so why don't we do it today?"

Herb didn't know it, but we were going to do it whether he wanted to or not. As the pilot, I was the aircraft commander. I had years of being pissed-off while I sat in the back seat when some guy in the front decided what to do with the airplane. Now it was my turn. I was a "fighter jock" and I damned well knew it.

I steepened our roll until the Phantom was in a 150-degree bank— almost inverted—and pulled the stick back to about three G's so that we did a "slice turn," descending and changing direction from our easterly heading to better align with the Canyon west of us. I turned the transponder to "Standby" so that most Air Traffic Control radars could not track us and put out the speed-brakes, the large flaps on the bottom of the wings designed to slow the airplane. They made a deep rumbling noise as they hit the fast-moving air flowing past the wings. The speed brakes did not slow us since we were in a steep descent, but they prevented the plane from accelerating. The F-4 rapidly dropped toward the earth just south of the Canyon. We rolled upright and leveled off just a few hundred feet over flat land. I pulled in the speed brakes when the plane had slowed to 350 knots (about 400 miles per hour), not especially fast for the super-sonic fighter but comfortable for sight-seeing. We zipped past sage-brush, dirt roads, barbed-wire fences, a few stray cows, and what appeared to be some small trees. In a few seconds, the land below us suddenly dropped as we crossed the south rim. I turned the Phantom the last 30 degrees to align with the Canyon and pushed the stick forward. We dropped below the rim. I turned off the noisy defroster.

I leveled the bird about half-way between the rim and the Canyon floor. I saw the winding Colorado River and followed it west through what was truly an awe-inspiring valley. The Canyon varied in width, sometimes narrow, sometimes vast, with occasional tall buttes like isolated towers rising in the wide portions. The horizontal lines of the various colored rock strata of the Canyon's walls provided a handy reference for maintaining level flight. Although we couldn't hear them, the roar of our engines must have echoed between those magnificent walls. Any tourists should have been properly impressed. Like most fighter pilots, I loved showing off for the lowly, land-bound people below. As the famous World War II Air Force General Carl Spaatz once said about fighter pilots, "We were a different breed of cat; we flew through the air while the others walked on the ground."

Few, if any writers could adequately describe the Canyon although I'm sure many have tried. But the beauty from my ejection seat, flying at 400 miles-per-hour below the rim was not the Canyon: It was that I could and was flying a jet fighter through one of the world's greatest wonders. And I loved what I was doing. I was in control of America's hottest fighter, cruising through perhaps nature's most resplendent wonder. It was as if I owned the place.

I was probably the envy of startled tourists, both the many who stood on the rim, and the braver few who hiked, rafted, or rode mules on the Canyon floor. My plane may have even starred in some vacation photographs.

Talk about a rush!

The Canyon's beauty was just one more of the vast spectra of vistas experienced by me or any fighter pilot on each trip into the sky.

The world, from my seat in the cramped cockpit, constantly impressed me with its splendor and the panorama, especially in the western U.S. But I had flown many other places in the F-4, albeit mostly as a lowly GIB: Over the Atlantic and the Azores to Spain and Germany; above the vast Pacific via Hawaii, Guam, and Okinawa to Korea; across the sea to Japan and around snow-capped Mount Fuji; low over the swamps of the Carolinas; high over the Rockies; down wide rivers and up narrow valleys; across cities, towns, and villages; you name it. The world of a fighter pilot has no limit, or it seemed that way to me in 1969.

We stayed in the Canyon across most of northern Arizona, generally following the Colorado River until it widened as it formed Lake Mead. Ahead was the Hoover Dam in southern Nevada, close to Las Vegas. At the eastern edge of the lake, we turned south and climbed to a more appropriate—and legal—altitude. For the entire trip through the Canyon, Herb and I said little. Despite my other adventures in the F-4, some things were too majestic to discuss. It was better just to do them.

The flight back to Tucson was quiet, almost boring. Our training at the RTU—Air Force jargon for Replacement Training Unit—focused on preparing us to fly the mighty F-4D in combat. I entered the school with a bad attitude typical of pilot-GIBs who were stuck in the rear seat for several years. I attended another RTU in California two years earlier as a GIB, flown the Phantom over half of the globe, and had even upgraded to the front seat at my squadron in North Carolina. But the Air Force had its rules, and no amount of any one pilot's experience would override them: All F-4 front-seat pilots must attend a six-month RTU prior to going to "the war." So, my training in Tucson was redundant as far as I was concerned. But, hell, Tucson was a great place for it.

***

Near the end of the training, a request came down from one of the many headquarters asking for a crew to volunteer to ferry an F-4 to Thailand. During the war, planes of all description regularly crossed the Pacific to replace combat losses. This was especially true for the F-4 fleet that, after the massive F-105 losses earlier in the war, now carried the brunt of the fighting for the Air Force.

The mission was simple: Go to Ogden, Utah, to pick up a plane and fly it to a base near Sacramento, California, where we would join with several other planes. Together we would fly to Hawaii, spend one night, fly on to Guam the next day, spend a night, then on into Thailand where we would drop our planes. We could then get on a military-contracted airliner for the trip back to San Francisco, then fly commercial to Tucson. The whole process should take a week or so; ten days at the most.

At the time, I was a single, twenty-five-year-old Air Force captain. After four years in the military, I could still put everything I owned—everything—in the trunk of my red Mustang convertible. While it was true that I was "chomping at the bit" to get into the war, I figured that it would not end soon—so, what the hell?—why not take the trip?

All my previous ocean crossings had been in the back seat, watching someone else fly and begging for what little "stick time" the guy in the front would give me. Here was an opportunity for me to be in charge of the plane, to handle the controls, to be "The Man." Better still, an Aircraft Delivery Group handled all the arrangements en route, everything from flight plans, coordinating air refueling, parking and maintenance, lodging, meals, and return transportation. All I had to do was fly the plane. It simply "don't get any better than that," to borrow an old saying.

Herb and I talked it over. We had no commitments to anyone back home. Our Vietnam tours would wait a week or so since the long war was not likely to end soon, if ever. The trip would mean more flying. An adventure. Fun.

We volunteered.

***

We moved out of our rental houses and dropped my car and our few belongings with some friends. Herb had a dog, a Dalmatian named "GIB" that he boarded with a friend. We packed just enough clothes for the trip in our soft-sided flight bags. There was little space for personal gear in the F-4. We were told our plane would have a "travel pod"—an empty napalm canister modified with a side door—that we could use to carry our gear. Still, there was only room for a couple flight-suits and two or three changes of civilian clothes each. But that should do it for a week-long trip.

It was late June.

We picked up the plane in Utah and flew to California. We joined with three other F-4s and launched for Hawaii. The F-4 had a range of about 1,200 miles with full internal fuel and three external tanks (called "drop tanks" because we could jettison them when necessary). The trip from the coast of California to Honolulu covers 2,000 miles over water, with no islands for any emergency landings. That distance discrepancy meant that we had to fly with KC-135 aerial tankers and refuel on the way. By this point in my flying career, I had refueled the plane many times, so there should not have been a problem.

Except there was. An axiom in fighter aviation that says that the farther from land the plane is, the more noises the pilot will hear, the more the gauges will fluctuate, and that more weird things will happen. Sure enough, about half-way across, just beyond the "point of no return," strange things started.

I noticed that occasionally the stick would kick, meaning that it would make a sudden up or down movement that changed the pitch of the plane. The kicks were random. I tried using the F-4's primitive auto-pilot but the kicks disengaged it. The longer we flew over water, the more distant the land was, the more bothersome the kicks. These kicks, these unpredictable "transient inputs" to the pitch of the plane, became more frequent.

When we flew loose formation on the tanker, the kicks were merely nuisances. When we were hooked to the tanker, flying formation just below its tail with the refueling boom connected to our plane, the kicks were terrifying.

After nearly seven nerve-wracking hours, we landed safely at Honolulu International Airport and taxied to the adjoining Hickam Air Force Base. That was the good news. The bad news was that the maintenance facility at the base was not staffed for any significant work on the then-modern F-4. Sure, they could refuel the planes, repack the drag-chutes, handle minor work such as changing a tire or adding oil. But working on the flight controls? Never.

The next morning, the rest of the planes left for Guam—and took the tankers with them. Herb and I stayed behind with a broken airplane and no way to move it—even if it were fixed—until another tanker arrived. Being two bachelors, we did not shed any tears. If a plane was going to break down, Honolulu was the best place on earth.

We had a great time. There was nothing we needed to do, even though the Aircraft Delivery Group required us to check in each morning.

We did, usually hung over.

A few days after we arrived, we got a call that the plane was fixed. We were told to take it for a test flight. Life just kept getting better for us. Stuck in Hawaii and now we had to take a fast fighter for a joy ride among the Hawaiian Islands. Talk about a hoot! We took off from Honolulu, did the grand tour of the islands, buzzed a few beaches—on the outer islands, of course—did flybys for a couple local cruise ships, then landed—with the same problem we had when we arrived a week earlier.

The maintenance folks went back to work; Herb and I went back to Waikiki.

Some days later, they found the problem. Since the F-4 was a high-performance fighter, it was built with "negative aerodynamic stability," which essentially meant that, left to its own devices—or even in the hands of an inattentive pilot—it could tear itself apart. That negative stability was intentional, designed into the plane to give it the best possible performance for the high sub-sonic and supersonic world of fleet defense, the Phantom's original role for the Navy.

To make the whole system work, it had flight controls that moved with 3,000-psi hydraulic pressure. There was no "feel" to the controls as in most light planes and some earlier jets. To provide the proper stick feeling for the pilot, the designers built an "artificial feel" system. This system sensed the flight conditions of the plane and fed the results to the control stick. Unfortunately—or fortunately, depending on one's perspective—some worker in Utah had left some foreign items in that artificial feel system: a pair of pliers and a large chunk of steel wool, to be exact. These items rattled around, which interfered with the airflow in the feel system and resulted in occasional kicks to the stick—and to my heart when we were hooked to a tanker, hundreds of miles from land.

The plane was promptly fixed, and we were told to test-fly it again. We did. We flew around the islands again then flew up to the northwest shore of Oahu and did some high-G maneuvers. All was well; the plane was fixed.

Herb and I had just finished our maneuvers over the Pacific when we saw a white cone form on the deep-blue ocean below us. It was a nuclear submarine surfacing. The bow of the sub breached the surface with white foam all around it, then the entire boat appeared. This was both beautiful to behold and too much of a temptation for any cocky fighter pilot.

We attacked!

Not with bombs or cannons, of course. The Navy was on our side despite inter-service rivalries. We decided to give the sailors a proper welcoming to the Hawaiian Islands. After all, they might have been submerged for months. Why not show them that the Air Force cared about them?

We used the rest of our available fuel making high-speed, low passes on the submarine. Many of the crewmen came on deck to watch. We flew by fast, pulled up for a "wing-over" and dove back at them. I don't think we got low enough to make a "rooster tail" on the water with our exhaust, but we gave them a great arrival show.

Now, after ten days on Oahu, we had an operational airplane—but no tanker to move it with.

Back to Waikiki Beach!

Herb disappeared for a few days, so I checked in alone each morning. One day, a tanker landed and was scheduled to go to Guam the next day. We were to go with it. Good plan, but the F-4 required a two-man crew, not one. Herb was nowhere to be found.

The next day, the tanker left without us. The Aircraft Delivery guys were livid. The progress of aircraft being ferried overseas, especially those going to Vietnam, was monitored at the highest level of the Pentagon. The Delivery guys were under severe pressure to get our plane on its way.

The Group's commander hollered at me. He even threatened me with disciplinary action if I didn't find my navigator. He really was wasting his breath. What could I do? Worse, from his point of view, was what could he do? We already had orders to go to Vietnam. What else could anyone do to us?

I entertained myself in Honolulu, searching for Herb—sort of. I sat at the outdoor bar at Fort Derussy, an Army recreation station next to Waikiki Beach. Drinks were much cheaper there than at the civilian bars. I sat under a banyan tree and watched the Apollo Eleven astronauts walk on the moon.

Herb was nowhere to be seen. For all I knew, he was on the moon with the astronauts.

After six days of being missing, and two passing tankers later, Herb surfaced. By this time, the Delivery guys were mad enough that, if they had been able, they would have put us under armed guard.

We took off for Guam the next day. We had been in Hawaii for seventeen days. Life was tough for this young, single fighter pilot.

Yes, the plane finally got to its destination, Ubon Royal Thai Air Base in southeastern Thailand near the borders of Laos and Cambodia. Herb and I spent the night there, caught a courier flight to Bangkok and boarded a military contracted airliner to Japan.

In Japan, we boarded another contract carrier, a stretched DC-8 filled with about 230 GI's, mostly Grunts (the riflemen who fought in the jungles and rice paddies) returning from the Vietnam war. Since our clothing was limited by our duty, our orders gave us permission to travel in civilian clothes. We were the only two people on the plane who were not in uniform. This fact was only important because of our destination: San Francisco, in July 1969.

The flight from Japan was nearly fourteen hours. Considering the all-male passengers returning from the war, it was quiet.

Until the wheels touched San Francisco's runway.

The men on that plane—the returning GI's—erupted with ear-splitting shouts and cheers. They were home. Safe.

Alive.

Herb and I didn't participate in the commotion, but we were touched by it. Though we couldn't really understand how they felt, we felt good for them.

Until we got off the plane.

San Francisco may be a pretty city, but it was a crappy place for any GI in uniform at this stage of the Vietnam War. There were long-haired protesters inside the terminal next to our arrival gate when the soldiers—our soldiers—exited the plane. The protesters booed or shouted obscenities at these young men. Even though Herb and I were wearing civilian clothes, we were in the middle of these arriving troops. We ducked through the obnoxious chanters and hid in a USO until time for our flight to Tucson.

I did not understand how that disgusting display could happen in our country, and I still don't to this day. It was a disappointing end to an otherwise fabulous trip.

Chapter 2

My Turn

THE SUMMER OF 1969 was two-thirds over. Dad, my brother-in-law, and I sat at a round table next to a large window with a panoramic view of Washington, D.C.'s Dulles International Airport ramp. An occasional Boeing or Douglas airliner taxied by.

"Robby, we have time for a beer," I remember Dad saying as he placed his ever-present gray fedora on the table. He still called me Robby although my Air Force buddies called me "Buff," short for "Buffalo," a nickname I picked up during a half-year deployment to Korea. His thin, gray hair curled more than normal, damp from sweat.

I tossed my blue flight-cap, silver captain's bars up, next to his hat. We had lots of time. In our family, we always got to where we were going early. Dad did not like to be late, and neither did I. I carefully sat my olive-drab helmet-bag on the floor next to me.

His voice seemed strained, as if he were tense. He did not like goodbyes at airports though we had done a lot of them during my four years in the Air Force.

Four years! I should have been to the war and back by then, maybe even twice. When I graduated from pilot training, my orders were to the F-4 as a pilot GIB. The GIB's job was to operate the radar and inertial navigation system—called INS in our slang—to assist the pilot, and to do limited flying. In my eyes, it was a second-rate job for a pilot. But at least my first orders as a rated officer would send me to the war.

Those orders entailed nine months of training. It started with radar school, continued with six-months at RTU, and finally to survival school. After all that, I would be off to Thailand and the war. From the moment I got those orders, I was excited.

Why be in the military if not to fight for my country?

About three weeks before the end of that first RTU, the Air Force cancelled the orders for the entire class. No explanation, no substitution, just cancelled. The training continued as scheduled, even the weekly intelligence briefings on the war, yet we had no idea what was to become of us. Sixty guys, trained and mentally prepared for war, waited. What would happen in three weeks? Would we just sit on our butts in California?

Finally, I got orders to Seymour Johnson Air Force Base near Goldsboro, North Carolina.

North Carolina! I was fired up and ready for combat, but I was being sent to North Carolina.

Dad asked if my flight would land in San Francisco. He already knew the answer as we had discussed my itinerary before leaving home. I had a few hours there before my flight to the Philippines, which, strangely enough, went through Anchorage. He knew all the travel details, but it made for unthreatening airport conversation. For him, any topic seemed better than discussing the war.

My time in North Carolina only made my attitude worse. Many of the front-seat pilots in my new squadron had been to the war. They walked and talked differently than the non-combat guys. They wore lots of ribbons on their uniforms and spoke of things foreign to me. The veterans gathered in groups at social events. If I tried to join them I always felt the outsider. I soon stopped.

A year after getting to North Carolina, I volunteered for and received another set of orders for Vietnam, this time as a Forward Air Controller, called a "FAC." A few weeks before I was to leave, again with no explanation, those orders were cancelled. So, I sat in the Carolinas, unhappier with each passing day. The air war in the North ended, Lyndon Johnson left office, and I rotted in the States. Well trained—hell, over-trained—anxious to go, but fuming on the sidelines. I knew how athletes felt when they sat on the bench and watched others play the game.

A lot transpired between leaving my first RTU and this lounge at Dulles. I was a fully qualified F-4 front-seat pilot with not one, but two six-month training courses under my belt in preparation for the war. I had flown the F-4 across both the Atlantic and the Pacific Oceans multiple times, flown air defense missions with live missiles in Korea, stood alert with 500-kiloton nuclear bombs, flown 1,600 miles per hour, soared near the edge of space more than 12 miles up, skimmed the floor of Death Valley 300 feet below sea level, dropped live bombs on numerous gunnery ranges, fired live rockets, shot a 20-millimeter Gatling gun at 6,000 rounds per minute, and as I had done with Herb, flown the length of the Grand Canyon below the rim. In short, I had done everything a pilot can do legally in the F-4, and some not-so-legal things, too. In my eyes, I was a shit-hot fighter pilot, a real hot-shot. I had done everything.

Except I had never been to the war.

Dad asked if I had packed all my gear. He evidently did not consider that it was too late to do anything about it if I had not. While I did not understand at the time, I now know he wasn't trying to make the time pass; he was clinging to every minute we had left together. I wish I had known that then.

I wondered about Dad. All the conversation since we left on the journey to the airport had been idle chatter. Not one word about the

war. I was anxious to get into the war, but I sure as hell did not say that
to him. As far as our discussions went, I let him believe that it was the
Air Force's decision. I never told him that I had volunteered, not once,
but three times. The third one appeared to be the charm.

Dad, born into a poor farm family, never served in the military, but
his generation lived through the Great Depression, Pearl Harbor, Korea,
the Cuban Missile Crisis, and now the seemingly endless struggle in
Southeast Asia.[1] He was well-informed about Vietnam. In the Kennedy
years—while I was still drinking beer instead of studying in college—he
favored our military intervention, but lately seemed unsure. He watched
the TV news stories, especially the brutal, graphic coverage during
the Tet Offensive in 1968, a massive battle that our Army and Marines
won in Vietnam, but our press lost in America. Walter Cronkite had
been to Vietnam and declared the war misguided and "unwinnable."
More than 40,000 Americans were dead, and hundreds of thousands
wounded. Hundreds of American airmen, including many F-4 pilots,
were prisoners in unspeakable conditions in North Vietnam, some
into their fifth year. Nixon promised to end the war, to turn it over to
the Vietnamese, and bring the American troops home. But hundreds
of thousands remained.

Now Dad sat in an airport lounge with his only son, his youngest
child, still a snot-nosed kid in his eyes, about to leave for that very war.
He must have suffered terribly, but he did not show it, not in his face
since he rarely showed emotion, and not at all in our conversation.
Not being a father myself, I was ignorant of his agony.

Still, I knew he wasn't happy about me going. As far as he would
know, I was going because it was my duty—which it was—not because
I had volunteered—which I had. I kept a lid on my excitement and
acted properly somber. As an experienced fighter pilot—looking back,
a better description would be a cocky son-of-a-bitch—I was ready for

the war. Any apprehension I had was only because I hated goodbyes at airports. Always have, always will.

We finished our beers and walked through the sparsely populated terminal to my gate. My khaki uniform or maybe the olive drab helmet bag attracted some attention from other travelers. Several frowned. After the social and political turmoil, much involving the war, that had erupted in 1968, I was not surprised. But I did not care, either.

We said our proper goodbyes at the gate, man-like, by shaking hands. Dad did not hug.

Finally, damn it, I was on my way.

***

The stop at Clark Air Base in the steamy Philippines was for Jungle Survival School, mandatory for all aviators on their way to Vietnam. Jungle School really wasn't about surviving in the jungle. At least not in the way one would think. Even though we referred to it as "snake school," we didn't eat snakes or drink from vines or coconuts. The school was about two things: Escape and Evasion—mostly evasion. It focused on how to get the hell out of the jungle if we got shot down. The seven days of training covered Search and Rescue (SAR) procedures, how to evade capture, dumb things to avoid (smoking for example, since the smell lingers in the jungle, or wearing deodorant or aftershave), and things to do, such as hide, don't run. And no gunfights. The .38-caliber revolver we carried was no match for the enemy's modern, rapid-firing AK-47 assault rifle.

Much of the training was devoted to rescue, not survival. We practiced signaling with radios, beacons, flares, mirrors, smoke, and ground panels. We reviewed and updated our personal identification data, which included questions with answers only we knew, and included the first PIN I ever had. This, of course, was long before the personal computer. All the then-unusual identification procedures were to keep the bad guys from luring our helicopters to a supposed rescue, then shooting them down.

We spent several days in the jungle for familiarization and to practice hiding. To check our concealment, the instructors sent some natives to find us. The Negrito tribesmen who worked for the Air Force could find Americans anytime they wanted. When they found us, we had to give them a chit that they later exchanged for rice.

On our evasion exercise, Herb, who seemed comfortable in the jungle, convinced me to hide in some elephant grass, a sea of thick, heavy stalks that grew to more than six feet high. Hide, hell! I got lost in it. We spent the night there, under ponchos, while rats ran across us most of the night. When a smiling Negrito found us at dawn, I happily gave him all my chits; anything was better than having rats run over me.

Herb thought the experience fun; I thought it sucked.

The jungle school had a large exhibit of every snake I could think of. There was a 24-foot king cobra and a 28-foot boa constrictor, which had been captured in a "klong" (canal) in Bangkok. The exhibit had the infamous "two-step" Krait, a viper common in Vietnam, whose venom is said to allow you two steps before you drop dead.

I did learn that though their venom was deadly, cobras were not as dangerous to people as I had believed. While a viper coiled, then struck quickly (such as a rattlesnake or copperhead), a cobra was slow. It had to raise about a third of its body into the vertical, then fell forward to strike. I watched a Negrito cleaning cages one day. He dumped an eight-foot black cobra on the concrete then turned away from it while he cleaned the cage. The snake rose as if to strike, but the Negrito calmly kicked the snake away.

That was not my last encounter with cobras.   -

When Jungle School ended, Herb and I were now teamed for the rest of this adventure, or so we thought. We flew to Bangkok, spent a night at the American officers' hotel there, then caught a ride on one of the local shuttles, a C-130, the venerable four-engine turboprop transport still around today. These shuttles—that all used the call-sign "Klong"—flew circular routes each day stopping at all the American bases in Thailand. We were fortunate to have only two stops, since riding in the back of a C-130, seated sideways on paratroop seats (sagging web straps and a seat belt) in the heat and humidity of Southeast Asia, poor air conditioning, the noise of the four turbo-prop engines, lots of sweaty men, cargo, and a hangover was not pleasant.

We landed at our destination, Udorn Royal Thai Air Force Base outside Udon Thani, in northern Thailand, about 50 miles from the Laotian border. It was hot in the back of the 130, and the cabin reeked of body odor, grease, jet fuel, and a bit of vomit. As we taxied toward the terminal, the 130 Loadmaster lowered the plane's rear cargo ramp. We were immediately hit with a blast of Thai summer air—even more heat and humidity.

As was tradition at Udorn, arriving flyers were met by their new squadron mates, given beer (when cold, a valued commodity), and taken by jeep in a mini-parade, sirens and horns blaring, around the base to the squadron headquarters. Survivors of the war left the same way.

I was surprised when two groups of pilots met us, one for Herb and a different group for me. I did not know it until that moment, but Herb had been assigned to the 13th Tactical Fighter Squadron, the Panther Pack, while I would fly with the 555th TFS, the Triple Nickel. We were not going to be a crew after our many months of intense preparation.

Herb and I would never fly together again.

One of the guys who met me was a friend from Tucson: Dave, a short, cheerful man later nicknamed "The Gnome." He was married and on his second tour in the war. He arranged to have me assigned as his roommate in our squadron "hooch," a long, narrow, teak-wood barracks with five rooms on either side of a latrine and small lounge in the center. The hooch stood on heavy stilts several feet above the ground, which seemed strange when I saw them, but was an effective design when the next rainy season started. A covered porch ran the length of the building on one side with doors that opened into each room.

My room, about the size of one in an economy motel, had a single window, which was usually darkened by a heavy curtain, next to the door. The small living area consisted of two lounge chairs (vinyl padded chairs with wide, wooden arms), a desk with a basic wooden chair, small coffee table, and four tall metal lockers like those found in most gymnasiums or high schools. The lockers were placed two on each side of the room with a space in between to walk through. A single mirror hung on one shellacked plywood wall. A heavy black curtain joined the lockers to separate the living and sleeping areas. The rear sleeping section had two parallel bunk beds, about four feet apart with a window air-conditioner centered on the back wall, which perpetually ran on the coldest setting. While there were four beds, only two pilots lived in many rooms. The upper bunks were available for any crews from other bases who might have to spend the night at Udorn (the primary emergency recovery base in northern Thailand). The sleeping area became pitch-black when the heavy curtain was closed. A small reading light hung at the head of each bunk.

We had several Thai house-girls who took care of our hooch and provided laundry service. We all chipped in a few dollars each month in exchange for clean rooms, clean sheets, daily laundry, and spit-shined boots. The job must have carried considerable prestige and pay, as there was no shortage of applicants. I doubt that any expensive American hotels had such a dedicated and efficient staff as these Thais.

I think they even liked us.

The day ended for me in the same way it did for every other new pilot or navigator (each was called "FNG" meaning Fucking New Guy)—with a "Welcome to the War" party at the Officers' Club, just across the street from my hooch. The squadron had a party when a new flyer arrived and another party when he finished his tour. About half of the squadron attended my arrival party since flying operations ran 24-hours daily. While I still had the gray cotton flight-suit that I wore on the trip up from Bangkok, most of the guys wore the Nickel party suit, a short-sleeved one-piece jumpsuit, dark green, with white embroidered name, wings, and rank. Everyone had the squadron insignia on one sleeve and the American flag on the other. On the right chest, opposite the name and wings, was a patch I was not familiar with: A pirate flag with "Yankee Air Pirate" embroidered on it. That patch originated earlier in the war when Hanoi Hannah, the communist version of Tokyo Rose from World War II, referred to our flyers as "air pirates." That term stuck, hence the insignia. Our aviators were proud of it.

Many of the men wore other insignia, depending on how far along each flyer was in his tour. The veterans had one that read "Nickel Night Owl," which signified they had flown night combat missions. A few wore large peace symbols in roundels on their backs. Instead of "peace," they declared "Participant—Southeast Asian War Games." I felt awkward in my stateside attire.

I received a formal introduction to the squadron. The emcee—I have no idea who he was—gave the introduction. I stood up, as if everyone in the room could not tell who the FNG was.

A voice from the group, in a ritual familiar to Air Force fighter pilots everywhere, shouted, "Let's say hello to Buff!"

In unison and with gusto, the squadron replied, "HELLO ASSHOLE!"

Another loud voice called, "Let's say hello to the asshole!"

Again, in unison, "HELLO, BUFF!"

Everyone cheered, and guys came by and shook my hand. The ritual really made me feel part of the squadron. It was a vocal recognition that I was now one of them. I felt proud to have joined the Nickel.

My last memory of that party—and that day—was when I stood on a chair with an iced-tea glass full of a concoction called "The Green Death." Triple Nickel aviators had to drink it on the day they arrived for luck, and on the day they left, in thanks. The Green Death was one-half Crème de Menthe and one-half vodka. The FNG (or survivor if at the end of his tour) was required to chug the entire drink, turn the glass upside-down on top of his head to prove it was empty, and then smash it against a wooden mock-up of a fireplace. If the glass did not break, the pilot had to repeat the process. If you weren't drunk when you got on the chair, you were when you got off.

That was the end of my first day in the war.

***

KA BOOM!

It was the loudest noise I had ever heard. The plywood walls vibrated, and the metal lockers rattled; the concussion nearly rolled me off my bunk. I hit the cold, vinyl floor with my bare feet and immediately swayed. I was so dizzy from the prior night's drinking that I almost fell over. The room was pitch-black except for a thin slit of glare from ceiling to floor where the two black curtains joined. My head pounded with the hangover from hell (and the Green Death), and worse, I had no idea where I was.

I stumbled through the curtains into the living area and was nearly blinded by the change in light. At least I knew I was in Thailand, not some drunken hell. My head felt like an axe was wedged in it; my hair stuck to my scalp. The front of my white T-shirt had a large green stain. I opened the door and staggered outside wearing only my underwear. There were other young men on the porch in attire from towels to shorts to flight-suits, pilots like me, squadron mates, but still strangers.

Like them, I leaned on the railing and looked across the street where the Officers' Club was. Above that teak building with its red metal roof billowed a dark cloud of dirt and ash.

My God, I thought, *they've blown up the O Club!*

Fortunately, it was an illusion. The explosion had occurred beyond the Club, next to the runway, but the Club blocked my view of that area. It turned out not to be an enemy attack either. An F-4 from another base had been hit by anti-aircraft fire in Laos so it flew to Udorn, the closest field, for an emergency landing. The damaged plane was escorted by another F-4, which, unknown to its pilot, had a "one-lugger," a 500-pound bomb that had not released, but hung on the bomb rack by the rear of the two suspension hooks. When the shot-up plane landed, the escort plane with the hung bomb accelerated to set up for its own landing. The acceleration from the F-4's mighty engines literally twisted the bomb off the airplane. The bomb hit the grass next to the runway and did what bombs were supposed to do.

Welcome to the war.

After I recovered from the day's rude start, I began the week-long process of FNG orientation. All new pilots were FNGs, no matter how old they were, how many hours of flying time they had, what they had done in other assignments, or how smart they were—or thought they were. Before they became a full-fledged member of any fighter squadron in Southeast Asia, they had to go through an orientation process that was often confusing, frequently boring, and seemingly endless. I was ready and anxious to get into the fray, but there were the damned FNG tasks to handle first.

It started with routine in-processing that all military people must do when assigned to a new base: pay and personnel processing, base orientation, medical clearance, security clearance, emergency notification procedures, and in Thailand, the infamous VD briefing, complete with a vivid slide show and dire warnings from the medics. If the show was designed to convince us not to have sex, it must not have been very effective. The advertised VD rate at Udorn was near 100 percent, a statistical quirk since some guys were multiple victims, some many times over.

The supply folks issued me jungle fatigues (I don't know why since we wore flight-suits), a steel helmet, canteen, and a web belt, all of which spent the entire tour in my locker. The items I did use, my green canvas jungle-boots, were welcome replacements for the all-leather boots used in the States. Jungle boots were lighter, vented, and had mesh insoles that helped keep feet cool and dry, at least when not sloshing through rice paddies.

After the base processing, Dave, my roommate, insisted that we go to town and get started on my party suit and try the local cuisine. The town, Udon Thani, was close to the base. It was the provincial capital and probably the most modern city in northern Thailand. Most tourists would have thought it primitive compared to Bangkok, but the Americans stationed there did not. I soon learned that a trip to town could take me away from the war, at least for an hour or two. The Thais always made me feel welcome.

We rode in a Thai taxi, always an adventure as I discovered, to a tailor who we nicknamed "Arma-Thief," a variation of his real name that I never could properly pronounce. He was a real Indian: beard, turban, and all. He made all the party suits, insignia, uniforms, and civvies for the Nickel. He knew everybody in the squadron by name. Some of the guys thought he was a spy.

He probably was.

His crowded shop featured sample clothing and bolts of cloth of every description. "Arma-Thief"—some of the guys called him that to his face—was friendly and talkative while he took my measurements. Despite my short time in Thailand, it was strange to hear his Indian-accented English instead of Thai. He measured me while his assistant, also Indian and probably a relative, entered the information into a green journal that must have had the names and measurements of every guy who ever flew with the Nickel. He measured everything from hat to shoe sizes. I had never been to a custom tailor before, or since, so this was a treat. Besides my party suit, I ordered some civilian clothes since I had brought few with me. Shirts and slacks were all exactly fitted to me, but as I discovered later, out of style.

Dave had already established his favorite restaurant, as far as I remember the only one he ate at during his tour. It was a place called "The Five Sisters," but the guys in the squadron referred to it as "The Ten Titties." The owners—I think they really were sisters—treated Dave as if he were some bigshot from Bangkok. His goal was to try everything on the menu. He went to town about once a week for dinner, but almost always to this restaurant. I tried a fish, rice, and pineapple dish that really surprised me in its quality. I would never have imagined that a fish and rice mixture would blend so well with pineapple.

One item, however, at the very bottom of the menu, did not sound appealing: Deep-Fried Small Birds.

The next day, I began the 432nd Tactical Reconnaissance Wing's new-guy school. It seemed strange to be in a reconnaissance unit since I always was, and always would be, a fighter pilot. In the earlier days of the war, the 432nd was a straight reconnaissance unit, but after LBJ's bombing halt, it had two F-4D fighter squadrons added to its

two RF-4C reconnaissance squadrons, but kept the Reconnaissance
Wing designation.

Udorn, officially a Royal Thai Air Force Base, flew the Thai flag along
with ours. While the base had a Thai commander, most of the military
people were American. The base was divided by the runway. On one
side was the housing and administrative area where I lived and ate.
It had the Officers' Club, Base Exchange, the various support offices,
hospital, radio and TV station, and the barracks for the thousands
stationed there. A shuttle bus, a school bus painted blue and aptly called
the "Blue Bird," carried people around the runway to the combat side
of the base, the flight-line.

The flight-line side teemed with activity, both day and night. Besides
the two reconnaissance and two fighter squadrons of the 432nd Wing,
there were an assortment of other organizations. These included the
40th Air Rescue and Recovery Squadron, the "Jolly Green Giants," heroes
who flew the big HH-53 helicopters and had saved hundreds of downed
pilots to date, and would save hundreds more by the time the war
ended. There was an AC-119K^2 gunship squadron, a modification of
the Fairchild "Flying Boxcar," an aging twin-boomed piston-driven
cargo plane. The 7th Airborne Command and Control Squadron had
the four-engine turboprop C-130s that carried large communications
pods filled with people to run the war. Two of these aircraft were always
in the air, one over the northern part of Laos, and one over the North
Vietnamese supply lines that led into South Vietnam.

The base also had a large, secretive compound that housed the
Central Intelligence Agency and its Air America operation. This
fenced compound was guarded to keep even U.S. military personnel
out. Through the flight-line gate to the compound flowed a real mish-
mash of aircraft including the AT-28, an attack modification of an
old single-engine piston trainer that sometimes bore Thai Air Force

markings, sometimes Royal Laotian Air Force markings, and sometimes no markings at all. The CIA also flew C-123 twin-engine propeller-driven transport planes, the Porter Storch, a strange looking high-wing single-engine "STOL" (short take-off and landing) airplane with a long snout, the Vietnam War's famous UH-1 "Huey" helicopters, and others. There was always activity in the CIA compound, but we Air Force folks knew little of what was going on in there.

Perpetual motion ruled on the Udorn flight-line: Planes roared off the runway every few minutes, planes loaded for combat, planes flown by warriors. Other planes taxied to or from the runway. Trucks, vans, and tugs scurried around the parked planes.

All this bustle and here I was, back in another damned school. If the Air Force trained me long enough, the war would be over. Dad would be happy; I would not.

I no sooner sat down for the school when I met an impressive lieutenant colonel, an African-American who I will call "Colonel Earl." We discovered we were both Penn State grads, so we had a common bond despite our differences in rank. He was assigned to the wing staff as the Director of Current Operations. He impressed me with his attitude and sense of humor about what were deadly topics. Colonel Earl was a combat veteran from both the war in Korea and an earlier tour in Vietnam, so his perspective was much different from mine. I sat next to him throughout the program. I probably learned as much from him as I did from the briefings. He paid close attention to the briefings and took notes.

Since he did, I did.

While I was anxious to fly, to really—and finally—get into the war, the intelligence briefings at New Guy School did seem relevant. While they covered the usual geography, culture, politics, and the war situation in general, to my surprise the main topic was Laos, not Vietnam. At that time, few outside the military knew much, if anything, about the war in Laos, still classified Top Secret. Most of what I had learned in RTU was about the now terminated air war over North Vietnam and the never-ending ground war in South Vietnam. I had prepared to fight in Vietnam, not some ancillary backwater skirmish in a primitive, jungle covered wilderness.

Laos had at least two distinct wars.[3] The Royal Laotian government, officially neutral, controlled little outside the capital of Vientiane and perhaps some of the territory along the Mekong River, the border with Thailand. General Vang Pao and the Hmong Army, made up of tribal people who lived in northern Laos, were our allies. They fought on a confused front—if you could call it a front—in the northern part of the country, with lots of help from the CIA, the U.S. Air Force, and probably others. Like the tides, the general's forces flowed back and forth each season over the grassy, open area known as the Plaine des Jarres[4] (Plain of Jars). The wide, flat Plain, which we called the PDJ, was mostly surrounded by rugged hills and karsts—sheer-sided mountains—some devoid of any significant foliage, others covered with jungle. The general was opposed by the Pathet Lao, communist forces allied with North Vietnam, who were increasingly being augmented by a substantial number of North Vietnamese "volunteers." We had a code name for this fight: Barrel Roll,[5] or simply "the Barrel."

Southern Laos was another, much different war. Laos bordered the North Vietnamese panhandle, the DMZ—the supposedly demilitarized border between the two Vietnams—and much of South Viet Nam. On its southern border, Laos met neutral Cambodia, though the North Vietnamese deployed a significant fighting force there too. The North Vietnamese firmly controlled the entire eastern half of Laos. Those forces maintained, improved, and protected their supply line that wove through the jungle from its origination at the several passes out of North Vietnam to its termination at various places in South Vietnam. The southern part of Laos had its own, quite appropriate code name: Steel Tiger.

While Americans back home fixated on South Vietnam, the air units in Thailand fought mainly in Laos, especially Steel Tiger. The FNG briefings covered the infamous Ho Chi Minh Trail,[6] where several roads out of North Vietnam radiated into the Laotian jungle and eventually ended in South Vietnam.[7] The Trail was not really a trail at all; it was an extensive network of often well-maintained dirt roads, mostly concealed under thick jungle canopy. It could probably be compared to the human body's circulatory system, where the blood vessels started at one side of the heart (North Vietnam) in main arteries, divided into smaller arteries and capillaries (in Laos), then came back together in the veins to end at another chamber of the heart (South Vietnam).

Our task was to stop the flow of blood (the trucks). Logic would say to do it at the heart, where it was concentrated. Unfortunately, the American strategy in Vietnam, directed closely from Washington, was illogical at best. Some military experts described it as "strategic defensive, tactical offensive." Most civilians would be at a loss to explain it.

Those fighting it had another description: "It's a fucked-up war." I soon learned why.

My Vietnam War would not be in Vietnam at all, or hardly at all. My war was going to be in Laos. I had to seriously revise my thinking. Three years of planning and dreaming of fighting in Vietnam had turned into flying over Laos, which in comparison sounded neither as serious nor as important. Worse, since the whole Laotian war was classified, I could not speak about it to anyone back home. To cap it off, there would be no combat pay for flying in Laos since we really weren't there.

Once each month, our pilots flew a mission in South Vietnam to qualify for combat pay.

What the hell was going on here? A war that did not qualify as a war? A war that didn't exist?

An important phase of New Guy School covered the enemy's forces in Laos, especially the defenses along the Trail, much of which were manned by North Vietnamese veterans. The briefings included considerable information on their anti-aircraft weapons.[8] The mainstay of the enemy defenses was the 37-millimeter anti-aircraft gun, which fired five- or seven-round clips of high-explosive ammunition. The rounds were not proximity-fused so they either exploded on impact, or air-burst at the end of a specific time if they did not hit an airplane. The 37's effective range was about a mile and one-half or so. Two other weapons were found in the higher threat areas. One was the Soviet ZU-23, a new, rapid-firing 23-millimeter weapon with ranges similar to the 37. Unfortunately, they did not fire seven-round clips: they fired like a machinegun. The other weapon was the 57-millimeter, another Russian model. This gun had an effective range of three miles or so, with airbursts well beyond that.

We also reviewed the SA-2, the famous SAM, the radar guided surface-to-air missile that had already brought down many of our aircraft. It was as big as a telephone pole, flew at nearly three times the speed of sound, and contained a large proximity-fused warhead of several hundred pounds that did not have to hit a plane to destroy it. That was the bad news; the good news was that there were no known SAM sites in Laos, but they were just across the border in North Vietnam.

FNG's received more training on survival equipment. While I was well-versed in the basics, including the ejection seat and parachute, I had to learn about new gear such as the device attached to the back of the parachute harness that could be used to lower oneself from the tall jungle trees. When I thought of trees, I imagined pines that went to 50 feet or so. In Laos, we were told the jungle canopy could reach 300 feet. Obviously, if a parachute hung up in the top of such a tree, getting down would be a problem. The Air Force solution was a lowering-device consisting of nylon webbing and some buckles that we could loop through the parachute risers, then connect to the parachute harness. After snapping it into place, the pilot unbuckled the parachute risers and, using a friction brake, lowered himself to the earth. It sounded good, but the system had only 250 feet of nylon webbing. I guess the pilot was to avoid getting hung up in trees taller than 250 feet.

I had another round of training on our various signaling devices. The best chance of survival in Laos was quick rescue. The faster the rescue, the more likely it would happen.

Finally, even though I was near the saturation point, I listened to briefings on the local airport traffic pattern, ground operations, jettison and bail-out areas, various controlling agencies, and many more procedures. All of this ended when I was given a booklet called "Nickel Standards." It contained the procedures that my new squadron used for the parts of the mission that were routine. The terms "routine" and "combat" did not seem to fit together in my mind at the time. They would later. The standards ranged from ground operations, arming and de-arming, join-up after takeoff, formations, air refueling, and much more. Each pilot was required to pass an examination on these procedures prior to the first mission.

My head was swimming plus I had still not accepted the idea of fighting in Laos. For three years, I had plotted, planned, and dreamed of fighting in Vietnam, specifically in North Vietnam. True, we weren't bombing there, but my mind had not adjusted to that minor fact. But my dream had been Vietnam, not Laos. Until New Guy School, I thought of Laos as someplace we flew over on our way to the war. I now had to get used to the idea that, for me, it would be the war.

I was confused and, I thought, terribly over-trained. When all this seemingly endless indoctrination finally ended, the squadron scheduler told me I would be flying combat—the next day.

Three weeks after I left Dulles International Airport, finally this warrior was about to teach the enemy a lesson.

Chapter 3

Combat

IT WAS EARLY SEPTEMBER, but still officially summer. Finally, after four long years of training and anticipation, I was about to get into the war. It really had seemed that I would spend my tour getting oriented. Well before the scheduled flight briefing time, I walked into the squadron building to the operations counter just inside the front door. The L-shaped counter was the first stop for the crews for all missions. Behind it hung a large, transparent plastic board where the schedulers posted the daily missions in grease pencil. The schedule shown on the board was our squadron's assignment from the daily "frag," a small part of the day's air-battle plan (frag was short for fragment, or a portion of the comprehensive air-battle plan that included all units in Southeast Asia). The board had the essential information, including the flight call-sign, mission number, aircraft tail-numbers, ordnance load, and the names of the front- and back-seaters.

There it was: Honodel! Number four in a four-ship formation. I did not recognize the name for my back-seater since I really only knew one guy in the squadron: my roommate, Dave. I was still learning the rest of them. The squadron's FNG checkout program consisted of ten missions with "old head" GIBs, although many of the old heads were younger than I was. These veterans were near the end of their tours, hence supposedly knew all there was to know. They were not instructor pilots as they would be if we were in the States, but just regular GIBs (some pilots, some navigators) with lots of experience under their belts. Once I completed the ten missions of the check-out, I would be cleared to fly with anyone in the squadron, not just old heads.

I wasn't sure exactly what I was supposed to learn. After all, in my mind I was already a shit-hot fighter pilot who certainly did not need more training. A lot of the material covered in the FNG School consisted of things I already knew. Sure, the part about the situation in Laos was new to me, but I had studied all the guns before, knew how to use the survival equipment, other than that tree-lowering device (strange name since it was for lowering the pilot, not the tree). As to flying the F-4D, I knew all that there was to know.

In my eyes, I was the world's greatest fighter pilot—God's gift to aviation.

I made my first mistake before I even started. I filled out my line-up card with all the information from the scheduling board, the way I always did in the States. I wrote down every name, tail number, all the various times, ordnance, and you-name-it, just like I had done hundreds of times. A regular encyclopedia of information was on my card.

Another guy in my flight stood next to me. He looked at my card, frowned, and said, "What the hell are you doing? If you get shot down and the gomers get that card, they'll know a hell of a lot about the rest of us. Just write down what you absolutely have to, nothing more." Gomer was a derogatory term for our enemy.

He seemed friendly, but his comment was more an order than a suggestion.

Shot down! What was going on here? Damn, I felt like a dumb-shit. The duty officer smirked from his seat behind the counter. Was I that clueless? I should have known better. I tore up the card and started over. This time, I wrote my call-sign, tail number, take-off time, mission number, and little else. (Later in my tour I would write even less, sometimes only the mission number.)

The rest of the flight preparation and briefing went more smoothly. As with all missions, preparation consisted of an Intelligence briefing followed by the flight briefing, and, in theory at least, ending with individual crew briefings. The crew briefing part was often just a few words while suiting-up for the flight.

The Intelligence briefing at wing headquarters dealt mostly with the ground situation in northern Laos (Barrel Roll, where my flight was going). The Intel officer discussed the situation, such as it was, in the PDJ. It seems that our friend, General Vang Pao, struggled with the seasonal battle to control this section of Laos. Since the full-blown dry season would soon dominate the country, the Pathet Lao were getting frisky, preparing to take back the part of the PDJ that the Hmong had secured during the past rainy season. It was a regular cycle that had begun years before and would continue until the war ended.

The Intel Officer, a skinny lieutenant dressed in a short-sleeved khaki uniform, stood in front of a huge, wall-sized map, which could have been the moon for all I knew. He pointed to several known 37-millimeter anti-aircraft gun locations. I tried to note their locations on my map as best I could. The rest of the flight members, including my GIB, seemed disinterested. It did not take me long to realize that the 37 was a mobile gun. Though it had to be towed, it was easily moved. Sometimes the guns would be in pits, sometimes hidden in trees, sometimes in the open. But then I had a lot to learn about that gun as well as the others in Laos.

As with most FNGs, I had no idea of what was important and what was not, so I considered everything important, which meant that nothing was.

Back at the squadron, the flight gathered around a rectangular table in a small briefing room for about ten minutes, about one-quarter the length of the briefings I was used to in the States. The flight leader did not discuss anything to do with most of the flight, things such as ground operations, takeoff, join-up, en route formations, recovery, and others. All that was "Nickel Standard." True, it would become second nature to me very soon, but for this flight I struggled just to remember where the planes were parked and other trivia. Yes, I had passed a closed-book written exam on the Standards, but they were still hazy.

For a moment—just briefly—in that small room, the world's greatest fighter pilot had self-doubts.

For this, my first combat briefing, the leader discussed what we would do in the target area in more detail than for my later missions. We were assigned to contact a Raven FAC in the PDJ area of Barrel Roll. Ravens were American Air Force pilots in Laos who our government claimed weren't there: pilots who weren't there in a war that wasn't a war.[1]

We had no idea of what the target was, since the FAC would find one for us. The leader said we would use a "wheel" in the target area if the defenses permitted. The wheel meant we would circle over the target, each aircraft spaced behind the one in front, ideally by about 90 degrees. We would then attack as directed by the FAC, usually one F-4 at a time. The wheel was a common tactic in low threat areas, but not so good when things got hot. After all, the gunners could see all the aircraft overhead, watch each aircraft start its dive toward the target, and hence had plenty of time to aim and fire. It did not take many missions for me to avoid the wheel.

The leader briefed our tactics if the FAC directed us to support "troops in contact," which meant that our guys were in rifle range of the bad guys. If the Hmong troops were in proximity to enemy forces, there were some special rules we would apply, to include lower altitude for bomb release and some specific identification techniques to make certain we bombed the bad guys, not the good guys. If we flew in direct support of friendlies, we would really be dependent on the FAC, so our leader would ask for colored smoke-markers so that we could identify both the bad guys and the good guys. We did not want to accidentally bomb our friends.

To finish the briefing, the leader spent a few minutes discussing what we would do if someone got shot down.

Shot down! Damn, that got my attention.

He said whoever got hit should get out of the target area, if possible, and head south toward Thailand. (At this point I imagined a flaming F-4 with me in it. Not a pleasant thought.) The wingman of the stricken aircraft would stay close to him. The other element (a four-ship formation has two elements of two aircraft each) would climb and call for whatever help the situation dictated. In the event of a bail-out, the stricken airplane's wingman was to be the low CAP, the covering plane responsible for keeping the parachutes in sight and contacting the survivors. The second element would orbit high, coordinate with the rescue forces and any aerial tankers that may be on station. The flight members were quite attentive to this part of the briefing.

I damned-well was, too.

My first challenging task on this first mission was suiting up in the PE (personal equipment) room. In the States, I flew with a G-suit, parachute harness, and helmet. Occasionally, when flying over water, I wore LPUs (underarm life preservers that inflated when they hit the water). On rare occasions, I wore an exposure suit (we called it a "poopy suit"), for long, over-water flights when the water was cold. On most flights, I had been comfortable.

But, Toto, we weren't in Kansas anymore.

This was combat. For this mission, I needed help. My G-suit had not changed except now I had to stuff two frozen water flasks in the leg pockets (just above the ankles) where I kept my check-lists and maps. Dehydration was a real problem since Thailand's hot and humid climate caused lots of sweat; breathing oxygen through a mask during flight produced more dehydration; and fear in the event of a bail-out—so I had heard—caused the worst case of dry-throat ever. We had a white, kitchen-style refrigerator in the PE room with stacks of water bottles in the freezer that were hard as rocks. In Southeast Asia, they thawed fast enough.

Like some old-west gunfighter, I strapped on my web-belt with my Smith and Wesson .38-caliber revolver in its black leather holster. I even tied the "fast draw" nylon cord around my thigh to prevent the pistol from flailing if I ejected. I loaded my pistol with five rounds, but left the chamber under the hammer empty. Rumor had it that the high G forces of ejection (about 12) could force the hammer against a round hard enough to fire it ... into the pilot's thigh.

Why the Air Force saw fit to issue us .38's was a mystery to me. While it might have been a great police weapon, the enemy here usually carried AK-47's, then a new and fearsome assault weapon. I guess it was because our pistol was a last—a very last—resort.

Next, I put on my survival vest. That was a struggle since it was bulky and heavy. It held two survival radios, emergency locator beacon, two spare radio batteries, first-aid kit, strobe light, signal mirror, two day/night flares, sea-marker dye, 24 rounds of .38-caliber ball ammo, six rounds of .38 tracers, and more. We even carried a cloth map of Southeast Asia and a Blood Chit. The Blood Chit guaranteed payment, $10,000 in gold so I heard, to anyone who helped a downed pilot to escape. I don't know if it ever worked.

The heavy vest was vital. While the F-4 had a hard-shell survival kit and life raft in the ejection seat just under the foam seat cushion, the vest

COMBAT   47

was our primary source of survival equipment in the war. On ejection, just after the parachute opened, the seat kit deployed first then the life raft inflated. Those two items then dangled under the pilot on a nylon lanyard. This was a great system for peacetime or for over water, but not for the jungle. The raft—useless over land—and the kit were likely to hang up in the jungle canopy creating major problems for a pilot attached to them. If the parachute caught the top of one tree and the raft and kit caught another, the pilot would swing between them—and not in a hammock. Worse, all that dangling gear made a nice target for gunners. Hence, most of us flew without buckling the kit to the parachute harness. In the event of an ejection, the kit would go its own way. We would depend on what was in the vest.

Since quick rescue was the key to survival, prior to each mission all pilots tested both of their survival radios. We tested "Guard," 243.0 megahertz, the common emergency frequency monitored by all our aircraft, and the secondary rescue frequency, 282.8 MHZ. Of all the survival gear we carried, nothing was more important than the radios.

My parachute harness was different now, too. The F-4, as with most modern fighters, had the parachute built into the seat itself, so I only needed to wear a lightweight harness. I had to lug a 40-pound parachute during my T-33 days in pilot training, so I was quite happy with the lightweight harness I used in the States. In the war, though, my harness had not just the attached underarm life preservers, but the 30-pound tree-lowering device on the back. By the time I had the heavy harness over my survival vest, I felt like I might sink into the floor.

My faithful helmet that I hand-carried from the States hung on a peg next to my gear. But it was no longer the neat, white helmet with the 336th Tactical Fighter Squadron "Rocketeers" decal from my old squadron on the visor cover. Now it was plain olive-drab. Even the nape and chin straps, normally a nice sterile white, had been dyed olive-drab (called OD). At least my oxygen mask was the same, but it was already OD.

With all that gear on I was already sweating, despite the air conditioning in the equipment room. When I went out the door, Thailand hit me. It was not raining so the humidity was somewhere below 90 percent, but not by much, and the temperature was about 90. I had trained in Tucson where 110 degrees, "dry degrees" as the Arizonans said, was not uncommon, but I did not wear a hundred pounds of gear then, and I was not about to go into combat for the first time. Now I was soaked with sweat, and I was just starting.

All eight of us boarded the crew van, a blue version of a truck that, painted brown, could be used by UPS Corporation for deliveries. It had wooden bench seats on both sides for the crews. We had similar vans in the States so at least that part of the mission was familiar. However, in the States the crews were usually talkative in the van, making jokes or side bets on various parts of the flight.

Not on this flight. There was little conversation. At most there were a few whispers between front- and back-seaters, in hushed tones like couples whispering secrets. The van driver, one of our Personal Equipment specialists, stopped at each plane, called the tail number, and the appropriate two crewmembers got out. My plane was last.

When I stepped out of the van, the sun, heat, and humidity seemed more oppressive. My F-4 stood before me loaded to the gills. It had two 370-gallon fuel tanks on the outboard wing stations. As it sat there, the bird had 17,000 pounds of fuel, nearly 2,500 gallons: 8,000 pounds in the fuselage, 4,000 in the wings, and the rest in the external tanks.[2] I was accustomed to that fuel load from my peacetime flying.

Today, though, a lot more hung on it. The two inboard wing stations each had three 500-pound MK-82 bombs and the centerline station had six of them.[3] The bombs, loaded on white ejector racks, were OD color with fuses on the front and rear and lots of stiff metal arming wires connecting them to the plane. Each bomb had 220 pounds of explosive material inside a special steel casing designed to maximize the blast and produce lots of fragments. This 500-pound bomb was said to have more explosive force, and more shrapnel, than did the 750-pound bombs used in earlier wars. Those twelve bombs represented 6,000 pounds of weight, three tons, that I was not used to flying with.[4] Finally, two white AIM-7E Sparrow radar-guided air-to-air missiles were flush-mounted to the bottom of the fuselage, with their guidance fins sticking out. The swept-wing Phantom was an impressive airplane in normal circumstances with its big black nose, giant air intakes, and green and brown camouflage, but now it really looked like a warrior.

The standard procedure in the Nickel was for the pilot to do the pre-flight inspection of the plane while the GIB examined the armament. I did my "walk-around" inspection in the same manner as in the States, except for my growing nervousness and profuse sweat. The GIB checked each bomb and bomb-rack for security, and checked each fuse, both nose and tail, for the proper time for arming, usually four seconds. The time setting was critical for our survival since it determined the number of seconds between the bomb's release from the rack until the fuse armed. That "safe separation" time prevented any bomb released at low altitude from destroying the plane that dropped it. Sadly, it still happened occasionally in the war.

Entry to the Phantom's cockpits was via a large, yellow, steel ladder that hooked over the edge of the front cockpit. From the side, the ladder looked like two large shepherd's hooks connected by the ladder rungs. I handed my helmet to the crew chief and struggled up the ladder. My gear made the climb a challenge, but the step down into the narrow cockpit was even more challenging. I felt as if I was being stuffed into a small barrel.

Strapping in to the cockpit, something that I had done with little effort for the past three years, now seemed daunting. The gear I wore made me feel like little Randy in the movie *A Christmas Story*. The tree-lowering device forced me out from the seat back while the bulky survival vest hampered my movements. When I leaned forward to attach the leg-restraints, the vest contents pressed against my abdomen, which made breathing difficult. The leg-restraints were buckled around each ankle and just below each knee. They were designed to allow free leg movement in the cockpit, but to forcibly retract the lower legs upon ejection to prevent flailing.

Normally, I would have attached my survival-kit straps next. The kit and life-raft were in the seat below a slightly padded cushion under my butt. However, since we wore survival vests and flew over jungle, that gear was superfluous. I attached my G-suit and oxygen hoses, both on the left side, next. The oxygen hose connected to a coupling on the left side of my harness. Both connections were designed to disconnect easily upon ejection, but not in flight.

My lap-belt was next. With all the additional gear, it was difficult to even see it. The crew chief had laid each half on the side consoles, well extended. I fastened the metal buckle just below where my belly-button should have been but for the mass of survival gear. I pulled both ends of the belt as tight as I could stand. While cinching it tight made the seat more uncomfortable, the last thing any pilot needed was space between his ass and the seat when the ejection occurred. It was well known that if the seat started moving before the pilot's body did, spinal injury, sometimes even fractures, were likely. I could stand the discomfort from the tightly cinched belt.

Getting to my parachute risers would have been impossible if the crew chief had not helped me. He leaned behind my head and put the right riser next to my shoulder. I pulled the metal, spring-loaded guard up with my thumb, and pulled the latch down with my index finger so the crew chief could insert the riser prongs. I released the latch and guard. We repeated the process for the left side. When we finished, as was my long-time habit, I pulled hard on each riser to make certain it was secured then jerked my torso forward to ensure that the automatic locking system (like that in cars today) would function. By now, I was soaked with sweat.

The crew chief handed my helmet to me and said, "Good hunting, sir!" That made me feel better. I did not see his name or rank since he wore a white T-shirt and green jungle-fatigue pants. From his calm and friendly voice, I guessed that he knew I was on my first mission.

I soon learned that those hard-working, unsung ground crewmen were really heroes. They busted their asses in grim working conditions to make sure we flew the best airplanes in the world. They sat and worried until "their pilots" brought "their birds" home safely. When a plane went down, they suffered, probably with worry that they may have done something wrong. The crew chief had a hell of a big responsibility for little pay. Some were barely out of their teens.

When the crew chief got off the ladder, another guy, our van driver, came up and snapped a picture of me. Seems it was the squadron policy to photograph each pilot prior to the first mission. That picture hung on the aircrew board in the squadron hallway until the pilot's tour was over. I did not realize it at the time, but it was also useful if the pilot was shot down. The rescue forces could use it for additional identification if necessary.

I'm glad I did not know that at the time.

When the photography was finished, I put my helmet on, snapped the chinstrap, connected my oxygen hose to the coupling on my harness, and slid the mask's bayonet into my helmet's connector. I took a couple of deep breaths to make sure the system worked, and perhaps, to relax me a bit. I even switched the system to 100-percent oxygen and took a few breaths of that cool, refreshing gas. Then I switched the system back to normal air.

Finally, I was in a familiar environment. The cockpit was my home. I knew every switch, every instrument, every lever. At eye-level was the thick combining glass where the gunsight would be projected when I needed it. Below that was my radar scope. To the right of it was a smaller scope, the Radar Homing and Warning system, which we called RHAW (pronounced "raw"). The control stick stood on a pedestal between my legs. The flight instruments—attitude, heading, altitude, airspeed, rate of climb, and others—were spread across the panel directly in front of me. On the lower right corner of the instrument panel were the many warning lights that told of trouble, such as hydraulic or generator failure, or of normal processes, such as when the external-tanks were feeding. Just above the warning lights was the handle that could lower or raise the Phantom's massive tail-hook. The landing-gear handle was on the left side of the instrument panel. On the upper right, mounted just under the glare-shield that stuck out over the instruments, were the "Master Caution" light that lit up when any abnormal warning light came on, and two engine-fire and two engine-overheat lights.

Directly in front of the stick, between my knees, was the armament panel. This was the business section for selecting and arming the various bombs, rockets, or guns that we carried. By my left hand were the two large throttles, contoured on top for my fingers. On the side of the right engine throttle were the radio/intercom and the speed-brake switches.

The radio, transponder, navigation panels, oxygen system, and other systems were mounted on the two flat panels to my left and right. It was all arranged so that the things I would need most were in front of me. For its day, the F-4 was a well-organized brute.

I performed my cockpit check quickly, from memory. As with most pilots, I did not need a checklist to get ready for engine start. When I switched the intercom switch to "Hot Mike," I heard my GIB breathing in my headset. He already had the inertial navigation system warming up.

"I'm on," I said into the quarter-size round microphone in my oxygen mask that just barely kissed my upper lip.

"You're fine. INS is aligning." He wasn't messing around; the airplane's Inertial Navigation System was busy locating us on planet earth.

A third voice said, "How do you read me, sir?"

It was the crew-chief. He stood on the concrete about half-way between the plane and the large yellow power cart that would start our engines. A large air hose, nearly a foot in diameter, ran from the cart to a connection under the plane. The young man wore a black headset that looked like overgrown ear muffs. He had a large black cup-like mask that covered his mouth where his mike was.

"Ready to start?" I asked my GIB.

"Roger."

"Give me air on two," I said to the chief. The young man stepped to the big yellow cart, and moved a switch. I could hear the cart's small jet-engine whine as it forced high pressure air through the hose and into the engine.

"Rotation," I said as the tachometer left the zero position. Almost simultaneously, the hydraulic gauges started to move up.

I pushed the ignition button on the back of the throttle. "Ignition," I said as I moved the throttle around "the horn," the indentation that prevented the throttles from inadvertently being shut off in flight.

I looked out at the chief. He had walked to the rear of the plane to check that the engine had actually started. He was walking back, holding the long, black ground intercom-cord in his hand. How the crew chiefs managed to do all their work and not get tripped by that cord baffled me.

When the engine reached idle RPM, I checked that the gauges—exhaust gas temperature, oil pressure, hydraulic pressures, and others—were normal, or "in the green" as we said. Each gauge had green markings to show when it was in its normal operating range. We repeated the process for the other engine.

The chief and his two assistants disconnected the air-hose and closed all the panels under the Phantom. We then checked each flight-control for proper functioning.

"Cleared to disconnect, sir?" the chief asked. He wanted to unplug his communication cord from the airplane.

"Cleared."

"Get one for me, sir!" The chief meant it. There was a faint click in my headset when he pulled his cord from the airplane.

My GIB and I finished our last few items. The chief stood directly in front of the plane. When I looked at him, he put both arms up in front, fists closed, with his thumbs pointing in, toward each other. He was signaling that the wheel chocks were still in. I nodded.

"Hammer Flight, check!" My flight leader's voice on the radio sounded gruff and serious.

"Two."

"Three."

"Four," I tried to sound as macho as the other three had. Suddenly, I felt nervous again.

"Udorn Ground, Hammer, taxi four Nickels," our leader on the radio again.

The ground controller responded immediately. "Hammer Zero-One flight taxi runway three-zero, altimeter ..."

I looked at my crew-chief. I held both hands up, fists closed, thumbs pointing outward, then moved them apart. He nodded and repeated the signal to his helpers who were under the bird next to each wheel. In my peripheral vision, I saw them move out from under the airplane dragging the large, yellow wheel chocks by their ropes.

The other flight members were to my right. The heat ripples and black smoke from their engines made finding them among all the other parked birds much easier. I did not have to bother, though. The chief knew his bird was number four in the flight, so he was not going to let me move until my turn came.

He stood well out in front of the plane, so I could see him over the black radar-dome. (We called it a "ray-dome.") He turned his head left to watch the other fighters pull out and turn onto the taxi-way. He turned his head toward me, held his right arm straight up and circled it in the air for me to increase the throttles. As I brought the throttles forward out of idle, the compressors in the air intakes began their signature howl.

I depressed the nose-wheel steering button on the base of my stick grip, dropped my feet from the tops of the rudder pedals to release the brakes, then tapped them quickly to check the brakes. The bird, all 54,000-pounds of it, started forward. I pulled the throttles back to idle. Once the Phantom started to move, it required only idle power to keep moving.

The chief, still facing me, raised his left arm straight out to his side signaling for me to turn right. I pushed the right rudder-pedal and the monster turned.

The chief moved to my left, out of the way and gave me a "thumbs-up," meaning that all was well on the outside. I returned the thumbs-up.

The chief saluted.

Damn, that made me feel good.

We taxied to the "arming area" at the end of the runway. There, more overworked and underpaid ground crewman, all wearing white T-shirts, jungle-fatigue pants, and big, black Mickey Mouse-style ear protectors, checked our plane for leaks and removed the various safety lanyards from the landing gear. They displayed the red lanyards to me. I was used to that from the States.

The arming process for the bombs was another matter. Several guys were under the plane for a long time, pulling safety cables from all the fuses. With 12 of the 500-pound bombs that meant twenty-four fuses. At last, they too came out.

It takes a lot of people to get an armed F-4 airborne, and I just saw part of the group. Many more had worked on it before I got to the plane.

"Hammer Flight, button three," the leader directed.

After each flight member acknowledged, my GIB, who handled the radio tuning said, "You're there."

"Hammer Flight, check." Again, we all acknowledged in sequence. Being a wingman means you get to say the same number over and over.

The Lead's GIB looked at the flight, tapped his helmet and nodded his head. As he did, his canopy, and all the other back seat canopies, were lowered together. The front seat pilot in the number one airplane did the same, and I lowered my canopy when he nodded his head. It was neat to see.

"Udorn Tower, Hammer is number one." We were next to the runway, four warriors ready to go.

I was one of them! This warrior finally was about to get into the war.

"Hammer Zero-One Flight, winds light and variable, cleared for takeoff, runway three-zero. Good luck!" The tower controller had not finished when Lead started to taxi onto the runway.

I was really going to war.

I managed to get airborne and into formation without significant problems. The Phantom seemed a bit sluggish to me with all those bombs hanging on it and required more power than I was used to, but I managed. The world looked strange given that northern Thailand was a blend of green woods and rice paddies, not the light-brown and reddish desert of southern Arizona. The roads north of Udorn, what few I saw, were dirt. No major highways or even what we call secondary roads to be seen.

Ahead, for the first time, I saw "the Fence." The Fence was our name for the Mekong River that separated Thailand from Laos. From altitude, it looked like a wide, medium brown ribbon. There were no rapids that I ever saw. It always appeared wide, flat, slow, and lazy.

Yet the Fence was more than a river. It was the dividing line. On one side was Thailand, the "friendly land of smiles" as the tourist posters used to say, where we lived a reasonably safe and comfortable life, at least considering there was a war going on. We had a BX, hot food, cold beer, showers, and clean sheets. We could walk through town without carrying a gun. The biggest dangers were strange food and aggressive taxi drivers.

Across the Fence was "Indian Country," as the veterans called it. Over there were a variety of people who wanted to kill us. Over there were many hundreds of anti-aircraft guns manned by veterans. Many of the guns were entrenched; others were mobile. All of them were difficult to see since our enemy had mastered camouflage. The North Vietnamese were entrenched in the south along the borders with the two Vietnams. The communist Pathet Lao were in the north. The neutrals were probably not too friendly either since they had been ducking our bombs for nearly a decade. Rumor had it that there were friendly Laotians in Vientiane, the capital, but we never got close to that city. Our only friends were the Hmong, the tribal people in the north, and a few Americans who were there ... but not officially there.

To cross the Fence was more than just crossing a river; it was passing through a gateway, the gateway to the war.

The flight leader called "Fence Check" on the radio. He must have done that for my benefit because Nickel Standards called for an automatic Fence check when crossing the river. It was the signal to arm our weapons and set our bomb sights. I went through the arming checklist although, even today, I probably could do all the steps by memory, blindfolded. Basically, it meant tuning the radar-guided missiles, selecting the bomb stations, fusing the bombs, and selecting the release interval and the number to drop for each push of the bomb release button (called the "Pickle Button"). The only switch I did not arm was the Master Arm switch. I kept it in the "Safe" position until I got to the target area. It was not appropriate to drop bombs accidentally, even in the war.

The flight leader checked in with the airborne controllers, the 7th ACCS guys from Udorn who spent 12-hour missions in the back of a C-130, then he contacted our Raven FAC. After Lead gave him our mission number (must keep the records straight, even in the war), the FAC gave us information essential to the mission including the wind direction, altimeter setting, target location and elevation, suspected defenses, and the run-in and pull-off directions. To me, the flight's FNG, it might as well have been a discussion of organic chemistry delivered in Greek. It was truly "information overload," at least for my first mission. Thank goodness, my GIB understood it.

I did, however, pay attention when he discussed the "best bailout" area. Here we go again, discussing unpleasant topics. Again, but only briefly, I had a vision of my flaming F-4 heading for the ground with me in it. Would I really wait to get to the best bail-out area, or would I jump as soon as I could? Fortunately, I did not have time to ponder that problem.

Our target was several trucks concealed in some trees near a "T" intersection of two roads. At least the FAC said they were roads. To me, it looked like two light-brown dirt trails that met near a large jungle area. Damn if I could see any trucks and I could barely make out the Raven in his light gray O-1 propeller-driven airplane.

The Ravens were Air Force pilots who lived with our allies, the Hmong forces. They wore civilian clothes and did not carry military identification. If captured, their fate would be grim. The O-1 was a small, high-wing, tandem-seat aircraft. The Ravens often carried a Hmong soldier in the rear seat to coordinate with any friendly forces on the ground. How anyone could fly over targets in Laos at barely 90 miles per hour in an underpowered Cessna was more than I could understand. The O-1 carried only four "Willy Pete"—white phosphorous—2.75-inch rockets that were used to mark targets for the fighters. While many Ravens carried M-16 rifles in the cockpit with them, their only real defense in the air was that the enemy knew that if they fired at a FAC, he would return the favor by directing airstrikes at them.

The flight leader signaled for us to enter the wheel formation with the FAC in the middle, well below our planes. For the first of many times, I watched the tiny, gray O-1 roll into a dive—or at least he pointed his nose down—and fire a single rocket. A thin, white smoke-trail followed the rocket on its journey. Seconds later, some bright, white smoke billowed in the trees near one of the intersecting roads. The intense white smoke was unmistakable against the green jungle foliage.

The FAC radioed, "Your target is 20 meters north, where the road enters the trees. Cleared hot! There is an active twelve-point-seven hidden in the trees."

What? Not only was everything about this day strange, sweaty, or disorienting, but also there was a heavy machinegun near the target. Things had deteriorated as far as I was concerned.

"Bombs triple" called the flight Lead. "One's in hot, FAC in sight."

As the Lead aircraft dove at a 45-degree angle, my GIB said, "Check bombs triple, Master Arm on."

I acknowledged that all switches were set. The Lead aircraft pulled off his dive as a line of three ugly explosions, red with dark gray and black smoke, billowed up from the edge of the trees. The other flight members moved into positions for their attacks. My plane wallowed as I moved around the wheel. The FAC radioed corrections, my GIB said something about being slow, sweat ran into my eyes, and there was an uncomfortable, acidy feeling in my stomach.

Where was my training? I felt like I was not in control, that things were happening, but I couldn't understand them. I really needed a "pause" button so I could sort things out.

"The gun's active! Jink hard, three!" The FAC directed the third fighter. Below I saw some red streaks, a stream like a hose squirting into the sky.

A "jink" is a quick, hard turn, usually followed by a reversal or perhaps several. It was designed to break the gunner's aim. Since bullets have a time-of-flight of several seconds or more, jinking could often cause the rounds to miss. Unless, of course, the gunner had guessed what jinking maneuver the pilot would use and shifted his aim accordingly.

"AIRSPEED!" My GIB shouted into the intercom. "POWER!"

The plane did seem to be mushing. I pushed the throttles as far forward as they would go, what is called "military power," where the engine RPM was 100 percent. It was a novice mistake. The J-79 engines actually produced more thrust at 96 percent power. Above that, the exhaust nozzles started to open in anticipation of using the afterburners. Every F-4 pilot knew that, but on this first mission, I did not remember it. Some shit-hot fighter pilot!

"Four's in hot, FAC in sight," I lied; I had lost sight of the O-1. I rolled the airplane left to position the target so that it appeared to be above and to the left on my canopy (for you purists, about 135 degrees of bank with about a three- to four-G pull).

Only something was wrong. The stick movement felt mushy, not the usual firm stick I was used to. It was loose, sloppy, in my hand.

"We're too damned slow!" My GIB, again.

My elbow was locked as I pushed on the throttles. The nose went down to about 45 degrees below the horizon. I tried to quickly roll the wings level, but the roll was much slower than I was used to. The stick was still mushy in my hand. It felt different; what was wrong?

"Nine thousand. We're slow! Dive angle's good. Eight thousand. We're slow!" My GIB was feeding me information, for whatever good that did as I was way behind the airplane at this point.

In front of me, my gun-sight glowed bright red through the combining glass. The sight was a circle with a diameter of 50 mils, four inner arcs 25 mils out, at twelve, three, six, and nine o'clock. In the center was the "pipper," a two-mil-wide red dot that I was supposed to put on the target. Actually, I did not move the pipper; instead, it appeared to "track" along the ground as the plane went forward.

"We're slow! Ready. Pickle!" Pickle means push the bomb release button on the top of the control stick.

The pipper was short of the trees, but I pushed the button anyway.

Thump, thump, thump. Three very fast bumps, less than two-tenths of a second apart as the ejector-carts fired, and three 500-pound bombs left the airplane.

"PULL!" The voice, very loud.

I pulled back on the stick and pushed on the left rudder to roll the airplane. But instead of the heavy four- or five-G's that I expected the airplane buffeted.

"BURNERS! We're too Goddam slow! Burners, you ass!" I think he said "ass"—it might have been worse.

In the F-4, the throttles went straight forward to accelerate the engine itself, like a car only the throttles were hand operated. To get to the afterburners, the four sets of 3,000-psi fuel-injectors that pumped gas into the exhaust chambers and lit the big blow-torches, the throttles had to be moved outboard, 90-degrees from the normal motion, and then pushed forward again.

I rammed the throttles outboard and full forward to light both afterburners. Normally there would be a kick of acceleration here, but since I had the stick back and some G's on the plane, there was little immediate effect. Afterburners worked best before they were needed, when the aircraft had normal G force on it.

"Four, you're taking fire!" It was the FAC this time.

"REVERSE! Jink right!" The voice in the back again. They were definitely not suggestions.

At this point several factors came to my rescue. The F-4's afterburners were pushing us hard; my maneuvering was erratic, at best, so I was not especially predictable for the gunner; the gunner was probably not well trained—maybe he was an FNG too—and he was probably a bit shaken by the exploding 500-pound bombs and accompanying shrapnel.

Mostly, I was damned lucky.

The Russian 12.7-millimeter machinegun, like the U.S. .50-caliber, was a nasty, rapid-firing weapon that could do great damage to un-armored vehicles. The F-4 had no armor at all. During the war, the 12.7 brought down many of our airplanes, in North and South Vietnam, and Laos too. Our advantage was that its range was limited to about a mile and one-half and most of the guns had sights more suitable for ground combat, not shooting at high-speed aircraft.

Anyway, it missed me.

I did better on the remainder of the mission, but not by much. My GIB continued providing instructions, but now he spoke like a drill-sergeant, not a subordinate crewmember. Every word sounded like a command. My bombs were anything but accurate. Where I aimed and where the bombs hit seemed to be completely unconnected. Fortunately, there were no friendly forces anywhere near the target area.

At the end of the airstrike, the FAC radioed our BDA (bomb damage assessment). It was more of that Greek chemistry for the most part. He did, however, say that we had "seventy-five percent on target." I thought about that for a bit: Gee, 75 percent of four airplanes equaled three. One of us must not have hit the target area.

That sunk in later.

On the way home, when things had calmed down for me, I got a real talking-to from my GIB. The thirty-minute flight back was mostly him talking and me listening. It wasn't a casual conversation, no discussion of life in Thailand, the menu at the club, or how did I like the squadron.

No, he laid it on the line.

He talked, I listened.

Boiled down, the lecture was: "Speed is life." We needed the energy that came with speed to maneuver the plane properly. The faster we flew, the harder we were to hit, and if we were hit, the more energy we had to get the hell out of the target area. My training had always emphasized fuel-economy; hence afterburners were only used occasionally in flight, and almost never on the bombing range. Gunnery patterns in the States were flown at set speeds, usually 350 knots in the pattern and 450 in the dive.

No more. From now on, 450 would be my minimum. Later, I upped that to 500.

We crossed the Fence and life became more comfortable. Thailand lay below us, and Udorn Approach Control gave us information for our landing. The air-conditioner blew cold, foggy air out of the vents. Best of all, my GIB had finished his "Are you trying to get us killed?" lecture and we were now chatting about mundane stuff.

Life was good once again.

An unknown pilot, who truly must have been a sage, once described a combat mission as: "thirty minutes of boring cross-country, five minutes of stark raving terror, and then thirty minutes of boring cross-country." It seemed that way to me on this day, and would again and again.

Back on the ground, the atmosphere had changed. When the crew-van picked us up at our planes, there was much chatter among the flight. The discussion ranged from complaints about our BDA from the FAC—he said we damaged a truck and told us we had several KBA (killed by air), but that he would confirm it later. FACs never did confirm it later; they just wanted us to shut up and go away. Several guys, short-timers, meaning their days remaining in the war were numbered, discussed their upcoming DEROS (Date of Estimated Return from Overseas—when they were expected to go home).

Life was good; life was as it should be.

No one, not even my GIB, said a word about my performance. It simply did not matter now. We had flown the mission, no one had been shot down or even hit. We were one mission closer to the end. I really did not understand that then. In the States, there were long and detailed debriefings that covered every aspect of the flight, often ad nauseam. In the States, there would have been a written report of my lack-luster—at best—performance as part of my check-out.

Not here. Back in the squadron, someone put a checkmark next to: Honodel—Mission #1.

One down, a lot more to follow.

Chapter 4

The War That Wasn't

MY FIRST COMBAT MISSION damaged my ego—big time. I had spent years building myself up, believing I was a super fighter-pilot. Not a mere mortal one, either. No, I believed that I could do anything in the F-4, and do it better than any other man who wore a flight-suit. But after that mission, humility set in—and it hurt. It was bad enough that my own GIB had screamed at me for most of the attack. That by itself stung. Worse, everyone that was involved in the mission, every pilot, every GIB, even the FAC had witnessed my inept performance. It was difficult to hide 500-pound bombs that explode far from the target; it was harder to explain why they did so. No excuse worked. No one said anything to me after the mission, but I knew the truth.

I had screwed up in a big way.

After my humiliating performance on that first mission, I needed help. My roommate, Dave, was easy to talk with, and I genuinely liked the guy. That evening, we settled into our room's institutional lounge chairs. He, with his disarming smile, pulled out a bottle of Tanqueray and two water glasses, and set them on the small coffee table. I had never tried it before but, hey, why not? We had no refrigerator in our room and there was no ice machine in the hooch, so we had to drink it "neat."

Dave was on his second tour in the war, having flown his first as a backseat pilot at Da Nang Air Base in South Vietnam. That alone qualified him as a veteran, but he had another advantage on me. He had been at Udorn a month longer than me, so he was finished with the New Guy program and had already checked out as a flight leader.

When we finished our training in Tucson, Dave went straight to Udorn after his leave. He had attended Jungle Survival School prior to his first tour, so he was the first of our class to get into combat. While Herb and I had frolicked in Hawaii and across the Pacific on our ferry mission, Dave fought the war. Therefore, he qualified as my mentor—at least so long as the Tanqueray lasted. (He never ran out—for the entire tour.)

It was much easier to talk to a friend about flying problems than it was to discuss the same matters with instructor pilots. All pilots have large egos, but fighter-pilots take the ego to the outer limit. Mine had gone beyond that. The adage "You can tell a fighter-pilot, but you cannot tell him much" was based on reality.

Since Herb was in another squadron, Dave was really my only friend. Now he would be my counselor. Throughout my tour, I spent many hours discussing tactics, and lots of other things, with Dave. I had no closer friend during my time at Udorn.

I described the first mission, especially the fiasco over the target. Not only had I wallowed around so much that I became a target for a heavy machinegun, but also my bombs had hit nowhere near the target. In fact, they hit far enough away from the target to be an embarrassment. What-the-hell was wrong? I was a good gunner on the bombing ranges in the States and I sure-as-hell knew how to fly the F-4D. I had the flight hours to prove it.

Why had I screwed up over the target and why was I so confused during the attack on those trucks?

He listened carefully and refilled my glass often so that I let my guard (and ego) down. Just 'fessing up was difficult for me. Perhaps to relax me, Dave chatted about combat flying and the purpose of the Nickel Standards. The whole idea was to keep the non-combat portions of the flight as smooth and comfortable as possible, yet get things done efficiently. All that made sense and, having done them once, the standards appeared logical.

More important was to get our job done, and survive at the same time. If we kept ourselves and our planes safe, we could deliver more punishment to our enemy. If a plane was lost, we risked the lives of lots of other guys attempting a rescue. So, as Dave emphasized while sipping his Tanqueray, we had to be offensive and defensive at the same time. His use of the pronoun "we" disarmed me. Sure, he was talking to me, but by putting me in a larger group, he neatly bypassed my ego.

As to my poor airspeed control, he had lots to say. In combat, we did not fly standard patterns with fixed airspeeds. In combat, nothing was smooth. Fighters constantly maneuvered when attacking targets. He reminded me, several times, that in the States we flew airplanes that were more than three tons lighter and, more significantly, had much less aerodynamic drag. Therefore, State-side airplanes responded quicker to engine power changes. The Phantom accelerated much faster when it did not have all those weapons hanging on the wings.

In combat, pilots had to be aware of airspeed from the moment they took their feet off the brakes to start the takeoff. In short, he stressed our need (still using the pronoun "we") to stay ahead of the airplane. If a tight turn was coming up, we had to increase the power well before the turn, not in the turn. He really hammered home the need to use the afterburners. There were orbiting tankers available for mid-air refueling. No one would criticize a pilot for running low on fuel in combat. This was not the States where some staff officers spent their careers monitoring fuel consumption.

This was no longer training; it was the real thing.

***

The next day I was back on the schedule, again in the Number Four position. As with the first mission, we were scheduled to go to Barrel Roll to work with a Raven FAC in the PDJ. The intelligence and flight briefings were almost identical to my first mission. This time, however, I felt a bit more comfortable. Even getting suited up for the flight did not seem quite as cumbersome.

I had some of my old fighter pilot confidence—but not the cockiness—back. When I got to the bird, I was no longer the FNG on his first mission. Now, I knew the ropes. If I did not know all the ropes, I at least knew where they were kept. The start-up and taxi out went great. I was into it. I was fast becoming a veteran. It was different on this mission; I knew what I was doing.

We taxied onto the runway, the first two birds in front, the second two—my element—500-feet behind, and stopped. I put my toes on the tops of the rudder pedals and pressed hard to hold the brakes. I shoved the left throttle forward and did a quick engine instrument check. The engine compressor made its loud, distinctive howl, like some badly wounded beast (the dinosaurs in *Jurassic Park* would have been impressed). The nose dropped as the engine thrust strained against the brakes. I snapped the throttle sharply back to idle. The right engine produced the same results.

The planes in the first element ran-up their engines for take-off. Black smoke billowed behind them. The turbulence from the exhaust buffeted my plane. After the tower cleared us for takeoff, our leader's plane rolled; simultaneously the black smoke stopped and two bright-blue cones of fire from the afterburners replaced it. The buffeting of my plane increased. His wingman followed a few seconds later. More buffeting.

My element leader, Number Three, pointed a finger straight up and circled it. That was the signal for me to run-up my engines. I did. I brought both throttles to 85-percent RPM, as much power as the brakes could hold. Any higher, and the thrust would overwhelm the brakes. The engines howled as if being tortured. The nose went down, compressing the shock-absorbing nose-wheel strut. Even at only 85-percent power, the Phantom strained to go.

Number Three released his brakes and lit the afterburners. The turbulence vibrated my plane. Because the F-4's engines were mounted with a slight downward tilt, the fire from his afterburners actually reached the runway and the tip of the blazing cone deflected up from the concrete. It looked like a Bunsen burner turned slightly beyond parallel to the ground.

"Ready?" I asked my GIB.

"Roger."

I dropped my feet off the brakes so that my heels were on the cockpit floor, the rest of them on the rudder pedals. I moved the throttles to 100-percent power as the Phantom started its roll. While quickly glancing at the engine gauges, I moved the throttles outboard and the first of the four afterburner stages in each engine lit. The engine nozzles opened wide for maximum airflow. I moved the throttles forward so the next three stages of the afterburners lit in sequence.

The 27-ton monster charged down the runway, two blow-torches pushing it and giant clouds of hot rippling turbulence following it.

For all the weight she carried, the Phantom accelerated nicely. Sure, it was not the "slam against the seat" acceleration I had felt in the States when she was tons lighter, but it was still a hard push.

"One hundred," my GIB called the speed. This was my maximum abort speed. We were going.

I pulled the stick aft at the computed takeoff speed. When I did, the Phantom leapt into the sky, accelerating rapidly. I quickly raised the landing gear handle with my left hand. Before the hydraulic system had finished getting the gear into the wheel-wells, I slid the flap-handle up. Even a heavy F-4 accelerates rapidly so I did not want to over-speed the flaps.

Ahead, I saw the smoke trails start as each of the three other planes in my flight came out of afterburner. The Lead aircraft turned in a 30-degree right bank. The others converged as the flight joined into formation. I turned my plane inside Lead's turn so that I could use geometry to join with the flight; it's called "cut-off." I moved smoothly up to Number Three's right wing, into close formation, meaning our wingtips were three feet apart.

Number Three's GIB glanced at me, so I slid down under his plane about ten feet below his bombs and checked his belly to ensure that nothing was loose or had fallen off. Everything was fine.

I pulled back up on Three's wing. This time the pilot looked at me, nodded, and slid down under my plane to repeat the favor. While he was gone, I maintained position on the first element. In seconds, Number Three popped up, gave me the thumbs-up signal, and resumed his position in the flight.

Damn, I felt great! I was doing everything I was supposed to and doing it well. This time, things were going much smoother. Now that I had gone through the routine parts once, I was comfortable. I knew what I was doing.

Until we crossed the Fence.

***

When the leader contacted the airborne controller, we were told that our mission was cancelled, and we were being diverted to a SAR in Steel Tiger.

SAR! That meant Search and Rescue. Damn, I was not prepared for that.

Steel Tiger! I wasn't ready for that, either. Wasn't that where the best gunners were?

There was an American pilot on the ground in enemy territory, and if that wasn't bad enough, Steel Tiger was the worst part of Laos. No rag-tag Pathet Lao there; it was defended by North Vietnamese regulars: well-trained, experienced soldiers. From my New Guy School intelligence briefings, I remembered that the defenses in Steel Tiger were more intense than those in the Barrel. In Steel Tiger, especially close to the borders with both North and South Vietnam, the guns got bigger, more numerous, the gunners better. Worse, if close to the North Vietnamese border, the enemy could fire SAMs at us from their side of the border.

The survivor was down somewhere near a town called Tchepone. I had, of course, little knowledge of the area but I had heard the veterans discuss the defenses there—always with respect.

Tchepone was the worst of the worst.

The controller ordered us to one of the airborne tanker orbits, called Anchors, for refueling. When a SAR was in progress, it was common for the controllers to stack flights of fighters which would then be called in by the SAR on-scene commander. The higher the threat in the area, the more fighters would be put in the holding patterns. Since a bomb-loaded F-4 had notoriously rapid fuel consumption, air refueling was the normal first stop.

In just minutes we approached the light-gray, four-engine KC-135 tanker, basically a Boeing 707 airliner with a refueling boom under the tail. I had refueled many times prior to this, but they were all dramatically different from what I was about to see. Air Force peacetime refueling operations are quite structured, with lots of procedures to complete, always in the same sequence. Everything from the initial contact, the approach to the tanker, flying with the tanker, and the actual refueling was done in strict compliance with the rules. Hence those operations usually took significant time to complete.

Not in the war.

In Vietnam, the objective was to get to the tanker as fast as possible, hook up as quickly as possible, get the fuel, and get-the-hell off so the next guy could hook up. That objective was the same for both the fighters and the tanker. The tanker crews, strictly controlled in peacetime, said "To hell with all that!" when they went to the war. Their mission, in their eyes at least, was to keep the fighter pilots alive; they did what they had to do to make that happen. There were many instances where the tanker crews intentionally left their anchors (in relatively safe areas) and flew their vulnerable aircraft into harm's way to get to a fighter that needed gas. During Rolling Thunder, one tanker crew famously went into North Vietnam to get to a damaged fighter. The crew was severely disciplined, but later (after the war) decorated for saving a fighter pilot that would have been lost.

The Triple Nickel had standardized refueling procedures that would have caused havoc and probably disciplinary action in the States. The fighters would pull up behind the tanker in close formation, called "fingertip," from whatever approach angle that was convenient. Numbers One and Three would go straight to the boom, which trailed behind the tanker at about a 45-degree angle down from the KC-135's centerline. Two and Four would go to the tanker's wings, one on each side.

The Lead would hook-up while Three flew close formation on him. As soon as Number One disconnected, Number Three would slide into position and hook up. Number One would go to the tanker's wing and

Two would immediately slide down and fly close formation on Three's wing. That process was repeated so there was always one plane refueling and one on its wing just a few feet away, waiting. This process cut the time to refuel dramatically. A four-ship formation could cycle through the refueling in about a quarter of the time needed in the States.

When One and Three took their positions behind the tanker, I pulled up a few feet from its right wingtip. I asked my GIB about any checklist items we needed to do. In the States, we would have to safe all the armament switches among other items.

He said, "Hell no, as long as the Master Arm is safe."

Wow! That was different.

When Two hooked up, I slid down next to him, my wingtip just three feet from his wingtip. I pushed a toggle switch behind the throttles to open the air refueling receptacle located on top of the fuselage, a few feet behind our rear canopy. When it opened, a "Ready" light came on above the instrument panel in my cockpit.

Number Two disconnected and banked slightly to the left and I quickly slid under the boom. Clunk! The boom latched into my refueling receptacle and we took on the gas. In just minutes we had on-loaded five-thousand pounds of jet-fuel. I hit the red disconnect button mid-way down the stick grip, closed the refueling door, and joined on Three's right wing. The entire process took just minutes.

We left the tanker and headed toward an orbit area, but never got there. The FAC, call sign "Nail," an OV-10 twin turboprop aircraft that was much faster than the O-1, wanted us to hit some 37-millimeter anti-aircraft guns a couple of miles from where the survivor was. The guns hindered the rescue forces, especially the HH-53 Jolly Green Giant helicopters.

This was a lot more serious—and dangerous—than the mission that I had prepared for. I had not yet encountered the 37, the gun that had already brought down hundreds of U.S. aircraft and would bring down hundreds more.

Worse, the life of an American pilot, stranded on the ground with the enemy all around him, was at stake.

Nail gave us the target area briefing, with the "best bailout" information that I eventually got used to hearing. The FAC rolled in and fired a Willy Pete. The rocket went into the jungle near a clearing.

"Your targets are along the tree-line," the FAC radioed. "Take 'em out! Hammer Flight, Cleared hot." He wanted lots of bombs on them and he wanted them now. The Nail had cleared us all at once. He turned his aircraft out of the area, back toward the survivor. He had more important things to do than to watch some F-4s blow up trees, and, with luck, some 37-millimeter gun crews.

The guns were concealed but their tracers, rising toward where the FAC had just fired from, gave away their locations. The light-gray tracers went out, followed in a few seconds by a series of white puffs as the rounds detonated.

So much for the idea that the gunners would not shoot at FACs. They had let loose a bunch of rounds at this Nail.

Our leader signaled echelon right and called, "Bombs ripple." The flight all moved to Lead's right wing.

"Two." "Three." "Four." Each of us acknowledged the instruction.

My GIB said, "One pass, haul ass. Keep your speed up." I must have had a reputation among the back-seaters.

Leader had briefed the echelon attack as one possibility during our ground briefing. He would go in first, followed sequentially by each of us with at least 30-degrees of heading difference to complicate the gunners' aiming problem. That meant that whatever heading Number One was on when he went in, Number Two would be at least 30-degrees different, same with the rest of us. The result would be bombs crossing the target area in some giant, exploding "X" pattern. If we did it correctly, we would create a big circle filled with bomb blasts and flying shrapnel.

The flight started toward the target, accelerating as we went. I had my elbow locked with the throttles at full military power, but eased them back to 96 percent for the best thrust. This time, since I already was going more than 400 knots, the stick felt firm and the plane responded nicely. The General Electric J-79 engines on the F-4 were more effective at higher speeds.

Lead started his dive heading about north. Two swung around so that he would attack heading about 330-degrees. Three turned even more to the west. Finally, I maneuvered so that I could roll in heading almost due west. There would be mere seconds between each of our roll-ins. I swung wide around the other three fighters as they fanned toward the guns.

Lead came off his dive with several hard jinking turns, vapor trailing from his wingtips. Some gray tracers arced through the sky, well behind him. The tracers disappeared briefly, then white puffs appeared as the rounds exploded. Twelve 500-pound bombs exploded in rapid succession, walking through the trees with their signature red flashes and dark smoke. The string of bombs seemed to cover several hundred yards. The noise and shrapnel must have been terrifying to anyone on the ground. It was impressive from my seat high overhead.

"Two's in hot." His plane rolled almost inverted and the nose plunged down steeply.

Two was well down into his dive when Lead's bombs detonated. Some 37-millimeter rounds were already coming toward him, this time a bit closer than those aimed at the first plane. The tracers appeared to come from several places, so we really were after multiple guns.

Two's string of bombs made an inverted "V" from my perspective.

Number Three continued turning to get the 30-degree heading difference.

"Three's in hot." His plane rolled and dove steeply toward the guns.

I watched Three dive toward the guns as I continued my turn. Finally, with my 30-degrees of separation from Three's heading, I started my attack: rapidly rolled the plane almost inverted so that the target appeared to be above my head, pulled the nose down hard using three or four G's, then rapidly rolled wings-level in the 45-degree dive.

"Four's in hot," I said on the radio.

A long string of bombs exploded below me. Three's bombs went straight across the "V." The target, with 36 bomb explosions all around and over it, was easy to see.

Not only did I have a better feel for what I was doing, my voice sounded strong and confident, at least it did to me. Damn, I felt much better than during the first mission.

"Forty-five degrees, eight thousand, speed's good." The voice in the back.

The gunsight's red dot, the pipper, seemed to move smoothly toward the center of the guns, just like it was supposed to.

"Ready. PICKLE. PULL." Even my GIB sounded more confident than the guy I flew with on my first mission.

I pushed the red bomb-release button—the pickle button—on the top of the stick and held it down. Thump—thump—thump…. The bombs came off too fast to count. I heaved the stick back in my lap and pushed the left rudder hard. With 500 knots on the airspeed indicator, the F-4 responded well with about five G's. That was much better than mission number one. I tensed my muscles against the G forces even as my G-suit's internal bladders inflated against my thighs and calves to keep my blood from pooling in my legs. I struggled to turn my head, which felt like it weighed 50 pounds, to look for tracers. I strained to see back over my left shoulder.

"We're taking fire!" That voice in my headset, my GIB. GIBs always saw the anti-aircraft fire before the pilots did. Pilots had to focus on the bomb run; GIBs focused on keeping us alive. A GIB's voice always told me when to pay close attention.

Burners, then harder left, fast reverse, hard right. Get away from the target area and get back with my flight. There was too much to do for me see where the bombs hit, but my GIB said they were "on target," whatever that meant. When the nose was well up into a climb and we were safely out of range of the guns, I looked back again. I saw lots of dark, black smoke where the 48 500-pound bombs had detonated.

Glad I wasn't on the ground there.

We headed west, toward the Fence and friendly Thailand as we re-joined. As was Nickel Standard, I joined with Number Three, slid down under him and checked his aircraft for battle damage or hung bombs. He returned the favor. Everything was fine.

In the de-briefing, the flight consensus was that there had been hundreds of rounds of 37s fired at us. I did not see anywhere near that number, and said that—aloud—in the debriefing.

Once more, dumb-shit FNG had opened his mouth. Leader explained—to me mostly—that we could only see the tracers when they were relatively close. When they were distant, we only saw the white airbursts. If the tracers appeared white or gray, they were getting close, but not really a threat. If we saw them as colors, red or green, they were too close. In short, the more distinct they were, the more trouble we were in. Each flight member saw a different picture than the others did. Also, the GIBs usually were better able to determine how intense the fire was because the pilots had to focus on the target and the bomb run.

Duh! I felt like an idiot, but I remembered what he said. Everyone in the flight saw things differently. Even my own GIB stated that he had seen tracers from several guns at once, coming at us. It helped if you knew what you were looking for, when to look, and how to look.

My big lesson was that I would always listen to my GIB, and I took it to heart. I'm glad I did not see the rounds coming at us: It surely would have screwed up my bomb run.

Okay, so that's why we had the FNG checkout program. There was a hell-of-a-lot to learn that was not learned in peacetime flying and not taught in the training schools. Some things must be experienced to be learned. No matter how realistic the training, nothing substitutes for combat, for getting shot at. The trick is to learn things fast and not die in the process.

As Dave had discussed the night before, I now knew that I had to devote 100-percent of my attention to the bomb-run. There was no time for distractions, even if the distraction was anti-aircraft fire. Once the nose came down in the dive, it had to be all business for me. Focus on the target and get the damned bombs on it.

If I had to risk my life, I might as well make the enemy pay for it.

I may have said and done some stupid things on my first two missions, but I was a fast learner. From now on, I would listen to, and trust, my GIB while I did what I was supposed to do—put the bombs on the target. My macho, fighter-pilot self-esteem was back.

Another checkmark: Honodel—Mission #2.

***

For the entire four years of my Air Force career I had worn the standard, dark-gray cotton flight-suit. In the heat and humidity of Thailand, the older the flight-suit, the better. Each washing made the fabric thinner, hence cooler. All the flight-suits that I had were veterans of many washings. They helped in Thailand's climate, so I was quite attached to them.

The only problem, according to the Air Force safety folks, was that cotton burned. Since the beginning of air combat, planes often burned when hit by bullets, especially incendiary or explosive rounds. When the plane burned, quite frequently the pilot did, too. We all knew the facts, but we figured that it would happen to the other guy, not us. That was my feeling. Yet by this stage of the war, the safety folks had reams of data that it could happen to anyone, and they finally had the fix for the problem.

We were ordered to turn in our cotton flight-suits, all of them, in exchange for the new Nomex suits, the same material that is used today.[1] These flight-suits were made of a synthetic material that, according to the manufacturer, could withstand more than 900-degrees Fahrenheit. The claim was that if the cockpit burst into flames, the pilot would not fry while going through the ejection procedures. Another plus was that the material was stronger than cotton so would not rip when a pilot had to run through the thick jungle.

All of us were issued new Nomex flight-suits and ordered to wear them. There would be no exceptions. Someone at some headquarters was smart enough to know that pilots were superstitious and, hence, their habit patterns were hard to change. Therefore, the orders that changed us into Nomex were strict and enforced. From that day on, even wearing a cotton flight-suit on the ground was cause for disciplinary action.

As an FNG, I could not—so did not—protest. I switched to Nomex.

Thailand's climate—one that made Washington, D. C. in August seem pleasant—was bad enough for me, but now besides sweating I itched from the brand-new material. It took me a while to adjust.

***

The rest of my FNG checkout program went smoothly—if I could call anything smooth in combat. The missions were back in the Barrel, mostly around the PDJ. It was back to the land where 37-millimeter guns were found, but not as common as in Steel Tiger. The 12.7-millimeter heavy machineguns were the main threat, but that changed as the dry season got going. The North Vietnamese "volunteers" brought more, and larger, weapons with them.

By the end of the FNG checkout program, I felt comfortable and had stopped scaring my GIBs.

One of the veteran guys in our squadron was shot down near the North Vietnamese border. Both crewmembers ejected and were rescued. Why would any fighter pilot eject from his airplane? The F-4, when not on fire, needed two essentials to stay in the air: at least one engine and one functioning primary hydraulic system. The engine was essential for flight, of course, and the hydraulic system was needed to operate at least some of the flight controls. Without both, the Phantom would not fly.

Battle damage to the F-4 could cause the crew to eject if it destroyed the engines or hydraulics, or caused a fire. The Phantom, when full, carried 12,000-pounds of fuel in its internal tanks: 8,000-pounds in the fuselage and 4,000-pounds in the internal wing tanks. Since most anti-aircraft rounds were either incendiary or explosive, a round hitting the wing (the plane's largest area) frequently ignited a fire in the fuel tank. While there were a few exceptions, most F-4s that caught fire from battle damage were doomed, often immediately.

The two-man Phantom crew rode on British-made Martin-Baker ejection seats. In its day, this was the most reliable ejection system in the world, although many believed it was also the most complicated. The pilot had two means of initiating ejection (bailing out): a "D-ring" on the seat between his legs, and a two-ringed face curtain at the top of the seat. Either initiated ejection.

There was much ado about the latest loss in the squadron until we heard that both guys had been rescued. When the two got back to Udorn, I heard first-hand about how dangerous the 37-millimeter was as an anti-aircraft weapon. The Russian gun, designed in the late 1930s, was still an effective weapon. One round could bring down the F-4. These guys had been hit by several rounds so were lucky to get away from the target before bailing out after the hydraulic system failed.

I fast became aware of the danger of ejecting in an area where we were bombing. After ducking bombs, the folks on the ground were not too hospitable.

***

Shortly after I completed my check-out I was scheduled to fly into South Vietnam to "earn" my $65 per month of combat pay. Our mission was a four-ship Combat Sky Spot. I had heard a little about it in training, but only in briefings. Essentially, it meant dropping bombs as directed by a ground-based radar. In theory, the bombs would fall into an area with known enemy activity, an area that also was clear of any friendlies. Essentially, we played a game of Battleship, but without the feedback of "hit" or "miss."

Oh yes, and we played it with live bombs, lots of them.

We launched out of Udorn, refueled using the now familiar Nickel Standard procedures then crossed into South Vietnam. We checked in with some controlling agencies with strange call-signs then were sent to a radar unit for the mission. All the time, we stayed at altitude, about 20,000 feet or so. There were broken clouds under us, so I only could see patches of the country.

The radar controller ordered us to fly a precise heading, altitude, and airspeed. As we flew his directed course, he made corrections to our heading to account for wind drift. We spread out enough so that the bombs would not all hit in the same place. The leader had briefed us to ripple-release our bombs when he did. Four planes, 48 Mk-82 bombs: 12 tons of explosives.

The controller gave us a countdown and finally, "Mark." The bombs started off the Lead aircraft and the rest of us dropped simultaneously. I saw these four strings of bombs falling, like the old films of the World War II bombers in Europe. The difference was that they had bombardiers aiming their weapons while we had a ground-based radar site that was far away from the target.

When the bombs were gone, we turned for home. I never saw any bombs explode thanks to the lower clouds. I never saw any anti-aircraft fire, either tracers or air-bursts. I never heard about any bomb damage from the attack.

Back at Udorn, the Sky Spot missions were referred to as "Sky Puke" missions since that seemed to reflect their accuracy.

But I had earned my combat pay on that benign mission.

Some war! We fought in Laos, planes went down in flames in Laos, people died in Laos, but Laos was not a war, hence no combat pay for fighting there. Hundreds of planes and pilots lost while fighting a war that wasn't a war. Go figure.

***

Despite that benign mission to earn combat pay, all the discussion of anti-aircraft guns, getting hit, bailing out, and getting rescued—or rather not getting rescued—really registered with me. There was a rumor—which I never confirmed—that one of our FACs had been captured in Laos. Apparently, he had been tortured to death, his body cut into pieces, then floated on a raft across the Mekong River near the American base at Nakhon Phanom. Like I said, it was a rumor, but, based on what I had heard about our enemy, one I believed.

When I heard that rumor, I was a two-pack-a-day Camel smoker and had been for a decade. Physically fit I was not. The next morning, I got out of bed and for the first time in a decade did not light up a cigarette. I quit.

Just like that.

I purchased some gym shoes at the Base Exchange and started running. At first, I could only do a few steps before I had to walk. What chance would a heavy smoker have if downed in the jungle with the Pathet Lao or North Vietnamese regulars on his trail? That was my motivation. And it was a damned good one. They may get me, but not without a fight—or at least a chase. I would do everything in my power to escape.

Our runway was 10,000 feet long, nearly 12,000 with the over-runs on each end, and it had a dirt road for security patrols around the side opposite the flight-line. That was the side toward the housing and administrative area. Hmm, measured, dirt, patrolled...a great place to run. So, that became my track. I could watch planes take off and land, deafening though it was, which was a diversion from the pain in my nicotine-clogged lungs. The guards provided security, if any were needed in friendly Thailand, and they quickly got accustomed to my presence. There were even a few other joggers.

It was a perfect track, except for the noise of the planes on takeoff, the occasional emergency landing, the heat and humidity (but I was getting acclimated to those), and the damned snakes.

Yes, northern Thailand had snakes, lots of them. It was not uncommon to pass three or four on a single run. Most were cobras, not vipers, so I just gave them their space—a lot of it. The snakes must have been accustomed to human activity because I never was attacked or even threatened by them. Most of them moved away from me, but I still weaved to keep them at a distance. Nevertheless, it was unnerving to have them around. But they kept me running a bit faster. Combat and the threat of going down in the jungle provided all the motivation I needed to overcome the pain in my chest from running and even the damned snakes. I ran four or five times each week for the rest of my tour. And no more cigarettes—not one.

I was no longer a new guy, I had improved my personal habits, and I felt like I was contributing to the war effort, even though officially it wasn't a war. Once again, I was a macho fighter pilot.

Believe it or not, I had settled in.

Chapter 5

The Golden BB

SETTLED IN, YES, BUT things were different in the war. One day I flew a mission into the Barrel. It was a non-descript mission after a normal briefing. Anti-aircraft fire was light, the weather—considering it was Laos in the dry season—was clear, and our flight flew the usual single-ship visual approaches for landing.

Back in the squadron, at the end of the short de-briefing, my flight leader said: "Congratulations, Buff. You passed your instrument check."

I was stunned. Instrument check? That was the first I had heard of it; I had not even used my flight instruments thanks to the cloudless sky. In the States, we had to fly an instrument check-ride each year during our birth month, mine being October. The check-ride was a formal examination performed by a pilot from the wing's Standardization/ Evaluation section, a group of hand-picked pilots with even larger than normal fighter-pilot egos. We had to attend an instrument refresher course, pass a written examination, and fly at least one simulator mission all prior to the actual check-ride. In short, the annual instrument check-flight was a big deal.

Not in the war.

I had no idea it was a check-ride, so I did nothing that was different, on the ground or in the air. I did not fly an instrument departure, transit any air routes, and did not make a high-altitude penetration and precision approach. But I had passed my annual instrument check. It was the last I heard of any check-rides while I was at Udorn.

I guess the squadron had more important things on its agenda.

That same attitude applied to lots of other training requirements, as well. In the States, each squadron had a ground-training officer that scheduled and supervised a myriad of requirements ranging from physical training to traffic safety to voting. There were times that I believed the Air Force could keep a squadron busy for an entire year with just the ground-training requirements. In the war, these items were properly recorded, but other than FNG school and our quarterly Gamma Globulin shots, ignored.

The "GG" shots were supposed to protect us from hepatitis or something. I took one of those shots in the butt and was sore for days—not good when flying while strapped to an ejection seat to say the least. Since we did not have computerized records, I simply recorded each future shot in my personal shot-record book myself, then told the ground-training officer it was complete. One of those was enough.

Like most squadrons, the Nickel was organized into four subordinate flights with about a dozen guys in each. The flights were commanded by majors who were the first-line supervisors of the officers in the flight. In the States, flights were typically close-knit units that met on a regular basis for the various duties assigned by the squadron.

Again, not in the war. On paper, we were assigned to flights, but in practice we were all one team of flyers. Meetings were rare, and when held, usually involved some specific, war-related project. There were many, many informal meetings: random groups of pilots who discussed the enemy, attack formations, ingress methods, or related issues such as how to better destroy a given target. Anything to do with flying the Phantom, getting the bombs on the targets, and surviving were topics for these often impromptu and sometimes lengthy meetings. Some would call them bull sessions, but the topics were anything but bull.

Every fighter squadron seemed to have at least one character, a guy who stood out for whatever reason. The Nickel was no different, but our character was valuable—and memorable—to me. He was a major, one of the flight commanders, whom we called "Ort."

Ort had flown B-58's, America's delta-wing supersonic bomber, prior to getting into the F-4. While we long-time fighter pilots normally didn't pay much attention to converted bomber pilots, Ort was different. He had been a professional boxer in civilian life, so he had a noticeably combative attitude. I don't mean that he was combative to other pilots; he was combative in his attitude about the war. His idea of fighting was to go after the enemy wherever he found them. The Rules of Engagement,[1] which we called ROE, those insane political restrictions put on us from our various headquarters, the top-level civilians in Washington, and who knows where else, irked him to no end.[2]

Ort was a regular at the O Club bar although he was not a heavy drinker. In fact, many times he did not drink at all. He had curly, dark hair, large hands and forearms, and his face looked like he had taken a few hard punches in his boxing days. He appeared to be a strong man with a large chest, but I never saw him act threatening to anyone. Ort spoke with a gravelly voice that I always thought fit a former boxer.

Ort often sat on the bar with his legs dangling from it. Sometimes Dave sat next to him: two men with combative attitudes and comparable reputations. The size difference between those two was dramatic. Dave was short, but certainly not scrawny. However, his legs seemed half as long as Ort's. Perhaps that was how Dave got his nickname, The Gnome. Whether Dave was there or not, usually a group of pilots surrounded Ort, either listening to his theories or discussing their own. We Nickels seemed to gravitate to him when he held court.

An occasional bar-room shenanigan was the "MiG Sweep." A Sweep started, usually in secret, when a few guys would gather at one end of the bar. Suddenly, they would charge down the length of the bar, sweeping everyone and everything out of the way. MiG Sweeps usually resulted in general bar-room chaos, spilled drinks, and pissed-off drinkers. Occasional scuffles broke out, but rarely serious fights.

One evening, Ort was holding court while seated on the bar. While he spoke, I noticed some guys from the Panther Pack, the 13th Squadron, had surreptitiously gathered at the far end of the bar. Sure enough, with lots of shouting they started a MiG Sweep down the bar, toward Ort. He turned his head toward the approaching commotion. He did not smile. He did not move. The sweepers got right up to Ort, paused, then went around him and finished clearing the bar. Ort sat there. Alone. Untouched.

When Ort spoke, people listened. Lots of the topics were lost to time, but one Ort frequently discussed has stayed with me: his concept of "gun seconds." All weapons have an absolute maximum range, but it was each weapon's effective range that concerned us. Without getting too technical, Ort's theory was that a pilot should limit the number of seconds of exposure to any particular weapon. When we cruised to and from the targets we stayed at a high enough altitude so that only the larger caliber weapons could reach us. Even if they did fire on us, we had lots of time to take evasive action due to an anti-aircraft round's time-of-flight. He also believed—and as my tour progressed, I did too—that even if a gunner tracked a plane, meaning that the gunner had solved all his aiming problems, the rounds simply might miss the plane. The dispersal of the rounds as they flew could work in our favor.

Unfortunately, we eventually had to expose ourselves to all the guns to get to our targets. Bombing with the F-4 in Vietnam was mostly manual. We did not have GPS (Global Positioning System) aiming devices—such as today's "smart bombs"—and even the early LASER aiming systems carried by some special F-4s stationed at Ubon Royal Thai Air Force Base in the southeast were still experimental. The F-4D had a radar bombing system, called "dive toss," but it was notoriously inaccurate, even on training ranges. That system used the F-4's radar to lock on to the ground and compute release parameters based on the range to the target. Some bombs would hit the target, or near it; others would be miles off. Late in the war, the F-4E squadrons at Korat, a base in central Thailand, reported to have used it successfully, but I couldn't verify that claim.

For most of the F-4s in the war, bombing was based on geometry, trigonometry, meteorology, and each weapon's ballistic characteristics. We planned the critical parameters of dive-angle, airspeed, and release-altitude, then computed a gunsight setting (measured in mils of depression from the centerline of the airplane) that should, under ideal, no-wind conditions, result in the bomb hitting the target. Of course, conditions were never ideal and even the best pilots often struggled to hit the planned aircraft parameters. Throw in the confusion of combat and inexact target locations, stir in some anti-aircraft fire, blend in a little nervousness, and bombs strayed from their targets, sometimes far from the target.

There was a saying among F-4 pilots that we "Measured it with a micrometer, marked it with chalk, and cut it with an ax." In Vietnam, the F-4, originally designed as an interceptor, had a reputation as an unreliable bomber.

We tried to offset our limitations by carrying lots of bombs. Maybe we could not hit a truck with one bomb, but if we dropped three, six, or even twelve at a time, strung out over the length of a football field, we greatly increased the odds of a hit, if not direct, then close enough for the bombs' lethal shrapnel to take out the target. When we put fuse extenders on the bombs (long poles on the nose of the bomb to detonate it three feet in the air), the deadly fragmentation pattern flattened and spread hundreds of meters from the point of impact. Finally, we had CBUs (cluster bombs) that spread hundreds of baseball-sized explosive charges over a circle about one thousand feet in diameter. A CBU provided something akin to a giant shotgun blast but with much bigger, exploding pellets.

What the F-4 lacked in bombing quality, it partially made up for in quantity.

Given all that, and more, Ort spent considerable time discussing ways to get the bombs to the targets, and actually hitting the targets without getting killed in the process. Like the other young pilots, I paid close attention to his theories. He was a warrior and we all knew it. Later, I adapted his theories with some ideas of my own.

Our discussions also included "the Golden BB." This concept was not new to us; it had been around since people started shooting at each other, maybe even before that. It has long been known by fighting men that there was an element of luck involved with combat. Sure, trained soldiers generally did things that would reduce their exposure to enemy fire. We fighter pilots liked to believe we were in control of our fate, that our handling of the plane would get us in and out of the target unscathed. Fighter-pilots thought they were invincible, that they were the master of their own fates. It was a powerful self-confidence. Maybe everyone else was vulnerable, but the "real" fighter-pilot was always in complete control.

Unfortunately, there was a limit to what any person could do to avoid being killed in combat. The Golden BB Theory said that if a bullet had your name on it, you were done for—period. Some pilots said they did not worry about it, but the Golden BB was not a theory at all; it was real.

***

I only flew with Ort on one mission, but it, too, was memorable. I flew on his wing in a two-ship formation in Barrel Roll. We attacked some non-descript target near the North Vietnamese border. During the attack, things changed.

"Hammer Flight, bandit, one-zero-zero, forty-five. Suspected white bandit, twenty west of Vinh," or some similar words came over the radio from an airborne radar-alert aircraft warning us of the bearing and distance to an enemy aircraft. "White bandit" was the common Vietnam War code name for the MiG-19, a twin-jet, barely supersonic fighter of 1950s vintage. The more common NATO code name for it was Farmer. It was 45 miles away.

Ort immediately pulled our flight away from the ground target and turned us east toward the MiG.

Ort radioed for me to "Green up" my missiles. We normally flew with our radar-guided missiles "tuned," (synced to the radar) but not armed. "Green 'em up" meant to arm the missiles. He then signaled for "fighting wing" formation, used for attacking enemy aircraft. In fighting wing formation, I maintained a position about 1,500 feet out and 45 degrees back from his aircraft. I was free to maneuver behind him, taking whichever side provided the best attack (or defense) position. My job was to clear his tail while he attacked.

"Contact!" my GIB said. "Twelve o'clock, thirty-five miles, slightly low. Closing, eight hundred knots." Our angle to the MiG meant we were closing with him faster than the speed of sound.

I could see Ort's head close to his radar scope as he watched it. He probably had the same information from his GIB.

"Hammer Flight, you are not cleared to attack." It was the airborne controller using his best official voice. The MiG was on the other side of the border, in North Vietnam, not in Laos with us. The Rules of Engagement did not permit us to cross the border.

Ort ignored, or did not hear, the call. I was almost at full military (non-afterburning) power trying to stay with him. We were about 500 knots and accelerating.

"Lead's locked." Ort's GIB called saying that his radar was locked on to the MiG.

"We're locked," my GIB said on the intercom telling me the same.

"Two's locked." My GIB said, this time on the radio for Lead's information.

Locked meant that our radar automatically tracked the target while providing us with range, closure, and steering information for a radar-guided missile attack. The radar automatically computed the best time to fire a missile given all the information about the target's movement. It did all that stuff with its computer for an air attack; we had to do it manually for ground attack. The F-4 had been built as an air interceptor, not a bomber. Air-to-air was its intended environment.

I looked at my radar screen. There was no sweep of the antenna now as it was fixed on the target. There was a bright blip, a dash really, almost centered on the screen. A small circle, called the "Allowable Steering Error" circle was in the center of the screen with a dot inside it. The dot was directing me how to steer for a firing solution for the missile. On one side of the scope were two dashes indicating maximum and minimum firing ranges. When the target was between the two dashes and if I kept the dot inside the circle, in theory at least, the Sparrow would hit the target.

We were still well out of range, but closing fast.

"Twenty-five-mile scope," my GIB said when he switched to a closer view. We would be able to shoot at about ten miles given our angle to the target and closing speed.

"Hammer Flight, you are not cleared to attack. Acknowledge." The airborne controller's voice was definite.

No response from Ort. He was fixed on the target. I believe that he meant to kill that MiG, rules or no rules. Ort was a fighter.

"Twenty miles." My GIB again. "Check missiles green."

"Roger, we're ready to fire. Do we wait for Ort or do we fire first?" I have no idea why I asked my GIB that stupid question. In combat—in fighting wing formation—my job as number two was to cover Lead's ass, not to shoot a target out from in front of him, even though that had been done already in the war.

"Hammer Flight, Hammer Flight, turn around NOW! You are not cleared to fire; you are not cleared to cross the border. Turn around NOW. ACKNOWLEDGE!" Those may not have been the exact words, but that was the substance. The controller sounded pissed.

There was no response from Ort.

We were almost at the border of North Vietnam.

Just as I thought we were going to cross the border, without any signal to me, Ort suddenly reduced his power and did a hard 180-degree turn.

I followed.

"Hammer Flight, wilco." Ort did not sound happy. "Hammer's RTB."

RTB means return to base. We were on our way home. I have often wondered if that MiG pilot had any idea how close he was to being on the receiving end of four Sparrow missiles. If Ort had disobeyed orders, crossed the border, and fired at that MiG, I would have gone with him and fired, too—when he directed, of course. I respected Ort as a leader. As my combat experience grew, I adopted much of his thinking. This was war, the enemy tried to kill us, so why should we not kill them?

When we got back to Udorn, Ort was livid. He had been seconds away from launching his missiles when the controller stopped him. The North Vietnamese were our enemy. He could have killed one of their aircraft but for, in his eyes (and the rest of us, too), an absurd rule that allowed them to sit safely on one side of an imaginary line, then, when they felt like it, to cross that line and kill us. If we were at war—all the shooting seemed to indicate that we were—we should be able to go after our enemy.

Ort was right. The way we fought was enough to make a grown man cry. In fact, it made thousands die, and millions more cry.

Shortly after that mission, Ort was informed that he was being transferred to some staff position—in Korea! The Air Force had often assigned field grade officers to flying assignments for the first half of their tours to get a taste of the war, then reassigned them to Saigon to help run it. We already had several 7th Air Force Headquarters staff officers attached to us for occasional flying.

But Korea? Ort must have seriously pissed off someone to get that assignment. I knew he wasn't too popular with the wing commander due to Ort's vocal opinions about the conduct—or misconduct—of the war. If Ort were being sent to Saigon, I could have understood that. After all, he knew how to fight so he could have been valuable there. Everyone in our squadron knew that 7th Air Force Headquarters needed some sensible help.

But Korea? To this day, even after a two-decade career in the Air Force, I can see no logic to that assignment. For all his strong and vocal opinions on the conduct of the war, he was a skilled, competent, aggressive leader. He had a reputation for getting to his assigned targets, destroying them, and getting his flight home safely.

What more could be asked of a leader or a pilot?

***

Early in October, Colonel Earl, whom I had met at FNG school, called me to his office in wing headquarters. He asked me to take a position as the Wing Tactics Officer on his staff. I was truly flattered that he asked.

Not only did I both admire and respect him, I simply liked being around him. He was one of those people that made everyone feel comfortable even when things were not. Since I was not doing anything in the squadron except flying, I had lots of time on my hands.

I eagerly accepted the job.

The two-story headquarters of the 432nd Tactical Reconnaissance Wing sat between the two fighter squadrons. My new office was on the second floor with a great view of the flight-line and the runway. Colonel Earl's desk was positioned so that he could speak easily to his subordinates. We had a Weapons School graduate, a major named Gary, who oversaw all matters involving how fighters were employed in combat. I had a desk next to him. There were three reconnaissance officers, two pilots and one navigator, who handled all matters dealing with that half of the wing. Colonel Earl, Gary, and I were the fighter guys in the office, so I would have guessed that we would click.

Not so. I got along better with the recce guys than with Gary, the weapons officer. I was not a Fighter Weapons School graduate, so Gary probably thought that I was not a credible Tactics Officer. The Weapons School was a prestigious and highly technical half-year program at Nellis Air Force Base near Las Vegas. Supposedly, only the best fighter pilots were selected to attend. We called them "Patch Wearers" for the distinctive insignia that they wore.

***

I was still getting accustomed to my new tasks when I heard the loud sirens indicating an inbound emergency aircraft. Udorn was a major emergency field so this was not unusual. Minutes later I heard that it was a Laredo FAC with battle damage.

The Laredo FACs were Triple Nickel F-4s with specially trained crews that operated in high-threat areas, ones that would be too dangerous for the O-1's that the Raven FACs flew. True, there were some OV-10's, the Nail FACs, that were fast enough to work almost anywhere in Laos, but there were few of them in Thailand.

A friend of mine, Rick, who lived two doors from me in the hooch, was a Laredo GIB. I checked the schedule and discovered that he was flying that mission with Pete, a veteran front-seater. Rick was a lean, handsome, dark-haired Texan, about my age. He was a Texas Tech grad who, like me a few years earlier, wound up as a pilot GIB. Unlike me, his first operational assignment was to Southeast Asia, not North Carolina.

Within minutes of the siren, an F-4 landed and snagged the approach-end barrier. Udorn had five barriers spanning the runway, steel cables that extended somewhat when engaged by the F-4's massive tail hook, a system like that used on aircraft carriers. This barrier could bring an F-4 from 200 knots to zero in only a couple hundred feet.

As quickly as the damaged plane stopped, emergency vehicles surrounded it. I was too far away to see what type vehicles were there, but it was far more than the usual fire trucks. Soon after the landing I heard that one of the crew was wounded.

It was Rick.

For a long time, perhaps an hour or more, the plane sat on the runway, exactly where it had stopped. The two canopies were open, and people moved about near the plane. Why, I wondered, did they not move Rick to the hospital? Why was he still in the plane? I heard others express the same concern.

Get him out of the plane! The wait was gut-wrenching.

Later that day, I learned the story. Pete and Rick were flying near the border with North Vietnam. Pete heard Rick groan, then say, "I'm hit!"

Pete immediately jettisoned everything from his aircraft and turned for home as fast as he could. He had little information from Rick, who must have lost consciousness. When they landed, Pete thought that Rick was still alive, but he died while still in his seat. One single 12.7-millimeter machinegun bullet had gone through a Plexiglas panel, a triangular unit about a foot on each side, that was just above the canopy rail, between the heavy metal of the front and rear canopy frames. The bullet hit Rick in the center of his abdomen just below the ribs. The bullet passed through an open space of about three or four inches between Rick's two survival radios. Had the bullet hit the canopy frame or either radio, Rick would be alive.

It didn't.

It was the Golden BB.

The next morning, I came out of my room at the hooch and saw two officers removing Rick's possessions from his room. The JAG—Judge Adjutant General—lawyers had inventoried and were preparing to ship his things home. Several other pilots sat on the porch railing, watching. I joined them. It was quiet; we just watched. I remember how sullen, how depressed I felt. Most of the time, when someone was shot down, the person would either be rescued quickly or simply be listed as "missing." In those circumstances, the pilot would be with us in the morning, in the evening he would not return.

This was different. Rick was dead. A lot of us had watched, albeit from a distance. He was with us in the morning, played darts in the squadron lounge, drank some putrid coffee, and then he was gone.

The worst part was that he was alive when the plane landed. I've always believed that, had he been pulled from the aircraft quickly, he might have lived. I knew I was probably wrong, but it seemed as if there was confusion as to how to treat him, which could explain the long delay with him bleeding while still in his ejection seat. My hypothesis of the situation was partially confirmed when the wing later developed a device to hook to a wounded pilot's parachute harness to lift him quickly out of the seat.

That afternoon, the squadron commander called a meeting of all crewmembers. About a dozen or so showed up, including me. He tried his best to give us a pep talk, some verbal motivation.

It failed. The guys just sat and listened. No one talked; they just stared at their hands or the wall. I was depressed when I went in, and I felt worse when I went out.

We gave the commander a sarcastic nickname from then on: Cheerleader.

There was a memorial service for Rick at the base chapel. The chapel was packed for the service, including most of the Nickel. I did not go. Rick was my friend, but his death must have made me realize that I, too, was mortal. He did not do anything wrong. That bullet really did have his name on it. They weren't attacking anything, just looking for targets. Even the world's greatest fighter pilot could not have survived that. Rick's death made me aware that there was only so much I could do to survive the war. The ultimate survival of any of us was not in our own hands. That was a scary thought then, and a sobering one when I think of it today.

The Golden BB theory was—and is—real.

I have always regretted my stupid decision not to attend Rick's memorial service.

Chapter 6

Hot Dog

ORT TRIED EVERYTHING HE knew to get out of his inane assignment to Korea. Being merely a captain, I thought that a major—a field-grade officer—could pull it off. After all, majors seemed fairly high in the rank structure. Little did I know. Anyway, if the wing commander, and probably others, wanted someone gone, that person was gone.

The Nickel scheduled Ort for a "Fini-flight." His end-of-tour mission was to be followed by a celebration on the flight-line with champagne, "well-done" words and handshakes from the squadron mates, and finally a party at the Officers' Club. Ort was scheduled to lead a four-ship formation into Laos. Two of his wingmen, both majors, were staff officers from 7th Air Force Headquarters in Saigon. Those two came to Udorn each month to fly a couple of missions and, I guess, see how the war was progressing. Ort's number four, a young captain, was a regular squadron pilot, a well-regarded veteran.

A policy in place during the war prohibited any sort of airshow at the completion of a tour, or any other time for that matter. The reason was simple from a headquarters perspective but irritating to pilots: There was always the possibility of undetected battle damage, so it was a matter of safety for the aircrews and the folks on the ground. In fact, the real reason was that air shows were dangerous if taken to extremes as some had been earlier in the war. A simple flyover was one thing; beating up the home airdrome was another. The complexity of the earlier airshows had progressed to the point that several airplanes had crashed in what seemed to be needless demonstrations. Celebrations on the ground were much safer, despite the hangovers. Looking back, the policy made sense.

Ort ignored the policy. He felt he was being exiled to Korea in a non-flying job, so what did he have to lose? He intensely desired to stay at Udorn, kill as many of the enemy as he could, and finish his tour in the normal manner. His purpose in life was being taken from him, and he was pissed. As far as I was concerned, he had damned good reason to be pissed, and I think every pilot in the squadron agreed. We wanted him to stay.

When he led his flight back to Udorn after the mission, he did not split the formation for single-ship, straight-in approaches as required by wing regulations. Instead, he put the flight in diamond formation, one plane in close formation on each of his wings and one in the "slot," close behind his tail. He flew over the runway at about 1,500 feet as if doing a fly-over.

But the flight did not just fly over the airfield. Instead, halfway down the runway Ort started a formation roll. This was a surprise not only to those who watched, but also to the pilots in his own flight. He was 1,500 feet in the air, parallel to the runway, in a diamond formation, and rolling. At about the 90-degree point, the two staff officers, shocked I'm sure, broke off from the formation. Number four stayed in position until Ort was inverted. Four could see the tail of Ort's aircraft and, seemingly, just above it the runway. That was too much, even for a veteran pilot. Four pushed his stick forward to climb (remember, he was now upside down), which separated him from Ort's plane.

From the ground, it appeared to be something like the famous "Bomb Burst" maneuver that the Air Force's "Thunderbirds" aerobatic team performed at airshows. Unfortunately, this was not the Thunderbirds, it was not an organized airshow, it was done parallel to the ground and quite low, not vertical. And worse, no one in the flight, except Ort, knew it was coming.

The wing commander, who witnessed it, did a Mount Vesuvius imitation. The shock wave engulfed the flight-line. He immediately grounded Ort and ordered a Flying Evaluation Board to determine if Ort should keep his wings or be permanently grounded—with loss of both his wings and flight pay. The flight-line celebration and squadron party were quickly cancelled.

Because of the time required to schedule and conduct the Flying Evaluation Board, a formal proceeding, Ort's assignment to Korea was cancelled. Some other major in Southeast Asia was suddenly reassigned. Who knows, maybe this whole scenario played out again at another base.

I'm sure the wing commander thought his problem was over.

Wrong. Now Ort was stuck at Udorn with nothing to do except voice his opinions about what was happening, about how poorly the military conducted the war, and anything else that crossed his mind. Worse, we had lost perhaps our best flight leader, certainly our most aggressive one.

This thing had gone poorly for all concerned.

I was befuddled about losing Ort, at least from a flying perspective. He would continue as an influence on me, but only on the ground.

***

About that same time, as part of my job as a tactics officer on the wing staff, I studied the plans that the Air Force had used for Operation

Rolling Thunder,[1] the air campaign against North Vietnam that LBJ terminated in 1968. Colonel Earl thought I might uncover some tactics that could be used in our battle over the Trail.

I did not. Instead, I learned that Rolling Thunder was a perfect example of how NOT to run an air war. From the dubious selection of the targets to the inane restrictions on the fighters to the predictable timing of the attacks, it was one blunder after another. These blunders, repeated almost daily, cost hundreds of lives and condemned hundreds more to torture and years of imprisonment. That study, along with discussions with other pilots—including Ort—and what I saw and did caused me much concern. Was this our best? The enemy trucked massive amounts of war-fighting material into South Vietnam then used it to kill our soldiers. We tried to stop that flow.

We were failing miserably.

The war was confusing, at best. The American media focus was on the fighting in South Vietnam and Nixon's Vietnamization policy.[2] That is, to gradually pull out American troops and turn the fighting over to the Vietnamese. Sounded good, but the ground situation was immensely complex. The war directly involved five Southeast Asian nations: the two Vietnams, Laos, Cambodia, and Thailand. North Vietnam was well supported by both the Soviet Union and China. The fighting in the South involved troops from South Vietnam, the United States, Canada, Australia, Korea, and others, versus an enemy that, after the Tet Offensive of 1968, was mostly North Vietnamese. Throw in the fighting in Laos, and later Cambodia, and the whole thing really did seem like a bucket of worms.

From our perspective at Udorn, we fought two distinct wars, wars that most Americans amazingly still knew little or nothing about. One was the battle in northern Laos supporting the Hmong against the Pathet Lao and, increasingly, the North Vietnamese.

It was not going well.

The other was the near futile effort to stop the trucks along the Ho Chi Minh Trail, far larger and, to America, more important.

It was going even worse.

At least the U.S. finally recognized that the two struggles we were fighting in Laos were actually a war. While it was still classified and supposedly hidden from the American public, we no longer had to fly monthly sorties to South Vietnam to qualify for combat pay.[3]

Getting shot at in Laos was now good enough.

***

If our involvement in Southeast Asia wasn't complicated enough, the Chinese were building a road in northern Laos. We did not seem to know what the purpose of the road was. Since the beginning of our involvement in the war, the U.S. had been concerned about China. During Rolling Thunder, there was a strictly enforced buffer zone to prevent our aircraft from getting too close to China. Sadly, the buffer zone gave the North Vietnamese a "safe area" where they did not have to worry about being attacked by our aircraft.

This Chinese Road in Laos added to our concern. What was its purpose? Where was it really going? The official story, from the Chinese so I heard, was that it was going from China to Burma. But why would the Chinese build the road in Laos when they could build it in their own country?

To find out what was happening, our Wing flew RF-4Cs over the road on a regular basis. There had been no anti-aircraft reaction to our reconnaissance planes, despite the presence of guns.

Until one day.

The recce crew that worked in my office, Chuck and Al, flew over the road expecting the usual quiet. Instead, they got shot down. Fortunately, the crew got well away from the road and ejected in a relatively safe area, if such an area existed in Laos. They were rescued quickly. They were the first aviators in my office to get shot down during my time there.

They would not be the last.

So now the Chinese Road presented a bigger problem. It was no longer something to just keep track of. Now it had cost us an aircraft. Should we respond by bombing the guns or the road? Was this road going to aid our enemy? Were the Chinese just sensitive to aircraft noise? The confusion level had risen significantly.

As seemed normal, we did nothing.

***

About this time, someone in our wing started thinking about better ways to fight. Our wing was unusual in that it had both reconnaissance and fighter aircraft assigned (Air Force wings are usually one or the other, not both). Why not use both resources together? Made sense. Reconnaissance aircraft find targets; fighters bomb targets. That much was obvious.

The problem was that the targets in Laos—both north in the Barrel and along the Trail—moved often, mostly at night. During daylight, the jungle provided excellent hiding places, especially where covered with double or triple-layered canopy. In many cases, the only way to find hidden trucks or supply depots was to follow the tracks made by the vehicles. Finding targets hidden in the jungle was possible, but required extensive reconnaissance-film study by intelligence specialists.

Once the photo intelligence specialists found the targets, the information went to 7th Air Force Headquarters in Saigon, then on to Pacific Air Force Headquarters in Hawaii, and perhaps even on to Washington. Targets in certain areas in Laos even required the approval of our ambassador in Vientiane.[4] Someone in this process eventually decided a target was worth hitting, so a "frag order" tasked one of the fighter wings to strike it. Given that process, it was not unusual for us fighter pilots to be assigned to hit a target that our own recce aircraft had found a week earlier. In far too many cases, the target was long gone when we got to it. Our aircraft were exposed to ground fire for non-existent targets. Being shot at while bombing trees instead of trucks was naturally offensive to us.

Such was the befuddling way of the war.

Since the targets, especially trucks, moved often and the normal targeting process took a week, why not cut out the delay? It was the beginning of a 432nd Wing operation that was dubbed "Hot Dog."

It seemed so simple. One RF-4C would fly over a designated area in Laos, usually along the Trail. The recce crew took their pictures, then hustled back to Udorn. A waiting truck met the airplane and the maintenance crews downloaded the film before the airplane even shut down its engines. The film was rushed to the Photo Processing and Interpretation Facility (PPIF) near the flight-line.

Waiting at the PPIF were the crews of two or four fighters. When the film came out of the development tanks it went directly to the viewing tables. The PPIF intel experts, using stereoscope glasses for 3-D viewing, picked out and identified any targets. The fighter crews located the targets on their maps and viewed the actual targets with the same 3-D stereoscope glasses. Not only did the fighter crews know exactly where the target was, they knew how it looked from the air. The reconnaissance aircraft had a variety of cameras, so the fighters could see the target from various angles. Better yet, they could locate nearby anti-aircraft weapons.

The fighter crews, having already been briefed and wearing their gear, then went straight to their airplanes, which were "cocked" for fast launching. When things went smoothly, the fighters could be airborne in about one-half hour, or even less, from the time the recce landed.

The fighters bombed the target about an hour or so after the recce passed, when the target was likely still there. Better yet, since the fighter pilots knew the target area, there was no need for a FAC. If there were no FAC in the area, the gunners were not alerted that a strike was coming.

Surprise was a wonderful advantage in combat.

During the preparation for the missions, I went to the PPIF to see the process up close. Using the stereoscope glasses, I clearly saw a road turn-off where trucks were parked in the trees. I counted the trucks and saw material and people near them. What startled me were the numerous fuel storage areas. These were small refueling pits near the roads. Each pit contained several 55-gallon drums of gasoline or diesel fuel and sometimes smaller cans, probably motor oil. These pits were scattered at varying intervals along the roads so that any one truck needing fuel could stop, refuel, then proceed quickly. None of these pits would be worth the risk of sending a fighter after it. Why risk a valuable aircraft and crew to blow up one or two barrels of gasoline? It was damned smart dispersal of their lifeblood.

The North Vietnamese were worthy adversaries; they used their resources well.

Hot Dog was a wonderful program and it worked. The teams hammered targets of value, instead of blowing down trees in vain attempts to hit something that may have been there a week earlier. The missions were efficient, too. Since the pilots knew exactly where their targets were, they did not need air refueling. The flights went directly from Udorn to the targets and back with no delays.

We loved it.

***

Shortly after Chuck and Al were shot down, the wing's weapons officer—Gary, who I think was one of the designers of Hot Dog—became the next member of my office to get shot down. He was hit while bombing a target in some dense jungle. When he ejected, he came down in a slippery jungle stream. As he tried to get his footing on the mossy rocks, he saw a rope dangling nearby. At the top of the rope was a CIA helicopter, an unmarked UH-1 Huey. Gary grabbed the rope and was hauled aboard the Huey. The helicopter then grabbed the back-seater and got them both back to Udorn safely.

Gary and his GIB had been on the ground only briefly. They were not even aware of the helicopter being in the area. It was often said that the quicker the rescue, the better. The longer our pilots were on the ground, the more dangerous the rescue. Gary's was a perfect example of a quick pick-up.

***

Perhaps it was Ort's influence or maybe it was just from observing and participating in the war, but I began to feel dissatisfied with its conduct. There were simply too many restrictions on us. A prime example was the border to North Vietnam. That imaginary line allowed our enemy to assemble his trucks and supplies in the open on his side during the day, then run them across the border at night. We had to wait until they crossed the border, in the pitch darkness, then try to find and destroy them. Why not hit them when they were assembled, open, and clearly visible?

On one of my missions my flight bombed some "suspected trucks" hidden under some trees quite near the border with North Vietnam. An OV-10 Nail FAC directed us during the attack. When we looked to the east from over our target, we could clearly see a long line of trucks on the far side of the border. One of our reconnaissance aircraft even had filmed them just before we arrived. They were waiting for nightfall to cross into Laos.

Near the end of our time over the tree-covered target, we started to receive anti-aircraft fire when several 37-millimeter guns fired on us. We must have gotten near some actual targets. As we were leaving after we dropped all our ordnance, the Nail asked if we had observed the anti-aircraft fire. Naturally, we said yes.

The Nail said that the fire had come from the other side of the border and that we should report that fact to the airborne controller when we checked out. As far as I could see, the fire came from the target area, not from across the border. But who was I to argue with a FAC? I reported the cross-border fire to the controller on the way home.

The controller promptly sent another flight of F-4s to the Nail. Under the Nail's direction, that flight crossed the border and attacked: not the supposed guns as the Rules of Engagement permitted, but the line of trucks. When they left, every truck in the column was destroyed or burning. Unfortunately, the controller also sent a reconnaissance bird over to film the carnage. He got some great pictures of the destruction.

Our wing now had both pre- and post-strike photos of the attack. One clearly showed a long line of trucks waiting at the border; the other showed almost all the trucks as wreckage. Our wing commander sent the pictures to 7th Air Force Headquarters in Saigon as an example of how well we were doing. He even had them included in a slide-show for visiting VIP's. It was a splendid example.

Until someone saw that the latitude and longitude shown on the pictures placed the attack in North Vietnam.

We were ordered to destroy the pictures and any reference to the attack.

We fought with one arm, while at the same time being shot at, shot down, going missing, or, like Rick, killed. That was not right! If we were expected to fight, to risk our lives, which we did every time we crossed the Fence, we should be allowed to hit the enemy where he lives. We didn't have to resume the quasi-strategic bombing of the North like we did in Rolling Thunder. No, not that World War II-type of air warfare, just let us cross that stupid border. Make them hide their resources both day and night.

This was not a small issue of interest only to a few hundred Air Force aviators scattered around Thailand.[5] Those trucks carried the weapons, ammunition, and supplies needed to wage the war in the South, a war that caused considerable turmoil back home. Our troops were on the receiving end of the material that came down the Trail. Our men were killed or maimed by the weapons in those trucks. Why not quietly remove the restrictions and let us hurt them before they hurt us? It made sense then, and it makes sense now.

But the restrictions stood, and woe be it to the pilot who violated them. That border was a giant impermeable wall. Cross it and get punished severely.

The situation was compounded by the difficulty of actually hitting meaningful targets. The ordinary targeting process produced poor results. On some missions, the FACs would find a real target to hit. Unfortunately, they had to have located the target when the fighters were available. Most of the fighters were F-4s, which had notoriously heavy fuel consumption. Without air refueling, a flight of F-4s might have five or ten minutes, at most, to work with a FAC. That was not much time to find and identify a target, brief the fighters, mark the target with a smoke rocket to help the fighters find it, then conduct the strike. The time available was further reduced if anti-aircraft guns were numerous or aggressive. After all that, the fighters had to actually hit the targets.

Some bright staff officer—we called them "staff pukes," although that term may be redundant—decided we could get better results if we spent more time going after known or easy-to-find targets. This guy had a knack for the obvious. So, what targets were either known or easy to find?

Guns, of course!

We were going to go out with the mission of destroying anti-aircraft guns. Think about it. The guns were used to protect things that the enemy thought valuable. The guns existed to keep us away from the important targets. The guns were small, mobile, cheap, plentiful, and as I discovered from film study at the PPIF, frequently dug in. It was not unusual for a 37-millimeter gun to be in a pit protected by high dirt berms to stop bomb fragments. To kill a gun, that is, to put it out of action permanently, required a direct hit, or at least a hit inside the dirt berm that protected it. To kill a gun required exceptional bombing accuracy, usually a hit within 10 or 15 feet. That kind of accuracy in the F-4 was uncommon on Stateside controlled ranges, much less in combat when the target shot back.

One factor that the staff puke missed was that when a fighter went after a gun, the gunner's job got easier. The gunner normally had to solve several problems to hit an airplane. He had to compute the range to the airplane and the elevation of the plane, then project its movement in reference to his gun. Range, elevation, and azimuth. It wasn't easy to hit an airborne target, especially if that target was moving at 500 knots.

But if the fighter attacked the gun, the gunner's problem was greatly simplified. No longer must the gunner traverse his barrel; he only needed to change the elevation of the barrel as the fighter progressed in the dive. When the gunner let loose his seven-round clips of 37's, the fighter flew right into them.

Attacking guns as part of getting to a valuable target was sometimes necessary. If the mission were SAR, it was often mandatory; we had to get our guy out no matter the risk. But there was another word for attacking guns for no reason other than to kill the gun and improve our bombing statistics.

Insanity.

Well, at least we had the Hot Dog program. The fighter crews that flew it scored some good hits on real targets, not just "tree parks." The daytime siestas of the truck drivers were rudely interrupted. From those drivers' perspective, the war had taken a sudden turn for the worse.

Our wing's bomb damage reports to Saigon showed a spike in the number of trucks destroyed. Naturally, 7th Air Force wanted to know why we were suddenly so successful. They found out that our wing had devised and implemented a nifty program that used only our own resources. It had no incremental cost, as it used missions already scheduled. Our wing coordinated the actions between the reconnaissance and fighter forces, hence reached a new level of efficiency and got results, all without the help of any higher headquarters.

The response from 7th Air Force Headquarters?

It ordered Hot Dog terminated immediately. Now go out and kill guns.

Chapter 7

Bad Moon Rising

WHILE FOLKS IN THE States were about half-way through the college football season, my turn arrived for the night-combat phase of the war: Nickel Night Owl. Our squadron conducted about one-third of its operations at night. Unlike back in the States, where a whole squadron flew at night for a week, then returned to day flying, Nickel Night Owl was always in progress. Long before I arrived, the squadron determined that the best way to conduct night operations was to put people on the night shift and keep them there.

When a pilot went on the night schedule, it was not just for a week, but for several months. As any shift worker would recognize, one goal was to allow the pilots to accustom themselves to working at night and sleeping in the day. Breakfast was no longer a morning meal; it was a sunset meal. Happy Hour was not at five p.m., but at five a.m. The normal routine was upside down.

The similarity ended there. Most shift workers have at least some light for their jobs. As I was about to learn, night work was dramatically different in the war.

As a new Night Owl, I received briefings from veterans of the program. I got a review of the physiological aspects of night flying, especially vertigo. I learned techniques to keep my night vision, such as wearing sunglasses after dark, dimming the lights in the squadron building, and never—never—look at my leader when he lit his afterburners on takeoff.

Nickel Standards changed for night work, especially the external aircraft lights. They were turned on only when necessary. The reason we flew with the lights off was simple, but excellent. The gunners could not see the plane. A gunner had a perplexing task trying to hit a target he could not see. He had to guess the position, speed, and altitude of the airplane. Hitting an unseen aircraft at night involved a lot of luck on the part of even the most experienced gunner. Therefore, no external lights.

Night combat entailed changes to our operations. The call signs of the various controllers were different; ordnance loads consisted of more "area-coverage" weapons, such as cluster bombs and fuse-extenders on the 500-pounders for fragmentation rather than penetration. The FACs were different, too. Instead of Ravens and Nails in their O-1s and OV-10s, there were Candlesticks which were old, twin-piston engine C-123 transports, and Blind Bats which were more modern four-engine turbo-prop C-130 aircraft.[1] The FACs were equipped with night-search devices such as starlight scopes, infra-red detectors, and other means of spotting trucks in the darkness. While day FACs carried smoke rockets to mark targets, the Candlesticks and Blind Bats carried both parachute and ground flares.

The biggest difference, though, was that the trucks that hid in the jungle during daylight moved over the roads in the darkness.

Perhaps the most important thing I learned was how to prepare my cockpit. In the States, I flew nights like most people drove cars—with the instrument lights on at a comfortable level for ease of reading. Not in combat. The front cockpit lights were on only for takeoff, the routine parts of the flight, and landing. In the target area—during attacks—they were off, completely off. Moreover, no lights could be allowed to come on. That meant the myriad of warning lights could not illuminate since a sudden bright light would distract and possibly blind me. Since it was not feasible, or even desirable, to disconnect the warning lights, I had to tape over them. All of them. Fuel transfer lights, caution lights, weapons lights, even the engines' fire and overheat lights had to be covered with dark tape. All that taping meant a lot more time in the cockpit prior to engine start. A half-hour extra was common.

My first night mission was with a veteran leader, Wes, who flew with his regular GIB, Fergie. Wes was a captain, about a year older than me, although he seemed more mature. He was a quiet, soft-spoken man who did not drink, or at least not much, so I rarely saw him at the bar. He had a patient manner, so he may have been a flight instructor at some point in his career. He separated complex processes into their simplest steps, which made things much easier to understand. He was one of those people that everyone got along with.

As we left the Personnel Equipment room and stepped into the darkness to go to the crew van, Wes told me to put on my sunglasses and, as soon as I got into my cockpit, to put on my helmet and lower the tinted visor. He explained that for night combat, seemingly trivial things such as protecting my night vision really mattered.

The flight-line at Udorn, like every base in Thailand, blazed with lights from all the maintenance activity. During the day, the business on the line was mostly launching, recovering, refueling, and rearming the planes. Night was when much of the repair and maintenance work occurred. Udorn did not have lights on towers like most U.S. airports. There were innumerable light-carts, each about the size of a Subaru, with two large, wide-area spotlights on top, run by internal gas generators. One of those carts sat next to nearly every airplane on the ramp. Add a fleet of pickup trucks, crew vans, and tugs, and the flight-line glowed with bright lights.

Wes advised me well.

We were no sooner airborne when I discovered that I had not taped all the necessary lights. Fortunately, Wes had instructed me to carry pre-cut strips of tape, so I had several stuck on the thigh of my G-suit. I scrambled to do some catch-up taping while I did a night join-up on his bird. I never made that mistake again.

Udorn was bright, but as we climbed away from the field, the world got dark. Or at least I thought it did. There were few lights in Thailand away from the cities, but there were a few.

When we crossed the Fence, there were none—I mean NONE.

We've all seen darkness, especially folks from rural areas. But I had never seen black like Laos at night. The stars were the only way to tell up from down. Even on moonless, overcast nights, the sky was always a little lighter than the ground.

No one showed a light at night in Laos. No electric lights, no head-lights, no campfires, no flashlights, nothing. About the only thing darker would be the inside of a coffin.

From the perspective of the people on the ground, darkness made sense. There were hunters in the air, searching for prey. Not only were there jet fighters roaming the sky, but also more fear-some hunters: the gunships.[2] Ubon in southeastern Thailand had the AC-130 Spectre gunships while Udorn, in northern Thailand, had the AC-119K Stingers. These cargo-type aircraft carried 20-millimeter Gatling guns along with lots of sensors to find things to shoot at.[3]

When I crossed the Fence that first night, I had no idea that I entered a new war, an environment that brought new terrors. Imagine fighting in combat, in a life or death struggle, and then doing it in the dark. I was about to learn a lot, about war and about me.

***

With a few notable exceptions, the missions that I flew at night, 53 with the Nickel, have blended into a dark, hazy mist of memories. Yet while the specific details have blurred, many incidents have not.

Besides the darkness, my first mission—my first lesson—revealed the volume of anti-aircraft fire in Laos. There was a hell-of-a-lot more of it than I thought.

During the day, we only saw tracers when they were relatively close. My rule was that if I could see tracers, they were probably shooting at me; if the tracers showed color, usually red or green, the gunner was either tracking me or soon would be.

At night, we could see anti-aircraft fire for miles. The lack of ambient light made the tracers stand out, like fluorescent paint on a black velvet canvas. It was like standing in Colorado Springs and watching the New Year's fireworks on Pikes Peak 20 miles away, only I saw tracers farther in Laos. Like fireworks, the tracers arced into the sky, neatly spaced depending on the size of the gun. They disappeared for a few seconds, then the rounds flashed as they burst—bright white flashes akin to flash bulbs. Of course, we could not see the smoke from them at night.

Aimed anti-aircraft fire was somewhat less dangerous at night simply because the gunner generally could not see a plane with no lights. Most of the guns in Laos were aimed visually, so the rounds often passed behind the target aircraft. When a gunner relied on sound, he almost always lagged the target.

So far, so good.

Unfortunately, the gunners knew this. Their veterans had learned to add additional lead to compensate. Some did successfully. They also recognized the sound change as a fighter started its dive. Pilots had to reduce engine power at the start of a dive since bomb-release speed affected accuracy. That power reduction changed the sound of the engines. From roll-in to bomb release also required that the plane fly a predictable path, which gunners loved.

Another problem was light. I learned that the darkness was my friend as well as my enemy. On nights with a bright moon, the gunners often would see a fighter, even when its exterior lights were off. The gunners' world was completely dark, so their night vision was at its best. If a fighter passed between a gunner and the moon, a cloud, or even close against a cloudless sky, it received a lot of gunfire. That may be the reason that "Bad Moon Rising" was the most popular song on the Udorn Officers' Club jukebox.

The darkness meant that our own afterburners could easily become our enemy, not friend. When the F-4 afterburners lit, they emitted long cones of bright bluish-white light directly behind the engine. In Laos at night, those burner cones were visible from the Barrel to Steel Tiger, and probably farther. Everything I had learned about using the burners during daylight missions I had to unlearn. The rule was to only use burners when necessary—absolutely necessary.

***

We did, occasionally, violate the no-afterburner rule. One night I was in a three-ship formation assigned to escort[4] a gunship. It was a bright, clear night with some moon. When the gunship aborted due to maintenance problems, our flight had nothing to do. The flight leader decided that we would troll for some guns to bomb. He told us to drop back from him in radar-trail formation with about two miles of separation between each airplane. We "stacked" higher so we would be looking down through his flight path. He flew up a valley known for having lots of trucks. He lit his afterburners, which made nice bright-blue flames above the road. Several guns opened fire on him, fortunately firing behind his accelerating Phantom. From the number two position,

I saw the approximate location of a gun, so I put some bombs on the area. Three did the same. We repeated the process until we were out of ordnance. I don't know if we hit anything, but it was fun dropping bombs on the guns. It was a little payback for all the shooting they did at us.

***

Flying at night brought an intense feeling of being alone. Other than during the safe parts of the mission—departure, refueling, and arrival—the other flight members were just voices on the radio. My GIB was yet another voice in my headset, a bit louder and without the radio's static tail. A GIB's job required him to keep his instrument lights on as well as his radar scope. When I turned my head, I could see the dim, red glow from the rear cockpit. So here I was, sitting in a nearly black cockpit with voices in my headset, but no one in sight anywhere. It was a weird feeling. I knew there were others with me, including the GIB six feet behind me, but I still felt alone.

***

In my Stateside night training, I almost always bombed using flares for target illumination. An aircraft would drop the flare, which hung under a small parachute. The flare cast a one-million candle-power light to the ground in a cone shape. The ground, and the target, would be illuminated as if under some giant flashlight. In the States, it was fun to bomb with them.

Not in Laos.

I was only a mission or two into the Night Owl program when I learned to hate flares. I was working with a Candlestick, an ancient, twin piston-engine C-123 along the Trail not far from the South Vietnamese border. The 'Stick had some trucks spotted moving down a road. The 'Stick would normally drop several "logs," bright green markers that burned on the ground and served as a reference. The 'Stick would use his Starlight Scope to track the trucks while giving us directions in relation to the logs.

On this night, the Candlestick dropped several flares. They lit high in the air and illuminated the road and some moving trucks—probably with terrified drivers—in a valley. During the dry season in Laos, there was considerable haze, most from smoke as farmers burned off fields or from the North Vietnamese trying to conceal their activities. The smoke settled into the lower areas, especially valleys. That was where those trucks were, visible from above under the flare light despite the haze.

I rolled in to attack.

The flares hung at about my bomb release altitude and they swayed gently in the air. The flare-light cast down into the haze created a "milk bowl" effect, somewhat like fog that you can still see through, though poorly. The sway from the flares hanging in their chutes meant the light cones, and the milk bowls, below them swung like overlapping, slow, unsynchronized pendulums. I released the bombs as I passed from darkness into the moving milk bowl. On my pull-out, I realized the gunners could see me, so I started a five-G jink. All the while the world swayed. I pulled the nose up hard toward the blackness above me. I thought I had recovered the aircraft and was now well above the flare light.

"I GOT IT! I GOT IT!" The voice from the backseat was demanding, to say the least. I felt the stick moving in my hand.

Since "I got it" was the standard call when changing control of the aircraft, I released the stick and responded with, "You got it." My response was habit from years in the F-4.

I felt the plane lighten, to less than the one-G of normal flight. My map light was clipped to the glare-shield above my instrument panel and pointed at my attitude indicator. I turned the knob so that it shone a dim, red light on the instruments.

We were pointed almost straight up.

As my GIB executed what pilots call an "unusual-attitude recovery" using his well-lit instruments, I stared at my attitude-indicator, perplexed to say the least. When he took control of the bird, I really believed that we were in level flight. Since it was pitch black, all my non-visual senses told me I had been in level flight. Without vision, it was easy to fool the body's sensory systems. No one could have convinced me that anything was wrong.

But I trusted my GIB. I never flew with a GIB that was not trust-worthy in flight, especially in the war. His ass was on the line just the same as mine.

I thanked him profusely, promised him a beer at the Club, and took control of the plane. We were still attacking those trucks, so I set up for another pass. I would be in better control this time.

No way.

The bomb run ended the same as the first one: "I GOT IT! I GOT IT!" in my headset. Another unusual-attitude recovery for my GIB.

Damn, he was good at them.

I adjusted my bombing altitude to stay above the flares. We finished the mission, but the higher releases did not improve the accuracy. At least the bombs must have deafened the truck drivers.

On that night mission, the two-seat concept—a concept that, as a pilot-GIB, I once despised—had saved our lives, not once, but twice in succession. Anti-aircraft fire could be deadly, but flying into the ground was always fatal. While we could never be certain, vertigo and disorientation probably killed a lot of guys at night, especially in Laos.

Thanks to my GIB, I was not among them.

Back at the O Club, a wiser me bought lots of beer for my newly admired GIB. I swore then never—I mean never—to fly under flares again.

I did not.

***

Night missions sometimes brought the unexpected. In the daylight, no life-loving truck driver would be caught moving on the roads. The only trucks I ever saw in the daylight were either parked in the trees, already destroyed, or across the border in North Vietnam. Not so at night. Using darkness as cover, the Ho Chi Minh "Interstate Highway System" bustled. From Mu Gia and the other passes, convoys of trucks moved along throughout Laos on their way to the various entry points into South Vietnam. Our sensors,[5] implanted and hidden throughout Steel Tiger, told us that the nightly truck traffic numbered in the thousands.

We flew above, they drove below, with only darkness between us.

One of the F-4's night missions (one of which I describe in more detail in a later chapter) was a gunship escort. The North Vietnamese feared the gunships more than any other aircraft that flew in the night war. Gunships—both the AC-119s and the newer AC-130s—as the name implied, carried several 20-millimeter Gatling guns along with what were then state-of-the-art sensors to detect targets on the ground. Being cargo-type aircraft, the gunships lingered for hours over an area making any movement under it dangerous or even suicidal.

Naturally, those gunships attracted lots of anti-aircraft fire. As escorts, we flew above the gunship and responded with bombs or cluster-bombs when any gunner opened fire. Hence, the gunship threatened the trucks, the anti-aircraft guns threatened the gunships, and we threatened the anti-aircraft guns.

It was the way of the war.

One moonless night I escorted an AC-130 as he orbited over some roads near the North Vietnamese border. Typical Laotian night, pitch-black below, lighter above from the starlight. A 37-millimeter gun let loose a clip in the direction of the Spectre: seven glowing rounds that reached into the darkness, went out, then seven white pops as the rounds exploded in the sky.

"Fighter, put something on him. He's a bit too close." The gunship's pilot made it sound like an order.

The gun must have pissed him off. The gunships, like the Blind Bat and Candlestick FACs, flew with their cargo ramps down. Most had an observer—tethered, of course—prone on the cargo ramp, spotting targets or threats. When the guns got too close and the gunship pilot had to do evasive maneuvers, those observers sometimes fell out of the aircraft. Of course, their crew mates would reel them back in. Some job!

Once the gun stopped firing, I could only guess at his location. In other words, I was looking for a dark object, against a dark background, while flying in the dark. Talk about a shot in the dark.

I selected some cluster bombs, one with instantaneous-fused bomblets and one with time-delayed fuses. They would cover a circle with a diameter of about a thousand feet with more than 1,300 baseball-sized bomblets, each with embedded pellets. I rolled in and dropped the bombs from a relatively shallow dive, about 30 degrees. On "pickle," the bomb canisters left the racks, fell for a couple of seconds, then an explosive cord separated the two halves of each canister. The bomblets then scattered like large shotgun pellets. Little ribs on each bomblet's case caused it to spin, which armed it. Most detonated upon impact. Then there were sporadic explosions from the bomblets with delayed fuses. Some of those with delayed fuses sat on the ground for anywhere from five to thirty minutes before they detonated. The delay-fused bomblets were especially good at night since no one could see them.

I pulled off in a left turn and did not jink. Instead, I looked back where the cluster bombs hit to watch the sparkles as the bomblets detonated. The instantaneous canister produced its 600 sparkles in a nice circle, then it got dark. There were occasional flashes at random locations as the delay-fused bomblets detonated.

I had my F-4 back in its normal position behind the gunship when a bright-yellow fireball erupted on the ground. Damned-well not a cluster bomb! The yellow fireball billowed upward and lit up the area around it. It appeared to be a tanker-truck, semi type like those that pump fuel into our gas stations at home. It produced a roaring fire.

That truck was the first in a convoy of about a dozen trucks, some also tankers. The rest had been forced to stop behind the burning truck. The now well-lit road wound through a narrow valley so there was no way for the other trucks to pass or to turn around. Backing up would be their only escape from the light.

"Fighter, pull off high and stay out of my way!"

You could almost hear the gunship pilot drooling in anticipation. His fangs were out. In seconds, streams of 20-millimeter tracers arced down toward the last truck in the convoy.

Smart pilot in that Spectre. I stopped the convoy—by accident I'll admit—and now he was going to pin them right where they were. In seconds, fire billowed up from the rear truck in the column. It was a beautiful sight: a string of trucks stopped on the road with fiercely burning trucks at each end. Lovely!

I can only imagine the chaos as the drivers fled their trucks (assuming they weren't chained to them as I heard they sometimes were) and ran into the jungle. The road had two tankers burning furiously, there were unfriendly aircraft overhead, and hundreds of exploding 20-millimeter shells, so the jungle must have seemed a haven to them.

Except, there were still about 600 cluster bombs popping off at random intervals sending their lethal pellets in all directions. Talk about having a bad night!

Unfortunately, I was low on fuel and had to leave the excitement. I doubt that the gunship, busy hosing the convoy with his 20-millimeter guns, missed me.

He didn't even say goodbye.

***

Not all the unexpected events were so rewarding. One night I worked with a Blind Bat, a C-130 night-FAC similar to the Candlesticks, in Barrel Roll. There was not nearly as much action there as on the Trail, but it could still be deadly. Some supplies coming from North Vietnam flowed through an area we called "The Fish's Mouth," named for the shape of the border with Laos. A major road, by Laotian standards—meaning dirt, but wide enough for trucks—supplied the Pathet Lao and North Vietnamese.

The Blind Bat had found something unusual in Laos at night: lights. There were some fires on the ground in the shape of a large triangle. Using his onboard sensors, the FAC was unable to determine what the fires were or why they were there. We were in an area where there were no friendly forces at all. Anyone on the ground likely hated us. Unlike the Spectre gunships, the Blind Bats carried no weapons, just sensors, marking logs, and flares. So, the Blind Bat told me to drop some bombs on the fires to see what would happen.

My GIB and I were not too excited about the idea. We could plainly see the target, three rows of fires that formed a triangle. I'd hate to guess how many fires were in each row, but it was probably six or more. The triangle was not small.

What-the-hell was going on? No self-respecting Communist fighter would build a campfire in Laos. In fact, no one would, friend or foe. But here it was, a nice yellow triangle glowing clearly in a black abyss.

My GIB and I reasoned that it must be some sort of trap. We looked around the area, but of course could see nothing in the darkness. No guns shot at us as we circled the triangle and the Blind Bat said the area had been quiet as far as anti-aircraft fire was concerned.

We decided to make one pass, and only one pass. We would drop the rest of our bomb load, six 500-pounders, three with fuse extenders that would add a lot of lethal shrapnel. If there was something there worth bombing, the Blind Bat could call in another fighter to hit it.

I turned on my gunsight and rolled into the dive. Through the round, red circle of the sight, I could see the yellow triangle as it appeared to move toward the dot in the center of my sight, the pipper. The pipper "tracked" smoothly toward the target. When the pipper reached the triangle, I hit the pickle button to release the bombs. At that moment, I saw something else in my gunsight, a blurry orange dot about 10 o'clock, between the outer gunsight ring and the pipper.

Without thinking, I reacted. I pushed the stick forward, putting about two or three negative G's on the plane.

My GIB screamed. Who wouldn't? He expected four or five positive G's. Instead we were shoved upward toward the canopy with dirt, maps, and loose objects flying up with us.

Some bright reddish-orange streaks went by the tops of our canopies.

Close! Too damned close! Probably 37-millimeter rounds.

The ground rushed toward us even if we did not see it. I did not want to be a fireball next to that triangle. I hauled back on the stick with at least six positive G's.

When we regained our composure, we told the Blind Bat that it was a flak-trap and to stay the hell away from it. We headed for home. We were both damned glad to be doing so.

***

It never paid to relax at night. One night I led a two-ship formation assigned to work with a Blind Bat. The weather, however, did not cooperate. Layered clouds prevented the Bat from finding any targets, so he turned for home. The airborne controller did not want to lose two attack sorties, so he sent us to a ground radar site for a Combat Sky Spot, or Sky Puke in our terms.

Our target would be an area—Sky Spot targets were always areas—on the Laotian side of the border, northwest of the infamous A Shau Valley[6] of South Vietnam. While it sounded dangerous, and would have been in the daylight, this was night, in bad weather, on a Sky Spot mission.

Piece of cake.

This would be an easy way to get a combat mission completed, without the usual tension. We found an altitude between cloud layers where my wingman could see me. I turned on my wingtip lights to give him a reference for formation flight. He moved out to a wide position to help disperse our bombs. I told the radar controller our altitude, which was significantly lower than normal, so that he could re-compute the release parameters.

We lined up on the bomb run, closely following the controller's airspeed and heading instructions. We were between the cloud layers, in clear air, and all seemed normal. This was a nice, quiet night flight.

About ten seconds prior to bomb release, number two radioed, "Lead, you're taking fire!"

My GIB shouted, "Tracers behind us, four o'clock." Then he added, with less volume, "They're not too close."

I looked back, and there they were. The rounds were behind us, so—relieved I'll admit—I did not take evasive action. As soon as we got the call to release from the controller and dropped our bombs, I called number two into close formation and we promptly climbed up through the next cloud layer.

In the de-briefing—at the O Club bar of course—we analyzed the mission. None of us had ever heard of a flight getting shot at on a Sky Puke mission. We decided that the clouds that were below us must have been a broken layer instead of a solid layer. The gunners probably saw my wing lights and decided to fire a few rounds at us. Bizarre.

I have no idea if those bombs hit anything or whether they even hit the earth. They just disappeared.

**

One night I attacked some trucks in Steel Tiger that one of the night FACs had found. When I pulled off from a pass, I looked up and saw several bright flashes over my plane. The flashes did not seem to be anti-aircraft rounds, especially since we had seen no tracers. I called the FAC to ask if he knew of anything that might cause them.

After a minute or so, he radioed back that a Navy A-6 Intruder (a twin-engine, two-seat attack plane) had been dropping cluster bombs in the area.

Damn! The flashes were the clamshell casings separating so that the bomblets could spread into their shotgun-like patterns. The A-6 had dropped them on top of us. My plane wasn't hit so I guess my Golden BB was not in the canisters.

Night combat was certainly different.

**

Night combat in Laos was an experience like no other. Some missions were dull, with the darkness being the major threat. Others, as I was to experience toward the end of my Night Owl time, produced major terror. However, no matter what happened in the air, they all ended at the O Club bar. Since only part of the squadron flew nights at any time, the group at the bar was like some clique of ghouls who were only out in the darkness. Creedence Clearwater Revival must have made a bundle on the money we spent playing "Bad Moon Rising" on the jukebox.

We kept the mission rehashing and comparisons going until dawn, when the first of the day flyers filtered in for breakfast. Weird: They were fresh out of bed, cleaned up, and stone sober, while we were smelly, exhausted, and loaded.

No problem. We'd sleep all day and meet them that evening, situation reversed.

Chapter 8

Dry-Season's Greetings

ONE AFTERNOON I WALKED into my room at the hooch and heard a man's laughter. The black curtains that led to the sleeping area were open and I saw Dave, lying on his bunk, reading. I naturally asked him what was so funny. He turned the book, a tattered, dog-eared paperback, so that I could see the title: It was *Catch-22*, by Joseph Heller.

Dave had his boots off and his flight-suit unzipped to the waist. The reading light above his head made his face glow and his white T-shirt shine. He usually smiled, but this smile was bigger than normal, more a grin. His face seemed bright; I think he was genuinely happy.

"Do you realize that these characters are here? At Udorn!" he said, or something to that effect. He could hardly contain himself. "I've got them all identified."

I sat on my bunk across from him and asked what he meant.

He said that every character in the book, Colonel Cathcart, Doc. Daneeka, Major Major, and all the rest were here. They were running the war, our war. It was a revelation of the first magnitude, and he was damned serious about it. He told me to read it and see for myself.

I did. In short order, we had matched the names of the characters in the book to names of people at Udorn and even to some at 7th Air Force Headquarters. Suddenly, the war made sense: It was senseless.

It was Catch-22.

***

Thanksgiving. Before I joined the Air Force, it was a special holiday for our family. Back in Pennsylvania, my family—parents, sisters, their children, and probably a few aunts and uncles—likely gathered for a day of turkey and all the trimmings. At Udorn, Thanksgiving passed with little notice. Someone said there would be a special turkey dinner in the chow hall, but few of us went. Especially us Night Owls. If not on the schedule for any night, I went to the office to handle my few duties. Colonel Earl, my boss at my Tactics Officer job at wing headquarters, knew that the night flying schedule made one's mind less efficient than in the daytime, so he gave me few projects.

One duty I had on a recurring basis was to schedule crews for an operation called "Combat Sage." Sage involved sending one combat aircraft and crew to Clark Air Base in the Philippines for a controlled missile shoot. During the war, our fighters carried missiles routinely, both radar guided and heat seeking models. These missiles endured lots of stress, much from the numerous take-offs and landings, but especially from the high G forces common during combat. Eventually, the stress took a toll on the missiles.

Hence Combat Sage. Instead of destroying the nearly worn-out missiles, why not have aircraft and crews from the combat units shoot them at drones under controlled conditions? That way, the Air Force and the manufacturers of the missiles and associated systems—such as the F-4's radar and fire control computer—could evaluate them. The assigned crew would fly one of its squadron aircraft to Clark, go through a series of system inspections and crew briefings, then fly the missile to a range and shoot it at a drone. The results were fed into the various data banks, the flyers debriefed, and finally the crew would fly back to Udorn or whatever base they came from. The entire process took less than a week.

When the Sage slots came our way, I assigned crews alternately from the Nickel and from our sister squadron, the Panther Pack. As fate would have it, one of the slots stretched over New Year's Eve. I decided to take that slot—to see how the program worked, of course. Colonel Earl chuckled when I put my name on the schedule, but he did not remove it. While I knew I would not be home for Christmas, at least I had a holiday treat, of sorts, to anticipate.

Early in December there was a major SAR in Steel Tiger. A guy from another base was shot down in a nasty area, near Tchepone.[1] The F-4 had gone down, one of the pilots was either dead or captured, and the survivor, named Woody, was doing his best not to join him. All the bases dropped most normal day-time operations and devoted full attention to the SAR.

It lasted three days. For a while, rescue looked doubtful as the North Vietnamese forces were nearly on top of Woody. Yet he was determined—and probably lucky—when one of our HH-53 Jolly Green Giants dropped a sling and grabbed him mere minutes before the enemy could seize him. After Woody was rescued, he described situations where our A-1 Skyraiders, propeller-driven aircraft that escorted the helicopters, strafed mere feet from where he hid. Until a famous rescue deep in North Vietnam in 1972, it was the longest SAR of the war. At least Woody got home for Christmas.

I became acutely aware of the approach of Christmas when Dave, my roommate, received a package from his wife. Dave was feeling down, and it showed. No one could blame him. This was his second tour in the

war and he had been away from his wife way too long. He had missed a
Christmas with her on his first tour and now was about to miss another.
That was too many for a young married couple. Being single, I was spared
that ache, but I listened to him whenever he wanted to talk. Besides being
my squadron mate and my roommate, he was my friend.

The package contained a small, porcelain Christmas tree with a
bracket inside that clamped on an ordinary lightbulb. The tree was
about a foot tall, shiny green with small plastic colored bulbs on the tips
of the molded branches. They weren't really the kind of bulbs that we
hung on our trees; they were pieces of plastic fixed on the porcelain to
allow light from inside the tree to filter out in an assortment of colors.
His wife even included the 40-watt lightbulb so all we had to do was
plug it in. Instant Christmas tree.

It was a perfect tree. Dave put it on our little coffee table with a
bottle of Tanqueray. The week prior to Christmas we had many discussions by that tree, about the war, about things we rarely discussed,
and about home. It was unusual because we normally did not talk
about home or anything other than the war. Combat was our world.
The sole focus of each day and night was to fly our missions and not
get killed in the process. We had to replace the Tanqueray several
times. Funny how something so simple could stick in my mind. I never
forgot that tree.

Christmas Season or not, the war continued. About a week before
Christmas, my office's recce crew—Chuck and Al—who a month earlier
had been shot down over the Chinese road, were shot down again. Like
the first time, they were rescued quickly. The Air Force had an unofficial
policy that any crew shot down more than once was to be sent home.
I guess they thought the crew was either doing something wrong or
were just damned unlucky. Since Chuck and Al were known to be an
excellent recce crew—that's why Colonel Earl had picked them—it must

have been bad luck. In any case, they packed and were gone quickly. They, too, would get home for Christmas.

I would not. On Christmas Eve, when my nieces and nephew were watching for Santa, I was on the night schedule leading a two-ship formation to go into the Barrel and work with a Blind Bat. It figured. What a way to spend Christmas Eve.

The night got off to a bad start before even leaving the dirt parking area in front of the hooch. As was common, we night fliers had the squadron crew-van available to drive to work. A bunch of us piled into the van, with my night-flying mentor Wes's GIB, Fergie, at the wheel. After we were loaded, Fergie backed up to turn around when one rear wheel went into a shallow ditch. This situation created a storm of hoots and various insults. The boys were rowdy that night.

Comments such as, "Fergie, where the hell did you get your license?" "Who taught you to drive?" "Have you ever heard of rearview mirrors?" filled the van. The last comment wasn't fair since it was dark and there were no street lights in the dirt parking lot.

I could not resist adding my two-cents' worth.

"Hey, Wes! You don't let him fly, do you?" I figured Wes must be responsible for his GIB, always. It seemed a wonderful way to harass Wes as well as Fergie. I gloated at my own wit.

With just a little wheel spinning, we got out of the ditch soon enough, but Fergie took more crap on the way to the squadron. He seemed irritated by it, unusual for him.

So much for the Christmas Spirit.

Things got worse after I got my own flight airborne. When we got up into Laos, we had to go through a line of thunderstorms embedded in thick clouds to get to our tanker. My GIB, using our radar, said he thought he could see a way through the cells. The F-4 radar was designed for air intercepts, so it was not the greatest for other functions associated with radar, such as ground mapping, or getting through rough weather. Not a problem though, since thunderstorm cells, being big and dense, showed up as bright images on our radars, usually well-defined.

I put my wingtip lights on "dim-steady" and had my wingman, a cheerful captain named Mike, join in close formation. My plan was to let my GIB direct us through the cells. The tanker, on the other side of the storms, reported that he was in cloudless sky.

So, we entered the line of storms. Since I was doing some serious instrument flying, I had my cockpit lights on as well as my radar screen, which glowed red in front of my face just below the bomb-sight. I trusted my GIB, but it reassured me to see on my own radar screen the massive thunderstorm cells he was steering us between. His headings looked good to me. We wove through the first few cells only to see more ahead. This was not a line of thunderstorms: it was more like a forest.

We were in the thick, cumulus clouds associated with thunderstorm cells and it was bumpy. I kept frequent checks on Mike, but he was tucked onto my left wing as if he had been welded there. The turns and the bumps did not seem to bother him. There was something comforting about seeing a wingman in proper position, especially in rough weather. It meant he was a guy I could count on.

We were exactly between two cells when a lightning bolt flashed directly between our airplanes. It was the brightest light I had ever seen. It was probably made brighter since it was night, in Laos, and I was trying to keep some of my night vision for the mission to follow by keeping my instrument lights dim.

I was flash blinded. Instead of my instruments, all I could see was a bright glare, as if I had looked into a camera's flash from a very close distance—only much worse. It almost hurt.

I expected to feel an impact as I was certain that Mike's airplane would collide with mine.

It did not. In a few seconds, I could see around the bright ball—now just a miniature sun—in my eyes enough to look out at my left wing. At the least I expected Mike would have executed the "lost wingman" procedure to get safe separation from my plane.

He did not.

Mike was still glued to my wing. I was amazed. How could he possibly see me well enough to fly close formation? The lightning bolt had literally passed between our planes. It was amazing that neither plane was hit. Mike later told me that he had the same bright ball in his vision, too, but that there was a small red dot in the center of it, my left wingtip light. He said he just kept the red dot in the middle of the big bright one. Eventually, he could make out my plane.

The lad was an amazing pilot.

We got to the tanker, but it wasn't quite as clear as we were led to believe. We were in and out of the wispy cirrus clouds, pitch-black as usual, but no problem after what we had passed through to get there. I pulled in behind the tanker and was about to hook up when the boom operator suddenly retracted the boom-extension and pulled the flying-boom up to its stowed position below the tanker's tail. He told me to get away from the tanker because I had fuel gushing over my left wing, at about the wing-fold.

My GIB shined his flashlight on the wing and, sure enough, there was a stream of gas coming up on the front of the wing, covering a good part of it, and flowing off the back. We had a fuel leak, one that looked big from the cockpit. Even bigger since it was night—over Laos.

The F-4 has internal fuel-tanks in the fuselage and both wings. We were, as normal, carrying two 370-gallon external fuel-tanks.

There was no way to tell where the leaking gas came from. It could have been from the external drop-tanks or the internal wing-cell, or both. In any case, this mission was over.

It was the only combat mission that I ever aborted.

I said goodbye to Mike, my wingman, turned back toward Udorn, and declared an emergency. To decrease the landing speed for the heavy, swept-wing fighter, the F-4 had a system, called "boundary layer control," that bled hot air off the engines and blew it over the wings when the flaps were lowered. Extremely hot air and leaking jet fuel did not seem like a good combination, so this malfunction required a no-flap landing. That meant landing much faster than normal.

I still had a dozen 500-pound bombs on board, with associated racks, and the two external fuel tanks. To make a no-flap landing with all that weight would require an approach speed of more than 200-knots. Above 200-knots, tires tended to explode causing loss of aircraft control. No way was I going to do that, at night, especially since 6,000 pounds of the load were bombs.

Udorn had a jettison area for this exact situation. I called the base and told them I was going to the jettison area to dump the bombs. Since we were not at war with Thailand, we jettisoned the bombs and the racks together so that the bombs would not arm or explode. The external tanks still contained fuel, so I decided to drop them, too. That would lighten the plane enough to use a reasonable speed for a no-flap landing.

After jettisoning the load, I swung around to final approach. Someone, probably my GIB, suggested that we engage one of the approach-end barriers instead of rolling down the runway. That way the fire-rescue vehicles could get to us quickly in the event of fire. Fire and airplanes simply do not mix.

One barrier was stretched across the runway about 2,000 feet from the approach end. I lowered the landing gear and the F-4's massive tail-hook, a vestige of the plane's original design as a Navy fighter. Without flaps, the approach was flatter than I was used to, but it was the faster approach speed that seemed the most unnatural. The bright yellow runway-lights and the slope indicator-lights next to the approach end of the runway stood out in the darkness. We both locked our shoulder harnesses in anticipation of an abrupt stop when the hook snagged the barrier.

The Phantom's wheels touched the runway and the big main landing gear struts compressed as the weight of the bird pushed on them. I pulled the throttles back to idle and intentionally lowered the nose-wheel by pushing forward on the stick. I did not want the nose in the air when the hook grabbed the cable as that would have slammed the nose down violently. Almost simultaneously, the hook grabbed the cable and we went from 180-knots to zero in a few hundred feet. The deceleration force pulled me forward hard against my harness. All-in-all, it was a smooth landing.

One good thing about the Navy was their cables. We shut the engines down as soon as the bird had stopped. No fire.

An old Chief Master Sergeant—he must have been at least 40—met us at the plane. I described the problem and he said he believed that, since the fuel gushed over the leading edge of the wing, the external fuel tank was probably the culprit. More importantly, he suggested that under these circumstances it was not wise to jettison the tank. The reason seemed obvious standing on the ground, but I had missed it when it mattered: The tanks were jettisoned with explosive cartridges that were about the size of a 20-millimeter cannon shell. If hot air and jet fuel did not mix, explosive charges and jet-fuel damned-well did not mix either. Somehow, we did not become a fireball when I hit the tank-jettison switch. That must have been my Christmas present.

It was a great one.

Considering that I was a know-it-all fighter jock when I got to Udorn, was there no end to the things I still needed to learn?

**

We stayed with the bird while it was towed back to parking. When we got there, a "Blue Bird," one of the school buses painted Air Force blue, pulled up next to us. My roommate, Dave, stood on the steps in the doorway, a beer in his hand.

He called for me to hop on. He said they were going caroling. He waved his beer at me.

Caroling? Oh, yes, it was Christmas Eve.

I got on the bus. There were about a dozen guys in flight-suits, both from the Nickel and the Panther Pack. Even Colonel Earl was there. There was also lots of cold beer, I think complements of the colonel. The bus stopped at both squadrons to pick up more guys, then proceeded down the flight-line. We gathered more stragglers as we went until the bus was nearly full.

We stopped every place we saw men working, which was every-where on a fighter ramp during the war, even late on Christmas Eve. Guys loaded bombs, pumped fuel, changed parts, and other functions. At each stop we serenaded them with probably the worst harmony ever. If we didn't know all the words, we faked it. We even stopped at the various shops to sing. Lots of the technicians came outside to listen. I guess all that time near the din of the flight-line had damaged their hearing enough so that we sounded better than we were.

After earlier events that evening, it turned out to be a terrific way to spend Christmas Eve. (I think of it every Christmas Eve and always tell my wife about that night. Each time, she pretends she has never heard the story.)

I spent Christmas Day in the office trying not to talk much. Colonel Earl was quiet, too.

* * *

A few days later, I was off to Clark Air Base for Combat Sage.

After refueling and flying over the coast of South Vietnam, the trip across the South China Sea to the Philippines became a pleasant cross-country flight. For a while it seemed like I might have been flying from Florida to Texas across the Gulf of Mexico. No lugging bombs, no anti-aircraft fire, just an overwater trip from one base to another. I really enjoyed the flight.

At Clark, our airplane and its systems were inspected by the various companies' technicians while my GIB and I received detailed briefings about what we were to do. Our missile shoot was scheduled for New Year's Day, of all times.

No matter, I was going to enjoy New Year's Eve.

As with every base in the Air Force, the Officers' Club hosted a proper New Year's Eve party. Clark Air Base was not in the war and they enforced dress codes, unlike Udorn. Unfortunately, I did not have the required clothing for a proper party.

Fortunately, there was a potentially better party at the Bachelor Officers' Quarters, open to all. My GIB and I attended and stayed well into the New Year. It was great. The place was packed with revelers and the well-spiked punch made for a festive night. The local officers had the latest music, wore normal clothes, and talked about things that we never even thought of at Udorn. The topic of conversation was not the war; it was anything but the war.

When I reported for duty New Year's Day, I was a bit foggy, to say the least. No problem, though. I could handle combat, so I could handle a controlled missile shoot. After all, there was no anti-aircraft fire here.

The mission was simple: I would fly to an over-water weapons range and intercept an unmanned drone. I would close to about three miles behind the drone. When in that position, I was to call "flare" on the radio. The drone's flare was mounted on its left wingtip and it would produce the heat source that the missile would see. The flare was much hotter than the drone's small jet engine, so, in theory at least, the missile would home on the flare. Even if the missile hit the flare, it would not damage the drone too much.

Once the flare was burning, I was to call "turn" and the drone would start a left turn. When the drone was at about my 10 or 11 o'clock position, I was to fire the missile.

No sweat.

We got airborne, somewhat dehydrated from the party and still not very clear-headed. I had the air-conditioner as cold as it would go, but I sweated alcohol. The missile firing-range was well out over the water, so the blue sky and the deep-blue water contrasted with the distant jungle-green of the Philippines, which made for a scenic flight. Best of all: no anti-aircraft guns.

My GIB got a radar lock on the drone and we pulled into range as planned. I called "flare" on the radio. I armed the missile, an AIM-9E Sidewinder mounted on the inboard station of my right wing. Its explosive warhead had been removed, but the rest of the missile was operational. The missile started a distinct growl in my headset, louder than I expected. The growl meant that the missile saw a heat source and was locked on to it. It was a threatening growl, so as not to be confused with our Radar Homing and Warning System that made a sound similar to a rattlesnake in our headsets when enemy radars locked on to our plane.

The flare's red smoke streamed from the drone's left wingtip. Growl.

"Turn," I radioed. The drone rolled into a left turn while I continued straight ahead. Growl.

When the drone was about 45-degrees off my nose, I fired the missile. Growl.

Or rather, I tried to fire it. Nothing happened.

What the hell? I stared at my switches. The Sidewinder growled, loud as ever, or even louder, in my headset. My GIB was talking, but I couldn't understand him. Why did the missile not launch? The drone was still turning, now passing my 10-o'clock position and working its way to almost abeam my plane.

Damn my fuzzy brain! Then I saw the problem: The "Radar/Heat" toggle switch was in the "Radar" position. I was so used to flying with the Sparrow radar-guided missiles that I must have, out of habit, put the switch in that position which told the airplane I wanted to fire a radar missile, not a heat-seeker.

I quickly toggled it to "Heat." Growl.

The drone was almost at my nine o'clock position, now well outside the advertised launch parameters for the Sidewinder. There was no way the missile was going to make that turn and get to the drone. Still, there was a loud, steady growl in my headset.

Oh, what the hell!

I fired the missile. The growl stopped. The Sidewinder shot off the rail, straight ahead with white smoke curling out of its engine, accelerating toward almost three times the speed of sound at a rate no human could stand. Almost at the same instant that the missile launched, the flare on the tip of the drone's left wing went out.

That did it, I thought. That missile was headed for nowhere.

Wrong again.

The missile started a hard left-turn in the direction of the drone. But the flare was out, so the missile must have been guiding on the memory of what it had seen last, in the direction of the drone, but with no target in its system. With the flare-less drone now abeam my plane, there was no way the missile would make the turn or find the drone. The state-of-the-art then was that we needed to be in a 60-degree cone behind a heat-source for the missile to track and hit a target.

Wrong yet again.

The drone was about 90-degrees off my nose and without a flare when that Sidewinder hit it—a direct hit—and knocked that quarter-of-a-million-dollar drone out of the sky.

Oh, crap! I might be in trouble now.

Back on the ground for debriefing, no one was sore at me. Instead, the technicians from the missile's manufacturer were quite pleased that their Sidewinder had worked far better than the company had promised. I may have shot down a drone, but I dodged a bullet.

**

The next day I flew back across the South China Sea, crossed South Vietnam, Laos, and landed at Udorn. In a weird way, it was good to be back. I had not been grounded or court martialed for destroying a valuable drone. It was a relief to get back.

Until I went into the squadron.

While I was drinking and having fun at Clark Air Base, Wes and Fergie had been lost. They were missing in Laos, and had been for several days. No contact with them at all. A recce had flown over the crash site and reported seeing two parachutes near it, but there was no contact with the crew. There was no SAR for my friends.

Wes and Fergie officially had been listed as "Missing in Action."

I was stunned. I looked up to Wes as a leader, mentor, and friend. And Fergie. Anyone who couldn't get along with him did not deserve to be allowed out in public. They were the best of the best.

There was some information as to what happened, but I have no idea how accurate it was. Wes and Fergie were on a mission in northern Laos when they saw some suspicious object on the ground. They reported it to an airborne controller. That controller, so the account went, told them to attack it. Wes radioed that he did not think that was a good idea. The controller repeated the instruction to bomb it.

Wes and Fergie were never heard from again. No contact of any kind. They had no wingman, so there was no one to see a fireball. Two of the finest guys to come out of America were gone. Wes was about the most patient guy I had known at Udorn. I don't think anything ever rattled him. Fergie was married and should have had kids as he would have been a terrific dad. Two more friends gone, and to what purpose?

I thought that 1970 had started with a hangover; instead, it started with a heartache. Losing those two guys cast a pall over the squadron.

My last memory of them was in the van when Fergie backed into the ditch. I just had to open my big mouth.

I have regretted it for forty-five years.

The Phantom Today. This Triple Nickel F-4D belongs to the Collings Foundation of Stow, MA. The foundation supports "living history of our heritage." The Phantoms at Udorn never looked so good.
Author's archives

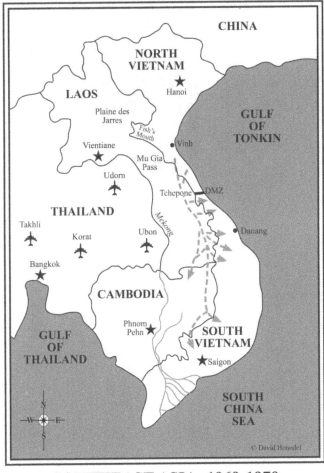

SOUTHEAST ASIA: 1969-1970

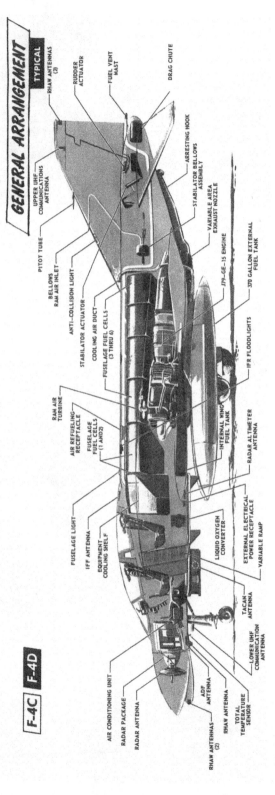

GENERAL ARRANGEMENT

TYPICAL

F-4C   F-4D

UPPER UHF
COMMUNICATIONS
ANTENNA

RHAW ANTENNAS
(2)

RUDDER
ACTUATOR

FUEL VENT
MAST

ARRESTING HOOK

STABILATOR BELLOWS
ASSEMBLY

VARIABLE AREA
EXHAUST NOZZLE

DRAG CHUTE

PITOT TUBE

BELLOWS
RAM AIR INLET

ANTI-COLLISION LIGHT

STABILATOR ACTUATOR

COOLING AIR DUCT

FUSELAGE FUEL CELLS
(3 THRU 6)

J79-GE-15 ENGINE

370 GALLON EXTERNAL
FUEL TANK

IFR FLOODLIGHTS

RAM AIR
TURBINE

AIR REFUELING
RECEPTACLE

FUSELAGE
FUEL CELLS
(1 AND 2)

INTERNAL WING
FUEL TANK

RADAR ALTIMETER
ANTENNA

FUSELAGE LIGHT

IFF ANTENNA

EQUIPMENT
COOLING SHELF

LIQUID OXYGEN
CONVERTER

EXTERNAL ELECTRICAL
POWER RECEPTACLE

VARIABLE RAMP

AIR CONDITIONING UNIT

RADAR PACKAGE

RADAR ANTENNA

RHAW ANTENNAS
(2)

TOTAL
TEMPERATURE
SENSOR

ADF
ANTENNA

RHAW ANTENNA

TACAN
ANTENNA

LOWER UHF
COMMUNICATION
ANTENNA

Inside the Phantom. The F-4 had every available space packed with fuel cells and other essential equipment. *TO 1F-4C-1, 15 December 1971. Author's archives*

"State of the art" describes the Phantom (in the 1960s). McDonnell Douglas's complex F-4 requires a tightly packed assembly of systems. The air-intercept radar dictates the size of the aircraft's black nose. Behind the two crewmembers are the six fuselage fuel cells, with one additional cell in each wing. No Phantom pilot ignored fuel, or at least I didn't. Chapters nine and ten discuss why. Two J-79-GE-15 engines (made by General Electric) each have four afterburner stages, selectable by the throttles. In "military power" (non-afterburning) each produces 10,700 pounds of thrust. With the throttles full forward to "maximum power," it increases to 17,000 pounds. Note that the engine exhaust tilts downward in the fuselage. This configuration enhances the plane's impressive supersonic flight characteristics.

The downward slope of the horizontal tail and the upward-bend of the wingtips are aerodynamic enhancements that help the Phantom perform well up to about 2.4 Mach, or nearly two and one-half times the speed of sound. The author's personal best was 2.25 Mach, or about 1,600 miles per hour. At that speed, the shock wave from the compressed air is visible in the cockpit as thick dark lines. The F-4's speed is possible because the plane has variable intake ramps that extend when the plane reaches about 1.7 Mach. When extended, the ramps narrow the air intake, preventing the shock wave from entering the engines. The aircraft's hydraulic flight controls need an artificial "feel" system that depends on ram air entering the bellows system. That system also creates problems as I describe in chapter one. Without artificial feel, a pilot could inadvertently rip the wings off the plane. Unlike earlier aircraft, the Phantom uses a liquid oxygen system which supports the crew for many hours. The author's longest flight, an ocean crossing, lasted more than 12 hours, but the oxygen system could have doubled that.

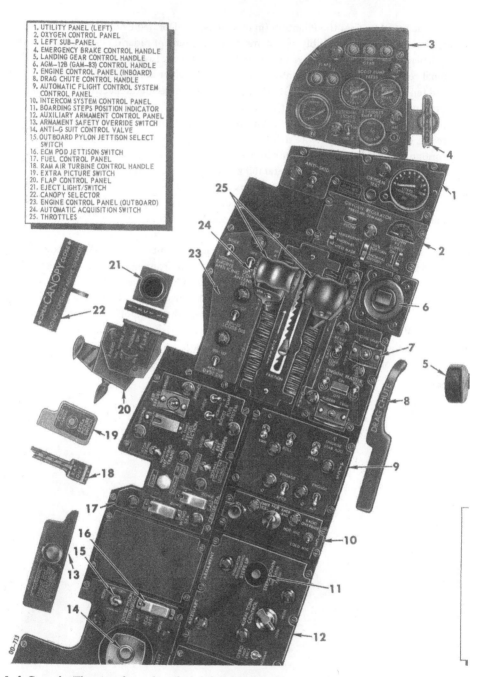

1. UTILITY PANEL (LEFT)
2. OXYGEN CONTROL PANEL
3. LEFT SUB-PANEL
4. EMERGENCY BRAKE CONTROL HANDLE
5. LANDING GEAR CONTROL HANDLE
6. AGM–12B (GAM–83) CONTROL HANDLE
7. ENGINE CONTROL PANEL (INBOARD)
8. DRAG CHUTE CONTROL HANDLE
9. AUTOMATIC FLIGHT CONTROL SYSTEM
   CONTROL PANEL
10. INTERCOM SYSTEM CONTROL PANEL
11. BOARDING STEPS POSITION INDICATOR
12. AUXILIARY ARMAMENT CONTROL PANEL
13. ARMAMENT SAFETY OVERRIDE SWITCH
14. ANTI–G SUIT CONTROL VALVE
15. OUTBOARD PYLON JETTISON SELECT
    SWITCH
16. ECM POD JETTISON SWITCH
17. FUEL CONTROL PANEL
18. RAM AIR TURBINE CONTROL HANDLE
19. EXTRA PICTURE SWITCH
20. FLAP CONTROL PANEL
21. EJECT LIGHT/SWITCH
22. CANOPY SELECTOR
23. ENGINE CONTROL PANEL (OUTBOARD)
24. AUTOMATIC ACQUISITION SWITCH
25. THROTTLES

Left Console. The view from the pilot's left side, all within arm's reach.
TO 1F-4C-1, 15 December 1971. Author's archives

Any fighter cockpit's left console should hold the most important controls since the pilot normally will have his right hand on the stick-grip and his left on the throttles (25). Sadly, the F-4 only partially met this ideal. Important items, such as the radio control, were on the right side, while the armament controls were on the front panel. The throttles have a friction control (the lever in the middle with the notched edge) so that the pilot does not always have to hold them, but in combat my hand rarely moved off them. Perhaps the most important item on this console—other than the throttles—is the fuel control panel (17). The three switches that have caps (covers) are jettison switches to release the external tanks. Some safety-minded person decided that the caps on the jettison switches should be safety-wired down. Before takeoff, I always broke any safety wire and raised the cover for the tanks loaded for that mission. In a tense situation I could just slap my hand back on the panel and get rid of the tanks. In the forward corner of the panel, shown next to the flap control (20), is the air refueling door control-switch (labeled "Extend" and "Retract"). I could reach that switch without ever looking, even in my sleep. That capability came in handy on the gunship escort mission described in chapter nine. On the left sub-panel (3) are the landing gear indicators (the three round windows at the very top). In a fighter, any landing gear that did not lock down was a major problem. Inboard from the console itself are two essential components: the landing gear control handle (5), and the drag chute control handle (8). While a drag chute might seem "nice to have," on wet runways it was essential.

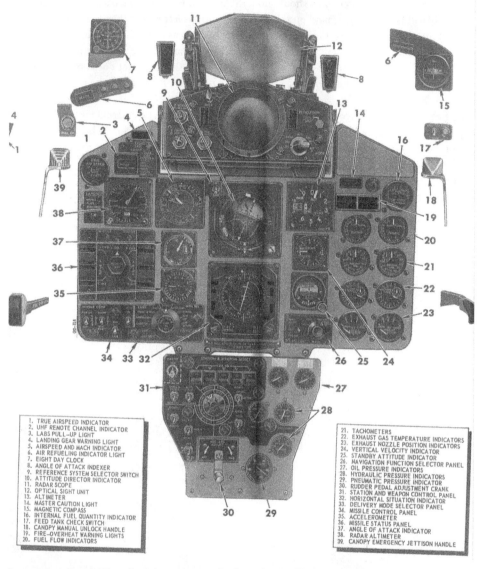

1. TRUE AIRSPEED INDICATOR
2. UHF REMOTE CHANNEL INDICATOR
3. LABS PULL-UP LIGHT
4. LANDING GEAR WARNING LIGHT
5. AIRSPEED AND MACH INDICATOR
6. AIR REFUELING INDICATOR LIGHT
7. EIGHT DAY CLOCK
8. ANGLE OF ATTACK INDEXER
9. REFERENCE SYSTEM SELECTOR SWITCH
10. ATTITUDE DIRECTOR INDICATOR
11. RADAR SCOPE
12. OPTICAL SIGHT UNIT
13. ALTIMETER
14. MASTER CAUTION LIGHT
15. MAGNETIC COMPASS
16. INTERNAL FUEL QUANTITY INDICATOR
17. FEED TANK CHECK SWITCH
18. CANOPY MANUAL UNLOCK HANDLE
19. FIRE-OVERHEAT WARNING LIGHTS
20. FUEL FLOW INDICATORS

21. TACHOMETERS
22. EXHAUST GAS TEMPERATURE INDICATORS
23. EXHAUST NOZZLE POSITION INDICATORS
24. VERTICAL VELOCITY INDICATOR
25. STANDBY ATTITUDE INDICATOR
26. NAVIGATION FUNCTION SELECTOR PANEL
27. OIL PRESSURE INDICATORS
28. HYDRAULIC PRESSURE INDICATORS
29. PNEUMATIC PRESSURE INDICATOR
30. RUDDER PEDAL ADJUSTMENT CRANK
31. STATION AND WEAPON CONTROL PANEL
32. HORIZONTAL SITUATION INDICATOR
33. DELIVERY MODE SELECTOR PANEL
34. MISSILE CONTROL PANEL
35. ACCELEROMETER
36. MISSILE STATUS PANEL
37. ANGLE OF ATTACK INDICATOR
38. RADAR ALTIMETER
39. CANOPY EMERGENCY JETTISON HANDLE

Instrument Panel. The pilot's instruments looking forward.
TO 1F-4C-1, 15 December 1971. Author's archives

The F-4 was the last of the "third generation" fighters. It did not have a computing bomb-sight, head's up display, or computer screens. It did, however, have more varied capabilities than any other airplane in its day. It could lug large amounts of virtually any ordnance then in existence. Delivering those weapons depended on using either the bomb-sight, projected through the combining glass of the optical sight unit (12), or returns displayed on the aircraft's air-intercept radar (11).

Conventional bombs were selected on the station and weapon control panel (31) that was placed just forward of the control stick. While not the best location, it was offset to the left, so the pilot did not have to take his hand off the stick. The five push buttons at the top of the panel selected the station; the other switches determined the sequencing, interval, and arming. I normally set up for my planned first pass when I crossed the Fence (Mekong River) except for the master arm switch in the upper left corner. I turned that on in the target area.

The missile control panel (34) could be a problem as I proved when I tried to shoot a heat-seeking missile with "radar" selected (see chapter eight for the embarrassing details). I've heard that I wasn't the only pilot to do that.

One critical instrument that I used more than any other was the fuel gauge (16). The F-4 guzzled gas faster than any plane I ever flew, especially in combat. As I proved during the SAR described in chapter ten, it was easy to focus on the target and forget fuel.

One last noteworthy switch that I—thankfully—never had to use was the round button on the delivery mode selector panel (33). This was the external stores jettison button, called the "panic button." It jettisoned everything that was hung on the aircraft.

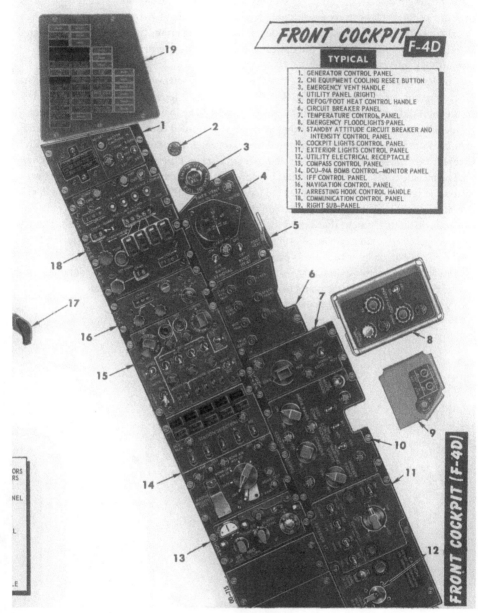

FRONT COCKPIT F-4D

TYPICAL

1. GENERATOR CONTROL PANEL
2. CNI EQUIPMENT COOLING RESET BUTTON
3. EMERGENCY VENT HANDLE
4. UTILITY PANEL (RIGHT)
5. DEFOG/FOOT HEAT CONTROL HANDLE
6. CIRCUIT BREAKER PANEL
7. TEMPERATURE CONTROL PANEL
8. EMERGENCY FLOODLIGHTS PANEL
9. STANDBY ATTITUDE CIRCUIT BREAKER AND
   INTENSITY CONTROL PANEL
10. COCKPIT LIGHTS CONTROL PANEL
11. EXTERIOR LIGHTS CONTROL PANEL
12. UTILITY ELECTRICAL RECEPTACLE
13. COMPASS CONTROL PANEL
14. DCU-94A BOMB CONTROL–MONITOR PANEL
15. IFF CONTROL PANEL
16. NAVIGATION CONTROL PANEL
17. ARRESTING HOOK CONTROL HANDLE
18. COMMUNICATION CONTROL PANEL
19. RIGHT SUB–PANEL

FRONT COCKPIT (F-4D)

Right Console. The view from the pilot's right side.
TO 1F-4C-1, 15 December 1971. Author's archives

The right console should, ideally, contain only "set and forget" items since the pilot flies with his right hand. At the top is the right sub-panel (19), commonly called the "tele-light panel." This panel contains a myriad of warning, caution, or information lights. Red indicates safety, yellow items require corrective action, green is informational. In the daylight, these lights could be easy to miss. Fortunately, all except the green informational lights cause the master caution light on the instrument panel to illuminate. Nights made things worse. Since I flew blacked-out in the target area, I taped most of the lights as discussed in chapter seven. Even so, some lights, such as the fuel level low light, were too important to tape over (see chapter nine).

Immediately behind the generator controls (1), is the communication control panel (18) for the UHF radio. The problem with this panel is that it is on the wrong side. Unless leading the flight, I rarely could take my hand off the control stick long enough to change radio frequencies. Clouds, formation flight, or other distractions could make a simple radio channel change dangerous. Fortunately, the back-seat crewman had duplicate controls.

While we did not use it in Vietnam, note the DCU-94A bomb control-monitor panel (14). These controls, in conjunction with a "consent" switch in the rear cockpit, arm nuclear weapons. These weapons could then be released using the method set on the delivery mode panel on the front instrument display.

The arresting hook handle (17), which lowers or raises the plane's large tail hook, is actually adjacent to the front instrument panel. I used it several times including Christmas Eve as discussed in chapter eight. That hook also kept me from sliding off the end of slippery runways on several occasions. Phantom flyers loved having the hook.

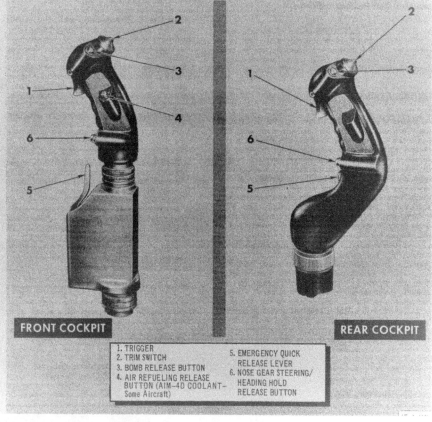

Control Sticks. The multi-function control sticks differ in the two cockpits.
TO 1F-4C-1, 15 December 1971. Author's archives

The business of fighters is fighting. I spent every combat mission with my right hand firmly around the stick and my left hand on the throttles, especially over a target. At the top of the stick is the trim switch (2) a four-way, spring-loaded button that sets the elevator and aileron trim positions (the rudder trim, rarely reset in flight, is controlled by a separate switch on the left console). Immediately to the left of the trim button is the bomb release button (3), commonly called the "pickle button." I can't attest to what other pilots did, but when I started a dive toward a target, my right thumb was always near the pickle button. Forward of those two is the trigger (1) used for firing the Gatling gun. I only carried a gun on several missions and never strafed. The F-4's 20-millimeter was no match for the heavier guns found in Laos.

On the left side of the stick grip is the dual-function air refueling release button (4). Normally, it releases the plane's connection to the KC-135's flying boom. However, when the aircraft is loaded with the AIM-4D heat seeking missile, it activates seeker-head cooling.

At the base of the stick is the nose gear steering/heading hold button (6). When depressed on the ground, the button allows the pilot to steer the nose wheel with the rudder pedals. The heading hold function, a feature of the auto-pilot system, is rarely used. At the bottom is the emergency quick release lever (5), also called the "paddle switch." When depressed, it releases the aircraft's stability augmentation system.

The rear seat control stick, to the chagrin of most F-4 crewmembers, has only partial functions. The odd curve of the stick prevents it from hitting the rear seat's radar display.

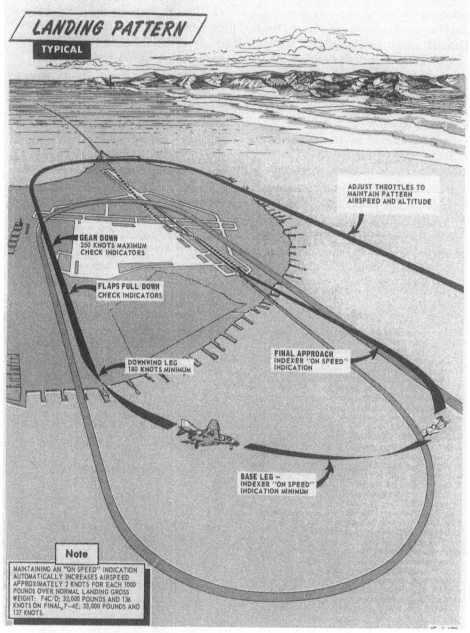

F-4 Landing Pattern. The overhead traffic pattern, devised many decades before the Vietnam War, is a fast and efficient procedure to get planes on the ground.
TO 1F-4C-1, 15 December 1971. Author's archives

EJECTION PROCEDURES

IF TIME AND CONDITIONS PERMIT

- ALERT OTHER CREWMEMBER
- LOCK SHOULDER HARNESS
- TIGHTEN LAP BELT
- LOWER HELMET VISOR
- ADJUST SITTING HEIGHT AS NECESSARY

BEFORE EJECTION SEQUENCE

SIT ERECT, BUTTOCKS BACK, SHOULDERS AGAINST PARACHUTE PACK, HEAD ERECT, SPINE STRAIGHT, LEGS EXTENDED AND THIGHS ON SEAT CUSHION. DURING A SEQUENCED EJECTION, THE CREWMEMBER NOT INITIATING EJECTION SHOULD FIRMLY GRASP THE LOWER HANDLE WITH BOTH HANDS, AS PRESCRIBED BELOW, WITHOUT PULLING.

1. EJECTION HANDLE-PULL •

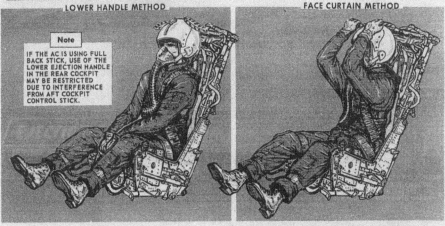

LOWER HANDLE METHOD

Note

IF THE AC IS USING FULL BACK STICK, USE OF THE LOWER EJECTION HANDLE IN THE REAR COCKPIT MAY BE RESTRICTED DUE TO INTERFERENCE FROM AFT COCKPIT CONTROL STICK.

GRASP THE LOWER EJECTION HANDLE, USING A TWO HANDED GRIP WITH THE THUMB AND AT LEAST TWO FINGERS OF EACH HAND. PULL UP ON LOWER HANDLE UNTIL STOP IS ENCOUNTERED. WHEN CANOPY JETTISONS, CONTINUE PULLING UP ON LOWER EJECTION HANDLE UNTIL FULL TRAVEL IS REACHED.

FACE CURTAIN METHOD

REACH OVERHEAD WITH PALMS AFT KEEPING ELBOWS SHOULDER WIDTH APART. GRASP FACE CURTAIN HANDLE. PULL FORWARD AND DOWN UNTIL STOP IS REACHED. WHEN CANOPY JETTISONS, CONTINUE PULLING FACE CURTAIN UNTIL FULL TRAVEL IS REACHED.

When You Can't Land. The excellent Martin-Baker ejection seat has two methods of activation. *TO 1F-4C-1, 15 December 1971. Author's archives*

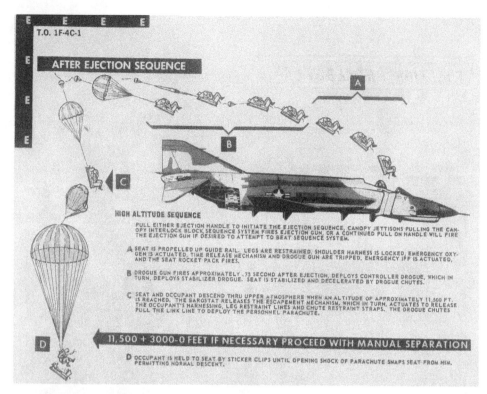

Ejection Sequence. While the system was complex, it worked.
TO 1F-4C-1, 15 December 1971. Author's archives

Every mission ends somehow. There are three ways: land, eject, or join the plane in a smoking hole. The first is preferred. The normal F-4 landing method is the fighter pilot's standard "overhead" pattern: fly an "initial" approach above the runway, "break" with a steep turn to downwind, configure for landing, turn a descending base leg, align with the runway then land. Simple, quick, effective—but forbidden at Udorn. Some authority decreed that all landings would be from straight-in approaches. Harder to perform, less familiar to pilots, longer time required—but mandatory. I don't know why.

If the pilot cannot make it to a runway, the best alternative is to ride the Martin-Baker ejection seat. In the Vietnam era, this seat is the best. Unlike earlier ejection seats, it is fully automatic. The pilot only need pull one of two ejection handles: the face curtain above his head, or the lower handle—called a "D ring"—between his legs. Once he pulls either, Martin-Baker takes over. The Phantom's seats are sequenced so that the rear seat goes first no matter who initiates the ejection. This sequence—rear canopy, rear seat, front canopy, front seat—ensures that the seats do not collide. Each seat has a rocket motor to ensure it clears the plane's tail. Once out, all functions are automatic until the pilot dangles under his parachute. Unfortunately, as Herb experienced in chapter 11, the helpless aviator sometimes became a target for anti-aircraft guns. While today's ACES (Advanced Concept Ejection System) seats are superior to the F-4's, they evolved from Martin-Baker concepts, well tested by Phantom crews.

The third method of ending the flight—joining the plane in a smoking hole in the earth—happened far too many times. I believe that it happened to my friend Andy (chapter 15).

Before the War: Tucson, 1969. The author next to a 20-millimeter Gatling gun. Prior to the war, it seemed like a wonderful weapon. By the standards of the A-10's 30-millimeter, it is a pea-shooter. *Author's archives*

Udorn Main Gate. Udorn was a Thai Air Force Base although in 1969 the Americans far outnumbered the Thais. Both flags flew over it, and, as seen here, both militaries guard it. *Courtesy of Tony Marshall*

Tailor Shops in Udon Thani. An early stop for all flyers was the squadron's preferred off-base tailor shop. Party suits, uniforms, and all manner of civilian attire were available, custom tailored, and reasonably priced.
Courtesy of Tony Marshall

Downtown Udon Thani. There were many excellent restaurants in the city, but crossing the street, even in the dry season, could be a challenge. The Thais were exceptionally friendly, so Americans always felt welcome.
Courtesy of Tony Marshall

Tony with Laser Bomb. Tony Marshall, who provided many pictures for this book, poses with a laser guided bomb. Tony flew 265 ½ missions. He was shot down over North Vietnam and finished his tour as a prisoner of war.
Courtesy of Tony Marshall

Waiting for Combat. Captain Vic Tucker, who also provided many pictures, poses next to a partially loaded Phantom. The inboard stations are loaded but the centerline rack is empty. Note the starting-air hose under the plane.
Courtesy of Vic Tucker

F-4s above Monsoon Clouds. The weather over Laos and Vietnam could be a challenge. While fighters easily flew above the clouds, getting down through them over enemy territory was another matter. The clouds also reduced the time available to react to anti-aircraft weapons.
Courtesy of Vic Tucker

F-4 with A-1 Skyraiders. This Phantom is taxiing past two heavily armed Skyraiders. The ancient A-1 proved itself to be a versatile and deadly weapon, and invaluable as an escort for the rescue helicopters.
Courtesy of Vic Tucker

F-4 Refueling Behind KC-135. The under-powered, unarmed KC-135 fueled the air war. The view here is from the boom operator's compart-ment. The war as we fought it would not have been possible without air refueling. *Courtesy of Vic Tucker*

Phantoms, Thuds, and Tanker. F-4Ds and F-105s follow a tanker on the way to war. This is likely an "Iron Hand" mission to destroy SAM sites. The F-105s find the missile sites, and the F-4s destroy them.
Courtesy of Tony Marshall

OV-10 FAC. The Rockwell OV-10 Bronco served as a forward air control aircraft, often with the call-sign "Nail." The Bronco carried five radios and had excellent endurance, almost unrestricted visibility from the cockpit, and twin-engine reliability. It usually was armed with smoke rockets but could carry other ordnance. *Courtesy Vic Tucker*

Nail OV-10 in Clouds. These planes were flying over Laos in the rainy season. Note that there are two crewmen in the OV-10, a pilot, and a rear seater who was frequently a navigator. Also, note the rocket pod on the OV-10, next to the centerline fuel tank. The closeup view of a rocket's nose on the lead aircraft indicates that the pod is wing-mounted, hence the plane was likely an O-2. *Courtesy of Vic Tucker*

AIM-9E Missile. The F-4 carried the Sidewinder heat-seeking missile along with the radar guided AIM-7E Sparrow. Both performed well below expectations although the AIM-9E was slightly better. The much-improved Sidewinder is still in service today as the AIM-9X. *Courtesy of Vic Tucker*

Air-to-Air with Falcon Missiles. This Phantom is equipped for aerial combat. It has three AIM-7E missiles in the fuselage wells, two AIM-4 Falcons in the inboard stations, and a 20-millimeter Gatling gun pod on the centerline. *Courtesy of Tony Marshall*

Wild Weasel. An F-105 refueling with a KC-135. The fighter's mission was to hunt down and destroy enemy surface-to-air missile sites, a deadly endeavor. It is probably akin to facing a nearby rattlesnake head-on.
Courtesy of Tony Marshall

HARM Passing Under Phantom. The F-4 was fast, but missiles were much faster. Here, a HARM anti-radar missile passes under a Phantom on its way to an enemy SAM site. The Phantom pilot likely followed up the missile attack with his 500-pound bombs.
Courtesy of Tony Marshall

Bomb Drop Through Clouds. Southeast Asian weather could be a problem. Fortunately, the Phantom had several alternatives for weapons delivery that did not depend on clear skies. Here, an F-4 releases a load of 500-pound Mk-82 bombs.
Courtesy of Tony Marshall

Headed North. Well-armed Phantoms accompany two F-105 Wild Weasel aircraft and a KC-135. Note the 13 TFS insignia on the air-intake of the closest plane, number 531.
Courtesy of Tony Marshall

Pre-Strike Refueling. An F-4E (far side), joined with other strike aircraft following a KC-135. There are many air-refueling photos because the author loved to see those flying gas stations, even if at the very last second as in chapter nine.
Courtesy of Tony Marshall

Udorn O Club. Access to an air-conditioned and well-stocked Officers Club was often stated as a reason to join the Air Force versus the other services. Udorn's club was a great example. Most missions started and, if fortunate, ended at the club.
Courtesy of Tony Marshall

The Liquor Store. The Officers Club was not the only well-stocked building on base. To keep morale up, our government made certain that all its troops could imbibe when off duty. It helped. *Courtesy of Tony Marshall*

Panther Squadron HQ. The 13 TFS sat on one side of the 432 TRW headquarters building, with the 555 TFS on the opposite side. During the monsoon season, the rain was a regular visitor. Note the squadron flag at half-staff. *Courtesy of Tony Marshall*

The Panther Pack Home. As described in chapter two, the squadron hooches were comfortable and well maintained. This photo shows the 13 TFS hooch on the right and the 14 TRS (recce) on the left. Note the house-girls in the center hooch porch.
Courtesy of Tony Marshall

Laundry Time at the Nickel Hooches. The hooch girls kept the rooms orderly, boots shined, and laundry clean, at least when fresh water was available. Note the wooden walkway, handy for avoiding an occasional passing cobra.
Courtesy of Tony Marshall

12.7 mm Machine Gun. Vic Tucker poses with an adversary. This Soviet weapon was encountered on almost every mission, either the 12.7 or 14.5 mm version. This rugged, rapid-firing gun could bring down an aircraft at ranges up to a mile or so.
Courtesy of Vic Tucker

Learning the Nemesis. The Soviet 37-millimeter anti-aircraft gun was every pilot's nemesis. A mobile and reliable weapon from World War II, it destroyed more American aircraft than any other. As described in chapter 12, it was simple to operate.
Courtesy of Tony Marshall

The Downed Pilot's Salvation. Sometimes the guns won the fights. When they did, HH-53s, flown by heroes and called the Jolly Green Giants, risked their lives to pull the pilots from the jungle.
Courtesy of Tony Marshall

A Happy Man. This flyer was pulled from the hostile jungle by a Jolly Green Giant crew flying the HH-53 seen in the background. See Earl Tilford's excellent history cited in the Suggested Readings for the story of air rescue in Vietnam.
Courtesy of Tony Marshall

Newly Remodeled Radio Station. Udorn was a large installation with many of the amenities of a non-wartime base. In the spring of 1970, the base radio and TV station was remodeled and enhanced. *Courtesy of National Archives*

Radio Station After Crash. On April 10, 1970, a battle-damaged RF-4C crashed into the base. The crew ejected at the last second, but the plane destroyed several buildings, including the radio station. Nine men inside died.
Courtesy of National Archives

Radio Station Building Remains. The remodeled radio and television station was destroyed. The nine men working inside did not receive combat pay because Thailand was not considered part of the Vietnam War. Still, they died.
Courtesy of National Archives

RF-4C Remains. There was little left of the Phantom after the crash. The author's memory is that the plane had about 6,000 pounds of fuel on board. While the plane struck the radio station, it missed the crowded base theater.
Courtesy of National Archives

RF-4C Crash Damage. The fire from the crash devastated the area around the impact point. Base fire-rescue crews and many volunteers fought the ensuing fire for hours. Many were injured. Chapter 11 has more on the crash.
Courtesy of National Archives

Recce Chase Mission Pre-launch. The author's final mission was escorting an RF-4C reconnaissance aircraft (center) over North Vietnam. Staying with the sleek-nosed recce was always a problem. Note the heavy ordnance, probably cluster bomb canisters, on the fighters' inboard stations.
Courtesy of Tony Marshall

Recce Escort. The RF-4C has OZ on its tail from the 14 TRS. The fighter's OY denotes a Triple Nickel bird. The author's final mission, described in chapter 14, was in the monsoon season, much cloudier than this photo.
Courtesy of Tony Marshall

Udorn Approach End. There are few more welcoming scenes than the view of the airfield at the end of a combat mission. But the best picture of all is the runway at the end of the last mission, as described in chapter 14.
Courtesy of Tony Marshall

Two Warriors Return. The author (left) and Vic Tucker smiling after a combat mission. Note the electronic countermeasures (ECM) pod under the left engine air intake. Vic ended the war with 1,018 combat hours in five different airplanes.
Courtesy of Vic Tucker

Nickels in Party Suits. Going-away parties were special events. Flyers donned their party suits and joined in the celebration. Given their orderly appearance, these two appear to be heading to the party, not returning to the hooch.
Courtesy of Tony Marshall

Pilots and Indian Tailor. Obviously, the "Triple Nickel tailor" (foreground) had divided loyalties. Here he is shown attending a function wearing a 13 TFS Panther Pack insignia. At least he has the "Yankee Air Pirate" insignia on his left pocket.
Courtesy of Tony Marshall

Going-Away Party. Every flyer in the Vietnam War dreamed of having a going-away party, and a peaceful trip back to "the world." Sadly, Tony Marshall, who took this photo, missed his own going-away party because he was a prisoner in Hanoi.
Courtesy of Tony Marshall

After the War— New Mexico, 1971. With his war seemingly over, the author enjoyed flying in beautiful New Mexico. This photo was taken prior to a deployment to Germany. Note the center-line fuel tank and the beat-up "travel pod" (an empty napalm canister) on the inboard station. *Author's archives*

In the OV-10 in Germany. Years after the war, the author flew as a forward air controller in the OV-10 Bronco in Germany. Here, he shakes hands with Steve Sollenberger, a high-school friend and forward air controller in Vietnam, who was stationed nearby. *Courtesy of Steve Sollenberger*

A-10 Days—Indiana, 1984. The author spent six years flying the A-10 Thunderbolt II, which is still in service today. The A-10's 30-millimeter Gatling gun would have changed many battles if the plane had been available in the Vietnam War. *Author's archives*

Career End—Hawaii, 1987. The author finished his Air Force career flying the Lockheed T-33, the same airplane he flew in pilot training. At graduation in 1966, the guest speaker said that the "T-Bird," as it was called, would retire in months. The author and the T-33 retired the same day, 21 years later. *Author's archives*

The Old Warrior Still Flies. The Collings Foundation F-4D, with bright Triple Nickel markings, launches with full afterburner power (notice, no smoke). It carries a 600-gallon centerline fuel tank and two "travel pods." Thank you, Collings Foundation, for keeping this plane alive. Thank you.
Author's archives

Chapter 9

God Said No

ONE THING I SHOULD have expected about night combat missions was they don't always go as expected. I was scheduled to lead a two-ship formation to protect a B-52 strike in Laos. Three of the giant, eight-engine bombers were going to bomb the Trail south of Mu Gia Pass, on the Laotian side of the border from North Vietnam. Each bomber could carry 108—yes, 108—of the same 500-pound bombs that we carried on the F-4. Each bomber would obliterate an area about one-half mile wide by three miles long. Multiply that by three for the night's attack.

My flight's assignment was BARCAP (Barrier Combat Air Patrol), meaning we were to screen the bombers and prevent any interference by enemy MiG fighters. For us, this mission meant no bombs. We would carry air-to-air ordnance only. We would be armed with four AIM-7E radar-guided Sparrow missiles, as usual mounted snugly against the fuselage of the Phantom. We would have two AIM-9E heat-seeking Sidewinder missiles on each inboard station. Since I had recently fired the Sidewinder, albeit at a drone, I felt quite comfortable with it. A similar day mission would have had the 20-millimeter Gatling gun-pod mounted on the centerline station, but, as this was night, we carried a massive 600-gallon external tank along with the two 370-gallon tanks on the outboard stations. Fuel should not be a problem.

My flight was to orbit about 40-miles north of the bombers' target area. I suppose the orbit was positioned so that we could be quickly vectored to intercept any MiGs that might try to get to the B-52s. At that time, North Vietnam would have bragged to the world if they shot down one of our bombers, especially in Laos. Our flight briefing was much longer than normal. We covered everything we could think of concerning air intercepts, radar-guided missile attacks, converting a radar intercept into a stern approach for attack with the heat-seeking missiles, and even what we thought a night visual fight with a MiG would be like, however unlikely that was.

We launched as scheduled, refueled, and went to our orbit position. For this mission, I had some instrument lights on as well as my radar scope, unlike almost all my other night missions. We set up our orbit, which was close to the border of North Vietnam. A radar controller made sure that we did not stray from the assigned orbit. I assume that he also searched for any aircraft approaching from enemy territory.

We had one well-stressed requirement: Do not, under any circumstances, lock on to the bombers with our radars. I guess that an air-intercept radar lock-on would have caused the bombers' Electronic Warfare Officers to shit their pants. As I remember, we even turned our radars to "standby" when our planes pointed toward the bombers.

Our GIBs diligently searched the sky with our radars when we faced enemy territory and especially when we were pointed toward the North Vietnamese port city of Vinh, the closest MiG airfield, the same field that had launched the MiG Ort and I pursued a few months earlier. Our radar-guided missiles were tuned and armed, the heat-seekers in standby. It was all business in our cockpits. We searched, watched, and waited.

Nothing happened.

After thirty minutes, a controller told us to return to base. The mission was over. The bombers had come and gone. We did not see the explosions; we did not see any MiGs. We went to an orbit, flew in a race-track pattern for 30 minutes, and went home. For all the pre-flight excitement, it was a dud. I expected combat; I got bored. It was, however, one more mission off the tour—and no anti-aircraft fire.

***

The night flying schedule meant I went to my office at strange times, usually afternoons. One day, as I was getting ready for work, there was some commotion on the runway. From the hooch, I figured it was some emergency recovery and nothing more. I did not think much about it since we had emergency landings on an almost daily basis. At Udorn, emergencies seemed routine.

I hopped on the Blue Bird shuttle that stopped in front of the O Club, wound through the administrative area, went around the end of the runway, then down the long flight-line to wing headquarters.

Before the bus reached the end of the runway, I saw aircraft wreckage. To a pilot, it was sickening to say the least. It was an F-105, or what had once been an F-105F. This was the two-seat version of the Thunder Chief, better known among those of us who did not fly it as the "Thud." The F-105 was a sleek, single-engine fighter designed in the 1950s for very high speed low-level nuclear bombing. Its mid-mounted swept wings accented the bird's sharp nose. It looked fast and, in fact, it was, especially at low altitude. This was the bird that had carried the brunt of the bombing during Operation Rolling Thunder, the air battle over North Vietnam.

The wreckage of this once sleek bird was covered with light-gray fire suppression foam, which had dried in the sun. The plane was not on the runway, the overrun, or even the grass at the end of the overrun; it rested on the far edge of the "klong," the deep, wide drainage ditch that paralleled the runway on one side and lapped both ends. It was obvious that the F-105 had slid off the runway, skipped almost—almost—across the ditch, and come to rest on the far side. What made the sight sickening was that only the rear cockpit was still on the plane. It was obvious that the nose of the plane had hit the far side of the ditch a few feet below the lip and broken between the two cockpits. The front cockpit, and its occupant, must have gone under the wreckage.

I got the story, bad as it was, when I arrived at the office.

The F-105 had been bombing a target when it got hit, probably by 37-millimeter rounds. The hits knocked out some of the plane's hydraulic systems, but not all of them. The crew nursed the bird back to Udorn, which they deemed the best emergency field due to our crash and rescue capabilities. Without all its hydraulics, the 105 had to make a no-flap landing, which required a much higher approach speed than normal for that big swept-wing fighter.

The pilot, using a final approach speed of about 220-knots, got the bird onto the runway. He knew the landing was above the limiting speed for his drag-chute—200-knots—so he did not deploy it. He did, however, lower his tail-hook.

That was a fatal mistake.

The F-105 tail-hook was a last-ditch device for stopping the plane if it ran off the departure end of the runway, not before. It was nowhere near as massive and strong as the hydraulically operated tail-hook on the F-4, hence could not be used for approach-end engagements. He must have forgotten that he was landing at an F-4 base, where the barriers, as I proved on Christmas Eve, would stop a 200-knot bird in a hurry. The problem was that the F-105's hook was simply not made for that speed.

The Thud's hook grabbed the mid-field barrier, which slowed the plane briefly, then the hook snapped completely off the plane. After the hook sheared off the plane, the crew rode in a 150-knot tricycle with no brakes due to the hydraulic-system failure. The pilot saw the end of the runway race toward him, then realized they would hit the ditch. I didn't know why the crew did not eject. The F-4's Martin-Baker ejection-seats would have given them a fighting chance. I guessed the Thud's ejection-seats were not as good as ours.

The nose dropped as the plane skidded from the flat ground beyond the overrun into the air above the ditch. It would be like a fast automobile that encountered a gulley; the front end would fall as the auto went into the air. Same here. Gravity took over, the nose dug into the far side of the ditch and the plane snapped. The pilot was crushed beneath his plane. The other crewman was rescued by our firefighters.

According to the survivor, the pilot's last words were, "Oh, Jesus!" I guess it was another form of the Golden BB. If he had been at his home field, or if he had not lowered the hook until after the mid-field barrier, he would have survived. It was more proof that sometimes, despite all that a pilot did to survive, the BB prevailed.

For reasons that I never understood, the wreckage stayed where it was for several days. Every trip on the Blue Bird had to pass it. It was depressing. Like every other pilot, I was superstitious about my flying. Was this an omen?

***

The next day, I was back on the flying schedule for more night combat. I had been flying night missions for several months, so I considered myself a veteran. One benefit of flying nights regularly is that pilots tend to get good at it. What was first a strange and threatening environment had become familiar and even friendly.

Anti-aircraft fire was easy to see at night while our airplanes were not. An ego-heavy, macho fighter-pilot—which still described me most of the time—could use the night environment to his advantage. All that was necessary was to avoid vertigo and not fly into the ground. Or at least that's what I believed. Rick's Golden BB was a distant memory. I believed that a pilot's fate was in his own hands. Good pilots flew into the face of danger and survived. Bad ones got shot down. I controlled my fate.

Of all the various night-missions we flew in the F-4, the one that stood out most was gunship escort. The AC-130 "Spectre" gunships were based at Ubon Royal Thai Air Force base, southeast of Udorn. The Spectre carried four 20-millimeter Gatling guns, each of which could fire 6,000 rounds per minute. While the F-4 could carry a Gatling gun, it had only a few hundred rounds of ammunition. The AC-130 carried many times that amount, so they literally could shoot for hours. One Spectre, called the "Surprise Package," had two of its Gatling guns replaced with two 40-millimeter rapid-fire cannons.[1] (They later added 105-millimeter howitzers, if you can believe that.)

The gunships had lots of what were then state-of-the-art detection devices, including starlight scopes, infra-red detectors, engine ignition detectors, fancy radar, and probably more gadgets, none of which we had in the F-4. To add to that equipment, the Air Force had air-dropped or manually inserted thousands of sensors into the Laotian jungle. These devices looked like small trees when they stuck in the earth or hung from the jungle canopy, but each carried a transmitter that sent information to orbiting C-47s. The detectors picked up movement, voices, body heat, and who-knows what else. All that information was available to the Spectres, who used it to locate truck parks, troop rest areas, fuel storage sites, ammo dumps, and other assorted targets.

The blacked-out AC-130s orbited in the Laotian darkness, using the outside intelligence sources and on-board detection devices to locate, then destroy, the various targets. Naturally, the North Vietnamese hated the Spectres, and employed massive effort to defeat or at least negate them. The enemy used extensive camouflage, decoys, and, of course, lots of anti-aircraft guns. Since the main part of the Ho Chi Minh Trail from North to South Vietnam went through a relatively small part of the Laotian panhandle, the North Vietnamese could concentrate their anti-aircraft guns, hence defend multiple points with dense, lethal fire. As the escorts, our job was to discourage the guns from shooting at the gunships, or at least stop them from shooting too much. The gunships were the enemy's primary targets, so we fighters did not receive much anti-aircraft fire.

On this night, I was one of a three-ship formation tasked to escort an AC-130 that would be working along the roads that ran near that nasty little Laotian town named Tchepone. To put things in perspective, our Intelligence folks estimated that there were more than 70,000 North Vietnamese in this area, whose center was once a town, but now was an expanse of bomb craters, blown-down trees, and rusting trucks destroyed in earlier bombing. There was a fair amount of aircraft wreckage, too. No one knew how many anti-aircraft guns were in that area, but we knew there were a bunch of them.

Being sent to Tchepone made even veteran F-4 pilots edgy. Fortunately, I was going at night.

The gunship's fighter escort was a formation in name only. The plan was for one F-4 to orbit above, and slightly behind the Spectre, one to refuel with a KC-135 tanker, and the third to transit to the gunship or to the tanker as the situation dictated. The critical part, as one might expect, was the orbit with the gunship. Each session with the gunship lasted about 20 minutes, depending on fuel and the extent of the action.

We usually cycled through this rotation three times on a typical mission. About the only time our flight was together was when we played darts in the squadron lounge before take-off. Once we left the squadron building, each F-4 launched at about 20-minute intervals. Other than at each change-over at the gunship's orbit, we rarely spoke to each other, and we never saw the other flight members until we got to the bar.

My navigator was a tall, lanky, first lieutenant, an experienced back-seater who was called "The Mayor" based upon his exploits in Udon Thani. As usual, we got to the bird well before our take-off time to take care of the extensive preparations for a night mission. I did a cursory walk-around the bird, then hopped in for my ritual of putting dark tape on every warning light in the cockpit, except two: The Missile Launch light on my Radar Homing and Warning system, and the Fuel Level Low light. I clipped my map light, an adjustable-intensity red light about half the size of a D-cell flashlight, to the glare shield over my instrument panel. The light pointed at my attitude-indicator, the globe-like instrument that told me which way was up. I was quite familiar with vertigo, the awful sensation of having no idea what position your body was in. Vertigo gets to all pilots at one time or another, and even though I was much more experienced at night flying, I was no exception as I had proved early in my night combat missions. While I kept my instrument lights on dim until after takeoff, I turned all of them off for most of the rest of the mission.

The Mayor did the pre-flight of the ordnance, three 500-pound bombs with fuse-extenders mounted on each inboard station, and five of the wide-nosed 800-pound cluster bomb canisters on the centerline station. Both ordnances had one purpose—to kill people. The goal, of course, was to convince the anti-aircraft gunners to stay in their bunkers, and stay off the guns. As normal, we carried two AIM-7E Sparrow air-to-air missiles and two 370-gallon external fuel tanks.

Things went smoothly for most of the mission. We crossed the Fence into the Laotian panhandle, joined with a KC-135 tanker, refueled, and then joined with the gunship. We cycled through our orbit with the Spectre twice, and dropped some bombs a few times on single anti-aircraft guns. Though long, the mission was relatively quiet.

After our third air-refueling, we went back to the gunship for our final orbit. It was a typical late dry-season night. No stars or moon because of the high clouds. Visibility was poor, due both to the darkness, and the haze and smoke hanging in the Laotian air. It was well after midnight and the strain simply from flying in the black night grew on me.

The gunship searched for targets over part of the Ho Chi Minh Trail road network that occasionally was not concealed by the jungle canopy. When we got back to re-join with him, we had difficulty locating him in the haze and darkness. The gunships flew in left turns, called "pylon turns" to keep their guns pointed at one spot on the ground. The AC-130 had a dim cross of lights, one leg running across the top of the wings, the other running down the length of the fuselage on top. Their pilots kept the cross of lights extremely dim to avoid detection from the ground. The only other lights anyone ever saw were the muzzle-flashes when the Gatling guns fired, followed by a long fire-hose of tracers heading for an unfortunate target. When the fire-hose hit the ground, there were hundreds of bright flashes as the rounds exploded on impact, frequently followed by secondary explosions of trucks or cargo that got hit. Overall, it was a sight that one would never forget, whether from the air, or, I presume, from the ground.

I finally got sight of the gunship and settled into an orbit, several thousand feet above and about 30-degrees behind the circular pattern he flew. Due to the poor visibility, and maybe because it was a routine mission and I was an old-hand at them, I kept the cross of his lights in one spot, from about 10- to 11-o'clock and low as seen from my blacked-out cockpit. In other words, I flew a nice, steady, predictable formation on the AC-130.

The Mayor, in the rear cockpit, could not see the Spectre since he kept his flight-instrument lights on, as well as his radar screen. Spatial disorientation probably had killed many F-4 crews, so he really had no choice but to stay lit-up. For the mission, I looked outside; for our survival, he looked inside.

We had only flown a couple of circles when a single 37-millimeter anti-aircraft gun fired one seven-round clip into the blackness, well behind the gunship. The bright reddish-yellow tracers arced up between the gunship and my F-4, went dark, then seconds later exploded in the night. Seven bright flashes—interesting to watch, when they did not threaten me.

One lousy gun; one lousy clip. But I was probably bored. I called the gunship to alert him that I was going to attack the gun-site, or at least the general area where I thought it was, with a couple of canisters of cluster bombs. If I could get within a thousand feet of where the gun was, maybe I could put a couple of those bomblets inside the gun's protective pit. That would teach them not to mess with us.

I pulled up to the apex of my attack, rolled over and pulled the nose down into a 30-degree dive, put my very dim bomb-sight, the "pipper," about where I thought the gun-site might be, and, when The Mayor called "pickle," I pushed the red button on the top of the stick which released the two cluster bombs. With the bird doing 500 knots, I started my pull-off with a slight left bank to get back into sync with the gunship and to watch the hundreds of sparkles from the exploding cluster bomblets.

That's when the proverbial "shit hit the fan."

When I looked out the left side of the canopy to find the gunship, I saw bright red tracers almost merged with my wing tip and crossing above my canopy, so close they sparkled. Not a few rounds, lots of them. I probably mumbled "Oh shit!" and when I turned my head away from the rounds, I could see my instruments from the red glow of the tracers. I reversed my turn to the right to get away from the threat when I realized that the tracers were coming from both sides. I was centered in a barrage of anti-aircraft fire. Every gun in the area blazed away at me. Tracers passed close on both sides of the Phantom and bright flashes of airbursts appeared above it.

Without thinking, I lit the after-burners. Wes had warned me about this before I ever started flying nights. With four sets of high-pressure nozzles behind each engine pumping fuel at 3,000-pounds-per-square-inch into the after sections of both engines, the result at night was two giant cones of bright blue light, like two huge Bunsen burners in the sky. It was an invitation for every gun in all Southern Laos to shoot—at me.

They did.

Thank God for General Electric, because the two after-burning J-79 engines pushed the F-4 skyward and away from the large and rapidly expanding mass of tracers, now arcing from every direction and to every direction. Rounds were bursting above, next to, and, I assume, below my plane. For reference, go to a Fourth of July firework display and picture yourself in the air at the center of all the action. I have never looked at fireworks without thinking of that night, ever.

I was pretty-well "maxed out" from the action, but as fate would have it, it wasn't over.

As I cleared the anti-aircraft danger zone, my Radar Homing and Warning System lit up. Both the Activity and Launch lights came on bright, and the loud rattlesnake sound in my headset warned of a surface-to-air missile launch. Another "Oh shit" moment. Without looking for the missile, I stupidly rolled the aircraft upside-down and pulled, hard, toward the unseen earth, how far below I did not know.

The ground kills just as well as—or better than—anti-aircraft guns. "Oops" number three.

The half-assed "SAM break" maneuver that I flew was designed to defeat a surface-to-air missile, but it worked best if the pilot actually saw the missile and performed the maneuver at the proper time. I did not see the missile, and, in fact, there probably never was a missile. In calmer times, and later in Cold War West Germany, I experienced situations when the Soviet surface-to-air missile radar operators would turn on the tracking and guidance radars without ever launching a missile. They knew that our detection systems in those days could only detect the radar, not the actual missile.

Those events took far longer to read than to happen in real-time that night. Between the glow of the tracers, the bright air-bursts in the black sky, the red glow from the RHAW gear's warning lights, the loud rattlesnake sound in my headset, and the high G-forces from my maneuvers, it was chaos—in my cockpit and in my once-macho fighter pilot's mind.

I came to my senses, rolled the F-4 upright, climbed, and tried to get a grip on myself. The world seemed limited to heavy breathing, my GIB's yelling, and sweat in my eyes and in my oxygen mask. I turned the knob on my map-light to check my attitude indicator, but all I could see was the ball aimlessly rolling around in its case. I asked The Mayor for help, but he said that the Inertial Navigation System, which ran both the navigation system and the primary flight instruments, had "tumbled." The gyros had lost their way. I asked him where we were, and got the same reply my own instruments had given me—he had no idea.

I keyed the radio's mike switch to call the gunship for help, but got no feedback. Damn! The radio—there was only one in the F-4—was dead. Another "Oh shit!"

Lost, over the Ho Chi Minh Trail in Laos near Tchepone, at night. Damn, damn, damn!

True to form, it wasn't over. With all that maneuvering, all that confusion, the unnecessary (some would say stupid, and I would be one of them) use of afterburners, there was only one naturally ensuing event: The red Fuel Level Low light illuminated.

That meant just 1,800 pounds of fuel remained in the tanks, enough for, at most, maybe 15 minutes of flight, but only if the bird was light and at altitude, not heavy and down low. Yet there we were—low, lost, out of contact, and, by now, befuddled. So, cut the flight time remaining in half, or more, maybe much more.

Finally, I got my act together.

The last thing I wanted to do was bail out, at night, in Laos, especially near Tchepone. So, with reference to the aircraft's standby compass, I turned the bird west, toward Thailand, and started a slow, low-power climb. My hope was that, before the fuel ran out, we could get to the Mekong River that separated hostile Laos from friendly Thailand.

When an F-4 ran out of fuel, the engines—naturally—quit. When they did, so did the hydraulic pumps that ran the flight controls. The bird would pitch up, then tumble to earth. There was no possibility of a glide because the horizontal stabilizer (the plane's elevator) would freeze in the full nose-up position. The best option was to eject just before the hydraulic pumps failed, so that the complex Martin-Baker ejection-seat system would have its best chance to function properly.

There was no doubt now: we were in trouble, big trouble. Sure, we had escaped near-certain death from the guns, but running out of fuel in Laos might be just as deadly. I was scared.

As we slowly climbed, we went through the pre-ejection checklist: we tightened our parachute-harness straps, zipped our pockets closed, and stowed anything loose in the cockpit (loose items would become missiles when the canopies were jettisoned). One of the items on the checklist was to put the Transponder (the radar identification system) to Emergency, which I did.

The Mayor and I discussed the actual ejection sequence. At that time, the F-4 did not have thrusters to push the canopies away from the aircraft. It relied on the aircraft's pneumatic system to open the canopy into the slipstream, so it could be blown away. That system was proven to be dangerous since if the rear canopy went first, there could be resulting suction on the inside of the front canopy, which might prevent it from blowing away. I did not want to be trapped in the cockpit, so I told The Mayor that I would jettison my canopy first, then he would eject both of us using his "Command Select" ejection option (he would pull his ejection handles, his canopy would go, then his seat, then mine). This sequence was to prevent me from being trapped in the front cockpit if something were to happen when his rocket-propelled seat left the airplane.

Last, with only minutes of fuel left, we discussed how we could get together on the ground; after all, it was pitch black. The reality of our predicament was almost crushing. It even seemed hard to breathe though the aircraft oxygen system was working fine.

For no good reason, I glanced outside. At my 10 o'clock position, slightly high, was a lone, bright star. That was odd, since I had not seen any bright stars that hazy night. We continued our pre-ejection planning, and I looked again at that star. It was bright, in fact, brighter than any star I had ever seen.

Then it was more. It was several stars.

And it wasn't stationary.

It was turning. And it had lights, lots of them. I could make out bright, white landing-lights, a red rotating-beacon found on the belly of airplanes, then the red and green wingtip lights, then the white engine-nacelle lights.

Then I could see that it was an airplane.

It was a KC-135 tanker!

That plane had every light turned on bright. I would have bet even the light in the john was lit. And the plane was in a 30-degree banked turn merging toward my aircraft's heading. As we approached him from slightly below, I saw the refueling boom, extended, swinging up and down, the radio-out signal for "You are cleared to connect."

With so little fuel, I was afraid to touch the throttles. Hell, I was almost afraid to breathe. But I didn't have to use the throttles. The tanker continued his turn in front of me and rolled out on my exact heading, no more than a quarter-mile away. He had slowed down so that I closed on him with no effort on my part.

It was definitely not a SAC (Strategic Air Command) approved join-up, but it was, without a doubt, the most beautiful rendezvous I had ever seen, and I had seen hundreds.

I opened my air-refueling door, slid the plane forward under the boom, so that the nozzle on the end of the extended portion of the pipe could get to my receptacle, located a few feet behind the rear cockpit. Then I felt the most wonderful sensation I ever experienced to that point in my life (yes, far better than sex), and one that I have remembered ever since: The "clunk" of that boom connecting with my refueling receptacle.

The boom operator sat in a little compartment above the boom with a small window. He had all his lights on, so I could clearly see him, earphones and all. He checked his gauges, then gave me a thumbs-up. We were taking on fuel.

My own fuel-gauge started upward, the Fuel Level Low light went out, and life started again.

God does forgive all.

Even fools.

I'm not sure of the exact events, but a radar controller at the big search radar-station at Udorn, call sign "Brigham," saw my emergency transponder "squawk" and figured that an emergency F-4 would certainly need fuel. The gunship relayed information about the fiasco to the airborne controllers, which must have confirmed the radar controller's opinion. The Brigham controller vectored the tanker on what must be the most perfect intercept ever flown—and not by a fighter, but by a tanker. (Somewhere there is a former Air Force radar operator who is a war hero in my book.)

I made it home, but the memory of that flight has never left me. For years, even decades, I relived it, dreamed about it, dissected it, and analyzed it. I have re-flown it more than any other in my Air Force career. It was my three screw-ups.

First, through my over-confidence I was lulled into flying a predictable formation behind the gunship. An anti-aircraft gunner did not need a college degree to quickly determine how many seconds I was behind the gunship. All that was required was for one gun (in this case a 57-millimeter) to fire; the others just fired toward where that lead-gun's rounds went. That produced the massive barrage I was in.

Second, it was insane to light the afterburners. No one could see me in the blackness, at least not until I lit the burners. Then everyone could.

Third, it was absurd to do a SAM break without first seeing the missile, especially at night. I should never have reacted to something until I knew what it was. Hitting the ground would have only added yet one more fireball to the scene.

So, there were three "Aw shits" that night, all within less than half of a minute. But I made it home, and any landing I could walk away from was a good one.

What did I learn?

Plenty! First, while it was great to have confidence in my ability, I should never have exceeded that ability. Everyone—even the world's best fighter pilot—has limits. Second, I learned to keep a sharp eye on my environment—situational awareness, called SA. Think first, then act. But the most important lesson was beyond me then, but it came to me decades later.

There was an "Override" switch for the Golden BB.

I could have died that night—and maybe I should have—but God pushed the Override switch and said: "No!"

Chapter 10

The Proudest Day

FEBRUARY WAS STILL THE dry season in Northern Thailand. I completed—survived might be a more descriptive word—my night missions, 53 in all, and was back on the day schedule. Night combat was exceptionally stressful, in part because the darkness and its associated spatial disorientation may have killed as many pilots as the enemy did. So, the squadron cycled people through that part of the operations. Though I no longer flew at night, I proudly added the "Nickel Night Owl" patch to my party suit.

Day flying meant that on non-flying days I could spend more time at my office. There had been some changes there. We had a new recce crew to replace the twice shot-down Chuck and Al: a friendly major named John, and his navigator, Joe. John was a long-time reconnaissance pilot with loads of experience. We also got a new weapons officer to replace Gary, another of the office members who had been shot down.

The new weapons officer, a major named Tom, was much more outgoing than Gary had been. Tom, unlike a lot of "patch-wearers" (Weapons School graduates), did not try to impress us with his extensive technical knowledge. He could discuss obscure issues in everyday fighter-pilot language, which meant no trigonometry or other obscure

165

math. That made my life in the office more pleasant, especially since we had adjacent desks.

***

In February 1970, the battle in the north of Laos was not going well for the Hmong Army. The added weight of the North Vietnamese "volunteers" meant that General Vang Pao's forces had to cede a lot of ground, basically most of the PDJ.[1]

I led a two-ship formation to Barrel Roll to work with a Raven FAC. When we joined up with the FAC, he gave us the usual information as to altimeter setting, winds, and bail-out area. He then directed us to a flat hill-top with small dirt strip with several shacks near one end, the entire area surrounded by jungle.

"That's a runway," he radioed to us. "Your target is there."

I seriously doubted that the short, reddish-brown length of dirt was a runway. What could take off or land on that? Besides, there weren't any enemy airplanes to use it. From my altitude, it appeared no longer than a football field, if that, and only a few yards wide.

His little plane was opposite the target from us. He radioed: "Your targets are the buildings at the end, especially the large one. Do you have the target in sight?"

Large? From my altitude, they looked like several shacks or huts. It could have been a very small, primitive farmhouse with a few, even smaller out-buildings.

I replied, "Roger, Hammer One has the target in sight; the buildings at the end of the runway." I maneuvered in a circle with the little cluster of shacks at its center.

"I'm not going to mark," the Raven said. Since we saw the target, I guess he did not want to waste a rocket because the little O-1 only carried four.

"Roger. Hammer Flight, bombs triple," I radioed to my wingman. No one was shooting as far as I could see—at least nothing big—so why not make multiple passes?

"Hammer, get the large building first. That's my hooch. We were overrun this morning and I don't want them to have my things. Hammer Flight is cleared hot."

Damn! It was his own room we were about to bomb. I knew the Ravens lived in a more dangerous environment than we did, but getting overrun in the morning, then bombing his own quarters at mid-day just did not make sense to me. My biggest dangers at Udorn were speeding taxi drivers and hangovers.

We destroyed the whole place, huts, runway, and all. I hope there were some North Vietnamese in his hooch.

When we left, the Raven thanked us. I wondered where he would spend the night.

***

Udorn had a C-47 "Gooney Bird" of World War II fame assigned for miscellaneous duties. It was like someone who owned a fleet of race cars but who kept an old pickup truck around for odd jobs. This twin piston-engine prop transport was parked outside our office, so it was clearly visible from our windows. Sometimes, when my mind idled, I speculated about the plane's history. Had it been in the Big War? Douglas Aircraft, the manufacturer, had built the first ones in the 1930s as passenger planes. When the Army Air Forces got hold of it, they adapted it to cargo and troop carrier duties. It had long since been mostly replaced with more modern aircraft. Still, it was rugged and versatile, so a few remained in service. Some of them were flown as electronics snoopers over the Ho Chi Minh Trail, the CIA boys flew some in the Air America program, and there were even some

AC-47 gunships in South Vietnam. In fact, it had been the original gunship that was replaced by the AC-130.

One day, the crew went out to our "Base Goon," as we called it, to fly some non-descript utility mission. They entered through the cargo door near the tail and walked up to the cockpit. They opened the cockpit door, and slammed it shut immediately.

In the cockpit was a king cobra. From their accounts, it was large, black, and alive. Did I say it was large? All snakes were large, and grew larger with each telling of the encounter.

Now they had a problem. There was no way the crew was going to fly with a cobra in the cockpit. There were no maintenance troops willing to get it out. The Security Police said they would shoot it, but any gunfire might do severe damage to the airplane. If only Thailand had Negrito tribesmen like those at Jungle Survival School in the Philippines. I'm sure they would have been able to remove the snake.

But we didn't have any Negritos, so we needed another plan. Some bright person had heard that a mongoose would kill any snake, especially cobras. A runner was dispatched to Udon Thani, the city next to the base, to find a mongoose.

One was located, so two cautious "volunteers" carried the small, furry weasel-like animal in its cage to the cockpit door. Quickly, they cracked the door open and shooed the mongoose into the cockpit, then slammed the door shut. They left the airplane and closed the cargo door. Now it was time for Mother Nature to take over.

The plane, completely closed, sat on the ramp directly outside our office window for the better part of a week. No one went in it; in fact, no one went near it. It just sat there.

Eventually, some more volunteers were sent in to see how the mongoose had done with the snake. The best guess was that the mongoose could only have eaten part of the snake, but we needed the airplane.

The volunteers opened the cargo door and carefully approached the cockpit door, checking left and right to make sure that the snake did not lurk nearby. They cautiously and slowly cracked open the cockpit door and peeked inside.

Nothing!

No snake, no mongoose.

They carefully—very carefully—searched the cockpit. There was no sign of either animal. Gone, without a trace.

The plane sat there for a couple more days with searches by cautious maintenance troops, but there was no sign of the animals. The rumor was that the pilots refused to fly the plane until they knew what had happened to the intruders. Finally—also a rumor—the wing commander ordered them to fly. They did.

How the snake got into the plane, and how it and the mongoose got out, remained a mystery. The best guess I heard was that the snake must have climbed up a landing gear strut and worked its way into the cockpit via the inside of the wing. If so, then it probably left the same way. Whether the snake ate the mongoose, or the mongoose ate the snake will never be known. Who knew? Maybe they both simply left the bird individually.

***

But never mind snakes and mongooses, the war still raged. One day, I was scheduled for an afternoon mission as number two in a two-ship formation to test a new ordnance. My leader was "Crazy," a Weapons School expert, a Patch-wearer, on temporary duty to Thailand to oversee the first-ever actual combat use of the Mark 20 "Rockeye" cluster-bomb.

This weapon, though its canister was white instead of OD, looked like any bomb when hung on the F-4's center-line or wing stations.

As with our cluster bombs, when the weapon was released, the outer clamshell split in half, releasing lethal darts. Because of their design, the darts formed a rectangle, about 200 feet wide and 300 feet long instead of the large donut shape formed by our other cluster bombs. Originally designed to fight the Soviet armored formations in Europe, the Rockeye contained several hundred darts, each about a foot long that looked a lot like lawn-darts: spiked nose and even fins. Each dart, designed to kill tanks, vehicles, and infantry, was fused to provide both a vertical armor-penetrating burst of molten metal, and a horizontal spray of pellets—sort of a 360-degree shotgun blast—to kill the infantry.

As far as I knew, there were few tanks anywhere in all of Laos, and most of the tanks in South Vietnam were ours.

No matter. The all-knowledgeable headquarters staff decided the Rockeye would be useful to destroy trucks, but would be great against anti-aircraft guns. That probably sounded logical to the staff in Washington, or even in Saigon, since an anti-aircraft gun was made of steel, and had a crew of several fleshy people. Sadly, the staff did not seem to understand anti-aircraft guns. You see, a gunner had a geometric problem when shooting at aircraft. That problem involved determining the range, azimuth, and elevation of the target airplane.

So why was this important? Well, every fighter pilot in Southeast Asia knew that attacking guns just for the sake of destroying the guns was stupid. Not just the "duh" kind of stupidity: I mean blind, raving stupidity. Anti-aircraft guns protected valuable elements of the North Vietnamese Army or its supplies. When we went looking for the guns, we, by default, ignored the valuable targets. Worse, when a fighter dived on an anti-aircraft gun, the gunners no longer had the azimuth problem. The target aircraft flew straight down the line of his gun barrel. Attacking guns in broad daylight, just to get at the guns, was a fool's errand.

But not for the folks running the war.

Crazy briefed the mission, which was to go into northern Laos. We were to contact a Forward Air Controller, probably a Raven. So, as with many of our missions, there was no preplanned target; we were simply going to bomb whatever the Raven could find. Since we had the new Rockeyes, we needed trucks or guns to get proper test data.

After our pre-flight arming at the end of the runway, we lit the afterburners on our 17,000-pound thrust engines and took off on this "routine" mission. Thailand was damned hot in the dry season, so by the time I pulled the landing gear up, I was already drenched in sweat. I joined into close formation with Crazy, we checked each other's aircraft for any problems, for loose bomb-arming cables mostly, and soon crossed the Fence.

The entire process of getting to the Fence involved gradually increasing stress, so breathing got a bit more rapid, and the sweat flowed more freely once over the Mekong River. I never understood how you could have cold feet and still sweat at the same time. Fighter air-conditioners left a bit to be desired.

The radio chatter picked up more than normal, and we heard an emergency locator beacon, a wailing—beep-beep-beep-beep—on Guard, the emergency frequency that all of us monitored along with our assigned frequency. Periodically, also on the emergency frequency, I heard a voice say, "Beeper, beeper, come up voice." It meant that the pilot on the ground should turn off his emergency locator beacon and use his voice radio. I had heard the plaintive call, "Beeper, beeper, come up voice" before and would hear it again, in the war—and in nightmares.

A short time after crossing the Fence, the airborne control aircraft contacted us and directed us to join up with a KC-135 tanker, refuel, and stand by for a mission change.

So much for our mission with the Raven. No circling while the Raven searched the jungle for hidden trucks or oil storage drums. No waiting for his bright-white Willy Pete smoke to filter up through the jungle canopy. That mission ended before it even started.

By the time we had rendezvoused with the tanker, we learned that an F-4 had been shot down in northern Laos. The pilot had not been heard from, but the back-seater was down, alive, in the jungle. It was common knowledge among F-4 pilots that, unless things went just right, the front-seater could be trapped in the cockpit after the back seat went out, and hence would ride the plane into the ground. I knew in my heart that the pilot was dead, although he, like many, would be listed as Missing in Action for the next few decades.

Perhaps he is.

But the GIB was alive. Unfortunately, he was on the ground in Laos, where no American who was not promptly rescued ever survived. (I lied. One Navy pilot was captured and later escaped, but that was early in the war. Most of the rest died, and probably not peacefully.)

We refueled, then orbited with the tanker. We listened to the Search and Rescue radio frequency while we flew on the tanker's wing. The airborne rescue force had located the survivor, but he was in the same area his flight had just bombed, never a good place to bail out. He was hiding in the jungle near a road, but had many enemy troops around him—probably pissed off—looking for him.

On the first attempt to get to the survivor, a Jolly Green Giant helicopter, the big, twin-engine HH-53, had been badly shot up by an anti-aircraft gun. The downed flyer was quite near that gun, so the anti-aircraft crew had little trouble hitting a hovering helicopter. That crippled helicopter, with a wounded crewman on board, was forced to return to Udorn. That left only one helicopter on scene. If that chopper could not complete the rescue, the downed American would likely die a horrible, slow death.

As we listened, we learned that the rescue force, with its A-1 propeller-driven Skyraider fighters, a throwback to the early war in Korea, had run into a 23-millimeter rapid firing anti-aircraft gun, a modern and deadly weapon. It could fire a virtual water hose of high-explosive rounds, and did so accurately. To make matters worse, the survivor was hiding near the gun—very near. He could not move with all the enemy troops searching for him. And there was no way that a helicopter could hover over him to get him out of that jungle.

Not with that gun firing.

Then we got the call to enter the fight. And why not? We were armed, so it was thought, with cluster munitions suitable to kill guns. Most of the airplanes airborne that day had 500-pound bombs. It was virtually impossible for an F-4 to take out an anti-aircraft gun with an unguided 500-pound bomb. In later wars, the smart bombs could do the job, but in 1970, it was all "Kentucky-windage" for us. Most guns were in pits, with dirt berms around them. It would take nearly a direct hit with a 500-pounder, and, despite our bragging, we simply weren't that good. I don't think that I ever hit a gun with a 500-pounder; close a couple of times, but not in the pit.

Crazy and I left the tanker and headed toward the fight. This was the time for the knot in the stomach, the tightness in the chest, the tension in the throat, and sweat in the oxygen mask, because the price of poker was getting quite high. But this was no damn game, there would be no room for error, no slack, no "puking off" the bombs just to get it over.

Damn! We had to kill the gun, or that kid on the ground was not coming home.

We reached the area and got a briefing from the SAR boss (the "on-scene commander"), a Nail FAC in an OV-10. He had moved the

SAR force out of the immediate area so as not to endanger the one remaining rescue helicopter. A road ran through a valley with steep hills on both sides, and a smaller hill on one end. The other end opened into a wider valley. There was probably a stream there, too, but I could not see it. The whole area was jungle, green except for the road of reddish-brown dirt. From our approach direction, the survivor was on the left side of the road in the woods, and so was the 23-millimeter anti-aircraft gun.

It was then that I noticed that the sky appeared odd. It was the dry season; low clouds were rare in Laos. Mostly there was the natural and man-made haze that hung over everything. But there were low clouds over this valley. Well anyway, they looked like clouds. It finally dawned on me that the "clouds" were made by the smoke from the air-bursts of what must have been thousands of rounds of anti-aircraft fire.

We were flying into one hell-of-a-fight, already well in progress. Now it was our turn.

Besides the 23 near the road, there must have been guns in the hills on both sides, to cover the road. Obviously, this was a main supply route, which was probably what the downed F-4 had been after. I never did find out what his target had been.

There was no end to the flying rules—the Rules of Engagement—during the conflict in Vietnam. But all the rules were ignored when one of us was on the ground. Every Air Force pilot knew that he could easily be the guy on the ground, so we tossed the rule-book and did what was necessary to get the survivor out. I had flown on several rescues earlier in my tour, but always on the periphery of the fight. Usually my role had been to prevent any enemy reinforcements, or to silence fringe-area guns.

This time was different. This time I was front and center, going for a target where a slip-up by me could kill our guy. This was pressure like

I had never felt before. I had been scared plenty of times. I had near misses with anti-aircraft rounds, the ground, and unbelievable vertigo at night, but this was different.

If I screwed up, an American airman would die. Son-of-a-bitch!

The FAC briefed us on the situation. He described the general location of the survivor, told us where the known defenses were, where the friendly aircraft were orbiting, and where the best place for us to go if we had to bailout. He described where the 23-millimeter was located, then rolled in and fired a Willy Pete rocket to mark the gun site, just in case we could not see the muzzle flash from that rapid firing gun. His mark was good, with the bright, white smoke from the phosphorous billowing up quite near the gun pit.

He did not have to bother; we could see where the tracers came from.

I turned on the Master Arm switch to complete the arming of the Rockeyes, and set up for release of three bombs at a time, in close interval (a bit more than one-tenth of a second between each bomb) to get as many of the darts on the target as possible. Crazy went in first and I followed. I tried to ignore the tracers arcing toward his airplane from several locations.

Thank God for training, for a fighter diving on a target had a predictable flight-path. The gunners had a much easier time trying to solve their geometry problem, because we could not maneuver while diving. Fortunately, the time going down "the chute," as we called the actual dive, required total concentration, so there were no spare brain cells for worry. I forced myself to focus on the glowing red gunsight with the pipper in the center.

My GIB avoided any mention of tracers during our dive. I assumed he looked for them, but perhaps not. Anyway, I'm glad he did not say anything to me.

On our first two passes we intentionally erred to the side of the 23 that was away from the survivor. We hoped that, with luck, a cluster-bomb dart or two might get the gun. As we should have expected, we did not hit it, but we had a much better feel for the wind, the terrain, and for the overall situation. Unfortunately, we were now targets for every anti-aircraft gunner in the valley and on the hills. Tracers flew through the sky, and those clouds got larger—much larger.

On my third pass, I reduced my dive angle, normally 45 degrees, to a shallow 20 degrees. That would allow me to get significantly lower as the pull-out would not require as much altitude. Still, I did not want to be too easy of a target, so I kept my speed at 500-knots. I released three more Rockeyes, lit my afterburners and did a five-G, left climbing pull off. By now, I was soaked with sweat.

The FAC radioed: "You got it! You got it!"

I kept my hard turn going to see the gun pit, but before I could bask in the glow of hitting it, the damned gun blazed away at me—again.

Hell's bells! Talk about a short-lived victory. Our Rockeyes must have hit the pit, maybe killed the crew, but did not hit the gun itself. The North Vietnamese were damn smart fighters. Most of their gun pits were dug so that extra crewmen would be safe from all but a direct hit. Most of their guns had multiple crews with them as the guns were more valuable to our enemy than were their people. If I did kill the first crew, the back-ups promptly took their places. That damned gun spit fire again, at me.

Only three Rockeyes left. Tracers crisscrossed the valley as every gun on planet earth seemed to shoot at Crazy. I don't think he cared, hence his nickname. Crazy never shied from a fight. The Air Force Academy should be proud of him.

I pulled up my visor, wiped the now-profuse and burning sweat out of my eyes, and rolled in again. Same thing for this last pass. Shallow dive-angle, concentrate on speed control, keep the pipper tracking steady to the target, and push down the "pickle" button a heartbeat before the pipper crossed the target. To hell with everything else in the world—FOCUS!

Nearly five years of flying, training, and combat experience came down to these few seconds. Talk about a time when failure was not an option.

Damn it! Why me? I had the last three cluster bombs and they had to hit.

This time they hit the pit, the crew, and, most importantly, that damned gun. I nailed that son-of-a-bitch! In fairness to Crazy, since I attacked close behind his last run, it would be better to say that one—or both—of us hit the gun.

It doesn't matter, though, the gun was gone. Our flight had destroyed it.

Unfortunately, now we had a problem. A big one. Crazy immediately started south toward Thailand, and without calling for join-up asked for a fuel check. That radio call brought on even more sweat. During the fight, I had not even thought about my fuel. Hell, I had used the afterburners after each attack. Now I was well below "bingo," our get-home fuel requirement, and so was Crazy.

He immediately called for a tanker.

It was almost too predictable; there were no tankers available, not in northern Laos, not anywhere we could get to them. Any SAR required lots of aircraft, most of which needed to refuel. We were literally SOL (shit outa luck).

There was not enough fuel to join up, not enough to do a battle-damage check of our airplanes. The only choice was to point toward home, do a reduced-power climb to medium altitude, so we could perform a long, gliding approach to Udorn. The F-4 did not really glide, unless one thinks a brick will glide. The technique we used to get as much range as possible was to gain some altitude, then use very low power settings that consumed as little fuel as possible. In the F-4, using little fuel was a pipedream. This was pucker-time. There was nothing to do but to watch the fuel gauge go down, relentlessly. No time to even think about the attacks on the gun, only to focus on getting to a runway. As a backup, my navigator and I planned the alternative—ejecting. The memory of that near-disaster on one of my final night missions was still on my mind. Damn! I didn't want to repeat that.

Would a stray tanker save us? I could only hope.

At about this time we heard the news on our radio: They got him out!

The survivor was safe on a helicopter, homebound. Now losing an F-4 or two didn't seem so bad, at least if the ejection systems worked as advertised. Still, the thought of trusting my life to a complex ejection system was not appealing. Being blasted into the sky with 12 G's by a rocket motor while flying at 200 knots, then falling through the sky waiting for an automatic parachute-opening system to function was not my idea of a proper end to an otherwise successful mission.

Finally, we crossed the Fence southbound. The muddy Mekong never looked so good. At least we would be in friendly country if we had to eject.

Crazy called Udorn Approach Control and declared an emergency for our pitiful fuel state.

Udorn Approach then made a reply that I had never heard before, or after. The controller said, "You are number SEVEN in the emergency pattern, with wounded ahead of you. Recommend you proceed south for bailout."

Good Lord! There were six other emergencies ahead of us.

Crap. With wounded men on an aircraft ahead of us, they were not going to give us priority, or even sympathy. That shot-up helicopter had just arrived at Udorn. With the other emergencies, it must have been a bad day in Laos. We were just two more problems, and evidently expendable. I don't blame them; the wounded always came first, especially the rescue guys. There were no braver people in the war, in any service, than the Jolly Green Giant crews. They never bought their own drinks at our bar.

God must have had pity on our fuel-challenged flight, for as we finally approached the runway, with damned-little fuel left, the other emergency aircraft had landed. We made angled approaches to the runway, the most direct route. Talk about a sigh of relief when we touched down. That was about all I could have handled that day. I would have hated to walk home after ejecting from a fuel-starved airplane.

Crazy's plane flamed out from fuel starvation in the de-arm area. The colonel in charge of the wing's operations was there when it happened. Normally, a pilot's ass would really be in hot water for cutting the fuel that close, but the colonel was thrilled about the rescue. Instead of chewing on Crazy's ass for nearly losing two F-4s, the colonel shook his hand.

Crazy had done a brilliant job leading the flight.

There was lots of happy chatter in the crew van on the way back to the squadron. Success was a wonderful, intoxicating feeling.

After the debriefing, I walked over to the shot-up helicopter. It had holes in the external tanks and ugly rips in the bird's skin with bent metal going in all directions. Inside, there was chaos, with gear scattered around, bullet and shrapnel holes in the floor and sides. Worse, there was blood spatter on the ceiling, on the armor plating that protected the rotor gears. It was a damned ugly site.

The wounded crewman, a PJ—para-rescue man—survived, I think. After the war, I heard that the most decorated Air Force airman from that or any other conflict was a PJ.[2]

That evening, as always, my GIB and I went to the bar for a few beers. As we rehashed the day's events, our Flight Surgeon walked over to us.

"You guys flew on the rescue today, didn't you?" he asked.

When we said yes, he said, "Did you know that kid is here in our hospital? He had a rough day and could use some company. You should go see him."

After the Doc left, I suggested to my GIB that we really should go see the guy. Like most fighter pilots, I get really smart after a couple of beers. So, I ordered some un-opened cans of beer. We each put a couple of cans in both of our lower flight-suit pockets, zipped them, and left the bar carrying—and drinking—some beer for the walk to the hospital.

Life's good with cold beer, and being alive and safe on earth.

We walked to the hospital, but were still each working on a beer when we went in. Naturally, an orderly in white hospital-attire stopped us at the door and said drinking was not permitted in the hospital.

Tsk, tsk! Air Force regulations.

We guzzled our beers, then walked down the corridor to the survivor's room. I have always wondered if anyone saw the cans bulging in our flight-suit pockets, but at the time I did not give a shit.

We went into the kid's room.

He sat on the end of his bed next to the boring, institutional-white wall, still wearing a quite dirty and muddy flight-suit. He could not have been more than 22, and he looked scared to death. But who wouldn't? His front-seater, probably a close friend, was missing and likely dead, and he damn near was. Given that, he probably was better composed than most of us would have been.

We told him we had flown on his rescue, and he sprang off the bed, shook our hands and thanked us profusely. At that point, we unzipped our leg pockets and produced the beers, for him and for us.

He protested, saying that it was against regulations to drink alcohol in the hospital, to which I said, "After what you've been through, who cares?" or words to that effect.

We sat with him, talked, and drank our beers. We left a couple of beers and an opener with him in case he needed help sleeping. I think he was genuinely glad we stopped in to see him.

Over the decades, the memory of many of my combat missions blurred, faded, or disappeared completely. Yet that day has never left my mind. Helping to save that guy was the greatest thing I ever did in my entire life, before or since. He went home, partly at least because I was there. I hope he lived a great life and had lots of kids and grand-kids.

It was February 18, 1970, and it was the proudest day of my life.

Chapter 11

R and R

ORT ENDURED MONTHS OF hanging around Udorn waiting to learn his fate from a Flying Evaluation Board that still had not met, or even been scheduled to meet. I had no idea what he did all day, but I saw him at the bar almost every evening. He spent most of his time lambasting the conduct of the war and the powers that be, from Washington, to Saigon, to our own wing headquarters. He had lots to lambast.

The latest would take us from the surreal to the inane.

Our wing commander (a colonel), perhaps in an attempt to get promoted to general, had decided he wanted better combat film. Our F-4s were equipped with KB-18 bomb cameras that started filming when we hit the pickle button and ran for some specified time. The idea was that the bomb camera footage would show the bombs leaving the bomb racks (which it clearly did), show the bombs dispersing in their fall (which it sometimes did), and finally show the bombs exploding (which it never did).

The result of all this photography was that we had lots of pictures of bombs in the air, and none of them hitting the ground.

The film did not show the bomb explosions because no fighter pilot in his right mind would do a straight-ahead pull-out for the camera field-of-view to stay on the bombs until impact. In the States, on test ranges, the camera worked great since the test planes always pulled out of their dives straight ahead. In combat, the pull-outs were always associated with jinking, usually lots of it. Pilots would pull and turn simultaneously, sometimes reversing the turn before the nose got above the horizon. The cameras, of course, filmed lots of jungle, but no explosions.

The idea in combat was to be unpredictable: to not allow the gunner to know where the plane would be at the end of the time-of-flight of his rounds. Back to Ort's "gun seconds" theory; when in range of a gun, move the plane erratically. With the unfortunate exception of a Golden BB, the more movement a plane made, the harder it was to hit.

But the commander wanted pictures of bombs exploding.

Somehow, he got word of a device we called a "Nellis Pod," a movie camera in a pod that could be mounted on the inboard station of the F-4. It was used at Fighter Weapons School at Nellis Air Force Base near Las Vegas to help analyze the performance of students when they dropped practice bombs on the gunnery range. An instructor, in a chase airplane, would follow the student in his dive, filming with the pod, and continue filming after bomb release until the bomb hit the ground. It was a great teaching tool, as all the various parameters could be studied to determine exactly what caused the bomb to hit where it did. The pod and all the detailed instruction helped most of the patch-wearers to be accurate bombers, at least on the gunnery ranges.

To my knowledge, no one shot at them back in Nevada, even the aliens rumored to be in Area 51.

But they damned-well shot at us in Laos. Nonetheless, the wing commander wanted film with actual bomb explosions.

Crazy had gone back to Nellis after the Rockeye test and returned to Udorn with a new, experimental land-mine. He also brought a Nellis Pod back, probably at the direction of our wing commander. Now our esteemed "wing king," as some called the commander, had a means of getting his film. All that was required was to hang the pod on the inboard bomb station, without the ejector carts of course, and put it with a flight going into combat. When one plane rolled in to attack, the plane with the pod would follow it down in the dive from a safe distance back. After the bombs came off, the pod-equipped airplane would continue down, filming as it went. When the bombs exploded, the pod aircraft would pull off.

Presto! Combat film of bombs bursting on target. It was simple.

Or should I say simple-minded? Instead of one plane flying a predictable path for the gunners to shoot at, now there would be two. The gunners could fire at the first plane. If they missed, it was usually from shooting behind their target. Now their problem turned into an advantage because a second plane might well fly into the rounds that were meant for the first plane. Worse yet, the pod-equipped plane had to recover from its dive, which meant it had to go through the same space as the bomber.

Gunners' heaven! Just put lots of rounds into that space. Shoot at two planes for the price of one.

The Nickel drew the short straw and had to fly the pod. First a regular pilot, a protégé of Ort, flew it. He came back and swore never to do it again. That word got around the squadron in an instant. Another tried—once. He swore it off, too. After only a couple of flights with the pod, no one in the Nickel would fly it. It was just too damned dangerous. The guys that had flown it swore it was only blind luck that had kept them from being blown out of the sky.

The problem was solved when Crazy said he would do it.

He wasn't called Crazy for no reason. He did fly the pod, and he lived through it. He probably should have gotten some Distinguished Flying Crosses for his work—or been committed to an institution. In any case, the wing king had his film. Now all that was left was to process it, make a narrated movie about how his wing was winning the war and—Shazam!—instant general.

But fate determined another outcome. The film, taken at significant risk to Crazy and the other crews, was damaged beyond use during processing. No movie. It was almost the reverse of Hot Dog, where a great program had been dumped for stupid reasons; here fate dumped a stupid program.

***

Besides the pod, Crazy brought another headache for us: The BLU-31B land mine. This 800-pound bomb had a blunt nose with a seismic fuse on it. When dropped properly, it was designed to penetrate downward into the earth, then as the pressure built, it turned upward and stopped below the surface, sort of in an underground arc. It then sat there out of sight and with no evidence of its presence (since it had entered the ground well away from where it stopped) until a train came by and created enough seismic disturbance to detonate it. It had no back-up fusing, such as a time delay, so if no train, no explosion.

To my knowledge, there were no trains in Laos, and never had been.

Whoever sent the bomb knew there were no trains, but there were bulldozers. The North Vietnamese used special road teams to repair the damage to the Trail done by our bombs.[1] These teams of various sizes lived in the jungle along the roads. Each was responsible for one segment of the supply line. They filled holes, repaired bridges, cleared land mines, and generally kept their segment of the road passable. Some of these teams had bulldozers that were detected by our sensors, which spied on a good portion of the Trail. Also, we knew that occasionally a light tank would move down the Trail to South Vietnam. Our troops in the South had encountered them already.

OK, so we had possible targets for the mines, although Crazy was not positive that a bulldozer would create enough vibration to detonate the mine.

That was the easy part.

The hard part was getting the bomb into the ground. It had severe restrictions on how it could be dropped. As I remember, it had to impact the earth at no more than 420 knots at a shallow angle, hence had to be released from the airplane from no more than a few hundred feet above the desired impact point. When a bomb left an aircraft, it had the same speed the aircraft had at release and the same angle to the earth. Gravity caused a bomb's trajectory to steepen as it fell. Therefore, we had to release the bomb from a shallow glide of about ten-degrees at low altitude to insure it entered the ground at the proper angle.

If anyone thought 420 knots was fast, he should have tried that speed with someone shooting at him. I had long ago set 500 knots as my minimum speed in combat. As for a ten-degree angle, that meant we could not dive with the mine, we would have to glide it in, at no more than 420 knots. In combat, with experienced gunners shooting at us.

Put this all together at low altitude, and Ort's "gun seconds" theory became more like "gun minutes."

Crazy had about 72 of these mines to plant. If the tests were to be meaningful, the mines must be planted in locations where there were likely to be bulldozers or maybe an occasional tank. That meant Steel Tiger, close to the North Vietnamese border. Ugly, dangerous places like Mu Gia or Ban Karai Pass, or around Tchepone. Places with lots of guns and lots of our wrecked airplanes littering the area. Once again, word got around the squadrons quickly. Most crews thought it was nuts. A few tried it and barely escaped. No volunteers came forward. Crazy was left to do most of the flying.

But not all of it. Colonel Earl said that, since I was the Wing Tactics Officer, I should participate, maybe even come up with some tactics to get this done. The obvious first thought was to put them in at night, when the gunners would not be as much of a threat. We rejected that idea due to the low altitude required. Too many airplanes would hit the ground. No, it had to be done in the daylight.

We knew that when a plane dropped mines that did not explode on impact, the gunners quickly realized that we could not immediately hurt them, so they would open fire with all they had. Sometimes we would mix a flight so that some birds carried mines and some carried cluster bombs to convince the gunners to keep their heads down. That was a possibility, but it did not offset the low, shallow, slow delivery required.

There was only one approach left: Surprise. Sneak in, drop, and get-the-hell-out before the gunners could react. In consultation with my office mate Tom, the wing's new weapons officer, we decided to use low altitude, high speed approaches, and stay behind hills or karsts until just before we reached the target area. We would then pop up and slow for the gliding approach to the target. Ort's gun-seconds theory should be short-circuited since the gunners would not likely be on their guns if they did not know we were there.

At least we hoped so.

Great theory: Sneak in fast, pop up at the last moment, drop the mines, and get-the-hell-out of the area. And, of course, no FAC. His presence in the area would alert the gunners.

I would have gladly shared it with others, but I was scheduled to lead the mission. My wingman was Mike, the same guy that could see a wing-tip light after a lightning bolt flashed by his eyes. We had flown several missions together and I knew him to be a steady, reliable wingman.

We planned our route into the target area, a well-traveled road inter-section on the Laotian side of notorious Mu Gia Pass. The pass had been bombed so much that no one could tell where the roads had been. It was trite to say that it looked like the surface of the moon; the moon never looked that bad. There were already plenty of other mines in the pass, so we were tasked to put our mines a couple of miles away.

With our ingress route and pop-up point selected from maps, we crossed the Fence and headed toward Mu Gia. Mike dropped into a fighting wing position, spaced well off to one side of my aircraft so he would not fly through any anti-aircraft fire aimed at me. We got as low as we could, probably a hundred feet or so, and used 480 knots, eight miles-per-minute, as our speed for ease of navigation. Our plan was to approach the target shielded by a hill, pop up as we rounded it, and do our mine-delivery glide after we passed it. Gunners in the target area would not hear us because of the hill, and even if they did, they would not be able to tell where the sound came from. Because we would be flying low, our camouflaged planes should be hard to see next to the jungle.

Everything went as planned. I got to the pop-up point, reduced the throttles as I pulled up to slow to the 420-knot speed-limit. The road intersection appeared before me, slightly to my left. I started the 10-degree glide as my plane rounded the hill, which was close off the left wing.

"OH, SHIT! GUN, 10 O'CLOCK." The excited voice of my GIB in the intercom got my attention.

I glanced left and saw something that looked like a gun with several people running toward it. But I had to look at the target and the sight. This was not the time to ignore the bomb run.

"Two, gun at our nine." This time my GIB transmitted on the radio.

The pipper tracked toward the target, airspeed was good, and I pickled the mines off the bird. When the next train came by, it was in for one big, loud surprise.

Burners. Hard-right pull. Being that low, that slow, that close to Mu Gia Pass was not where I wanted to be. We started up and away from the road.

"They're shooting!" Again, my GIB on the intercom.

I looked back but did not see any rounds near us. Those gunners must not have been too accurate. Mike pulled off his glide and we got the hell out of the area.

Back at Udorn, the pieces came together. My GIB saw the gunners running to their 23-millimeter. They did not, however, shoot at us.

By the time they were on the gun, Mike had started his glide. They let him have it. Mike said that the stream of tracers was aimed too high and that he flew just barely under them. Both he and his GIB said they were just a few feet above their canopies. The gunners must not have been accustomed to shooting at low, close aircraft. In any case, they missed Mike.

Thank God.

We had a few beers to help him recover from the trauma.

***

April finally arrived, and my R and R was next, and probably none too soon. I did not want any more of those low and slow bomb deliveries. Except for my short trip to the Philippines over the New Year, I had been at Udorn since August. It was time for a break, or so the squadron scheduler told me. There were several locations to pick from. Since I had spent weeks in Hawaii the prior summer but wanted somewhere that the natives spoke English, I chose Sydney, Australia. It sounded good and I had never been there.

All R and R's started from Camp Alpha, part of giant Tan Son Nhut Air Base just outside of Saigon. It was ironic that I had to go to Saigon which lay at the very center of the war, to start my R and R to get away from the war. One of the available destinations was Bangkok, which meant that people stationed in Thailand would have had to go to South Vietnam to go on R and R in Thailand.

Just one more insanity in the war.

I got to Camp Alpha the afternoon before my scheduled departure for Sydney. I was assigned a lower bed in a large, open, air-conditioned, gymnasium-style room that would sleep 120 men on the 60 nice, neatly organized stacks of military bunkbeds. It had a large shower room and a latrine on one end. As I stowed my bag, two Army officers walked by. These guys must have just come out of the field because their jungle boots were caked to the tops with red dirt. They raved about how great the air-conditioning was.

Damn, I was suddenly very glad to be in the Air Force. We thought everything was air-conditioned. I did not sleep well in that room with a hundred guys snoring, most of whom had not slept in a real bed, with clean sheets, in months. Back at my hooch, even if Dave did snore, the window air-conditioner drowned out the noise.

The next morning, I had breakfast at the O Club. It was a large, busy dining area with people in just about every uniform imaginable, but mostly flight-suits or jungle fatigues. Many of the patrons carried side-arms, which we never did at Udorn.

Different world, same war.

I was shocked to see my old roommate from pilot training walk in. We had roomed together for almost a year, until he washed out of the program and I subsequently lost track of him. He had gone to navigator school and now flew C-130s. We had years of catching up to do, so after breakfast we moved from the dining room to the bar. In Saigon, like Udorn, the bar was always open.

We had a couple of drinks when our old flight commander from pilot training came in. This would have been too much, but minutes later another member of our pilot training class walked in. Who would have thought there would be an impromptu reunion of a 1966 Alabama pilot training class in a 1970 Saigon bar?

By lunch time, I had consumed a fair amount of alcohol. It was time for me to check in for my flight, so I said my goodbyes and walked, or staggered, back to Camp Alpha. There were about 220 guys on my flight, and, as is the way of the military, we had to check in three hours prior to departure.

Then wait.

The waiting area was outdoors, in the hot sun. I sat on a padded bench among the hundreds of others, mostly enlisted Army troops. I was one of only a few officers and the only one wearing Air Force khakis.

Did I say the sun was hot?

***

When I woke up, the area was deserted, except for me. Not a soul in sight. My watch said that the plane should still be on the ground, so I rushed back to the sign-in desk. There, an Army second lieutenant, wearing khakis not jungle fatigues, told me that, since I had not reported when called, my seat had been given to a stand-by passenger.

The plane was still at the terminal. I could see it. And the passengers had not yet boarded! I insisted that I be permitted to resume my place in the line. Here was some REMF (that means Rear Echelon Mother Fucker, the Army Grunts' term for those not in actual combat) telling me, a fighter pilot with about 100 missions, that I could not board a plane that I had a ticket for and that sat on the ramp where I could see it. He said that I would have to check in the next day as a stand-by passenger for the next Sydney flight. With luck, maybe some other screwball would miss his call.

I guess I lost my cool.

Actually, I did. I proceeded to call him a few seriously offensive names and generally told him what I thought of how he was treating me.

I left when he called the MPs.

***

The next day, there was a different officer at the check-in desk, fortunately for me. Some other scheduled passenger did not show up, so I lucked out and got on board the flight to Sydney.

I had no idea that it was so far from Saigon to Sydney (more than 4,000 miles). The plane, a stuffed DC-8, had to stop at Darwin for fuel. We got to Sydney and received a briefing about how to conduct ourselves. No uniforms were allowed, which was a rule I was thankful for since mine badly needed a trip to the laundry. These people were our allies, so we were to conduct ourselves so as not to discredit the United States. Fat chance!

The final part of the briefing I remember well. The briefing officer said that, of any flight of 220 men that arrived, only about 200 made the return trip. He reminded us that failure to return was considered desertion and that the penalty for that was severe. Some Army infantryman next to me opined that Australia had no extradition treaty with the United States.

Several nearby Grunts chuckled.

The contrast between Sydney in April and the war was so sharp that I felt like Alice being dropped into Wonderland. Sydney was a beautiful city with people who spoke English, did not carry guns, and liked Americans. It was green, lush, not humid, and simply lovely to behold. People called me "Yank." Most did not even have to wait for me to talk; I must have looked like I came from some time warp. My GI haircut stood out and my Arma-Thief clothes looked like they had been made by an Indian tailor in Thailand—three or four years earlier.

Everywhere I went, people treated me as if I were a special guest. I met a young woman, Judith, I think, who showed me some of the city. We went to see The Battle of Britain at a nearby theater. For some strange reason, the poignant World War II movie did not remind me of my war. History, by its nature, was over, so it made sense.

My war still raged, and it no longer made sense.

When I traveled by cab, the taxi drivers frequently said, "No charge, Yank. We're with you up there." I sometimes forgot that Australia had troops fighting in South Vietnam. The contrast between the life I left at Udorn and this one in Sydney was too stark to comprehend.

One afternoon I was in the hotel bar. Oliver's "Good Morning Starshine," a huge hit in Australia, played on the jukebox. I noticed that the bartender had an accent different from the other folks around me. I asked him where he was from.

"San Bernardino," he said.

"Really? How'd you get here?" I had a knack for asking dumb questions.

"Same way you did. I just didn't go back." He said he had been there three years and that he was never going back.

I did not argue with him.

***

One warm evening, I went out for a stroll in the beautiful city. Along the sidewalks of a main thoroughfare, crowds faced the street, lined two- and three-deep along the curbs. I had no idea what they awaited, but they seemed excited. I walked between them and the shops until I came to a corner. The polite crowd had not blocked the crosswalk, so I waited there for the light to change. I was next to the street with no one in front of me.

The crowd behind me cheered, a rolling cheer that got louder as if following some moving object. An open limousine made a right turn at the corner and drove slowly by. In the back sat a man in a British military dress uniform and a formally attired woman, both smiling and waving at the lines of people. It passed within six feet of me.

It was Queen Elizabeth and Prince Philip. I waved.

***

There were about 20 empty seats on the trip back to Saigon. On the long flight back, I thought about how much better life was in civilization than in the war. I really did not want to go back. The war was not just dangerous.

It was run by fools.

From Saigon, I flew to Bangkok but got there too late to catch the C-130 to Udorn. I checked into the American Officers Hotel for the night. In the bar, I ran into some guys who had just come down from Udorn. They gave me some horrible news.

Herb, my friend and once would-be crew mate from Tucson, had been shot down in northern Laos. He was flying a fast-FAC mission—like Rick was the day he was killed—and was in the process of marking a target with a smoke rocket when the plane was hit. Herb and his pilot, Ralph, had ejected safely and were on the ground, but the rescue forces could not get to them due to the defenses. They were there for the night and it did not look good for their rescue. They had ejected in the same area where they were attacking. It is well known in the fighter business that if you bail out in an area you were bombing, the enemy would not take kindly to you if captured.

I was shocked and damned worried. Herb was special. Our Tucson time had made us a good crew and better friends. The thought of him being captured in a land where American captives were often tortured, killed, and dismembered, and maybe not in that order, appalled me.

The next morning, I got on the first C-130 headed for Udorn. Those C-130s stopped at every base in Thailand, so my arrival wasn't until afternoon. I don't know what I thought I could do; I just knew that I needed to be there. If there was to be a big SAR, maybe they would need me to fly on it. It seemed like an endless flight to reach the base.

I arrived at Udorn at almost the same time that Herb and Ralph were rescued. The base was abuzz with the news. I stowed my gear in my hooch and headed for the bar to get the details of the rescue.

The Club was packed, literally. Never had I seen so many guys in flight-suits, and they were loud. Many had flown on Herb's SAR, so stories flew everywhere. The enemy must have put up a big fight. The descriptions of the guns seemed to grow with each story. I even heard that Herb had used his survival radio to direct airstrikes on some of the guns.

All the stories agreed on one fact: It was one hell of a fight.

And we won.

The Panther Pack's commander (a real gentleman and future four-star general) called for silence in the bar. Due to the crowd and the excitement, that took some time. Finally, he could make his announcement. Herb and Ralph were in our hospital since both had been burned. The doctors had agreed to let them come to the club for exactly 30 minutes. They were on their way as he spoke.

The crowd erupted.

A few minutes later, minutes filled with bar noise almost as loud as the F-4's engines, two strange creatures entered. It was Herb and Ralph wearing dirty flight-suits but bandaged like the "Invisible Man" in that old sci-fi movie. They had the upper parts of their heads bandaged with only holes for eyes and noses.

The place erupted, again. It got even rowdier when Herb—I could tell it was Herb since he was shorter than Ralph—climbed up on the bar and walked to the brass bell hanging above it, and rang it with gusto. The eruption volume doubled. In those days, ringing the bell meant that the person ringing it was buying a round for everyone. It must have cost Herb a bundle.

When things calmed some, I cornered Herb and got the story. He and Ralph had found some targets and were preparing to direct an attack. They were under a high overcast, so they had their visors up. Herb did not mention it, but the F-4 engines smoked, making it easier to see from the ground. Add high clouds and the F-4 was visible for many miles. The gunners would have had no difficulty in keeping their target in their sights.

Ralph rolled in to fire a Willy Pete rocket to mark the target. As they started down in their dive, Herb felt rounds hit the bottom of their aircraft followed immediately by raging fire blowing out of the air-conditioning ducts on each side of his instrument panel. He said it felt like two blow-torch flames had hit him in the face.

Staying in the cockpit was not an option. He reached over his head and pulled the two face curtain handles that initiated the ejection sequence. Ralph did the same thing. There was no opportunity to make any calls or to get the plane away from the target area.

Herb's seat worked as advertised so within two seconds, he dangled helplessly under his parachute. The aircraft hit the ground and exploded well below him. Unfortunately, now he was an easy target as he swung under his chute. The gunners redirected their fire toward him.

I could only imagine how vulnerable it would feel to hang under a parachute as a target for 37-millimeter anti-aircraft guns. The guns had fired at both him and Ralph. Fortunately, they missed.

Herb said that, despite the gunfire, the parachute descent went quickly since they had been in a steep dive when they ejected. He came down in the jungle and immediately hid his parachute and himself. I remembered how good he had been at hiding when we went through Jungle Survival together just a few months earlier.

Enemy troops searched for the two aviators even as the fighters overhead tried to keep them away. The SAR forces got there quickly, but the guns prevented a fast rescue. At dark, Herb and Ralph were condemned to spend the night as prey in the jungle. Herb's face and neck were badly burned so he had to improvise some first-aid while hiding in the jungle. When we were in training in Tucson, Herb had taken some pre-med courses at the University of Arizona. He wanted to be a doctor, so he now had a patient before he even entered medical school.

The next morning, the SAR—and the fight—resumed. Herb was close enough to the guns to locate and identify them for the rescue forces. He used his FAC training to help silence the guns, and get himself out. The Jolly Green eventually got in, hovered, lowered its sling, and hauled Herb and Ralph on board.

Both flyers had serious burns, second- and third-degree, on their faces and necks. Herb even had burns through the vent holes in the armpits of his flight-suit. Fortunately, the Air Force had trashed the old cotton flight-suits and ordered us into Nomex. That material was advertised to withstand 900-degree fire. It must have worked.

The next day I went to the office. It seems that about the same time that I renewed my acquaintance with civilization in Sydney, Colonel Earl had gotten his plane shot up over Mu Gia Pass. He managed to get his bird back across the Fence and tried to get to Nakhon Phanom, commonly called NKP, an American base near the Mekong River. Unfortunately, he did not make it. He bailed out about five miles short of the runway. He was still a bit sore from the 12-G kick of the ejection seat.

Too many planes, flown by my friends, were being shot from the sky. After seeing what life was like "back in the world" as the Grunts in Vietnam said, I felt uncomfortable. In Sydney, there was no war. In Sydney, people were friendly; they lived the way people were supposed to live. There were no Rules of Engagement, Fence checks, tracers, or SARs. There were shops and restaurants, theaters and night clubs, busy streets and quiet parks.

There was no war.

***

In less than a week, though, it got worse.

Our office's recce replacements (for the two guys that were shot down twice) named John and Joe, were sent to film the progress on the Chinese Road in northern Laos. Like their predecessors, they were hit. They nursed their damaged RF-4C back across the Fence and it looked like they would make it to Udorn. The battle damage had taken out one of the primary hydraulic systems of the two that powered the flight controls.

As they approached the runway, only a few seconds from landing, the other hydraulic system failed.

Without hydraulics, the plane's flight controls froze, except for the elevator that controls the pitch of the plane. That control, due to the air flow on it, drove the plane full nose-up. John and Joe found themselves in a bird that suddenly pitched up hard and then, due to the slowing speed, rolled to the right; they went from being right-side up—in total control—over the approach to the runway, to being upside down—completely out of control—over the administrative and housing part of the base, only a few hundred feet in the air.

They had no time and they had no choice: Both ejected.

The two crewmembers landed on various roof tops, suffered some injuries, but survived.

The plane was another story. It crashed into the base; first it hit the top of a two-story barracks setting it ablaze, then it crashed through the base TV station.[2] The plane had several thousand pounds of jet-fuel on board, which immediately erupted in flames. The fire spread through the mostly wooden buildings around the wreckage.

The barracks, miraculously, was empty at the time, since it was mid-day.

The TV station was not. Nine people in the building were killed. There were more people in the vicinity that survived through the grace of God. One of our pilots who was walking out the front door of the hospital was shocked to see a fireball rapidly billow along the ground toward him. It stopped short, but he felt the intense heat.

The base burned for several hours. All our firefighting equipment, a considerable amount, was used to eventually get the fire controlled. Unfortunately, since it was the dry season, fighting the fire consumed the base's water reserves, even that in the swimming pool.

Thailand was not considered part of the conflict in Vietnam. Therefore, the non-flyers stationed there did not receive combat pay. Something was wrong with that policy. The airplanes and crews flying from Udorn were fighting the war. Those planes could not fly without the people on the ground. Now nine of them were dead, more injured, all because of enemy fire.

Still, no combat pay. Catch-22?

***

Things could not get worse, or could they?

Since the firefighters had used all our water reserves, the entire base now had a problem. It was still the dry season, so we had a severely limited supply of water for the thousands of Americans stationed at Udorn. The commander had no recourse but to implement water rationing. We would have running water from six to seven, mornings and evenings. We could shower and shave normally during those two one-hour periods. At all other times, there would be no running water. It seemed like the rational thing to do.

If we worked normal shifts, it would have been rational. But our flying operations ran around the clock, which meant that many people, both flyers and ground crews, had duty schedules that did not fit the hours. We had the beginning of a rapidly growing body-odor problem. It was hot and humid in the day, and almost as hot and more humid at night.

It was not just our showers that suffered. Our hooch girls, who did our laundry, had the same problem. They would gather the laundry in the morning and had fresh water for washing at the start. As the day progressed, the mass of usually sweaty uniforms had to be washed using the same water. I, unfortunately, looked inside one of the wash tubs; the water was black, pure black. That explained why my normally clean flight-suits seemed a bit stiff and stale. My underwear turned medium gray.

Yet by far, the worst problem was the toilets. They, too, only worked from six to seven, twice a day. Outside those times, they could not be flushed. Our hooch toilets filled fast. The latrine area, usually kept clean by our hooch girls, now reeked. Just to walk by it was disgusting. Using the toilets was even worse. Too quickly, the toilets filled to the top, so even those with strong constitutions could not use them.

It was a memory that defied escape.

To compound the problem, monthly most of us came down with three- or four-day cases of diarrhea, probably from the food or, as some believed, from the common-use water flasks we carried on our missions. It was normally not a major problem, just grumbling and cramps in the lower intestines—unless on a long mission, of course. That monthly problem was worsened by the water shortage. It was a vicious cycle. Some of the guys tried to hold it, which must have made things worse. A few had to go to the hospital.

The water shortage started a base-wide search for little-used toilets. If someone found an unfilled toilet, he shared that knowledge with no one. In short order, U. S. military personnel knew the location of every toilet on or near the base.

Many of us determined that the only solution was to cut down on eating. The urinals did not require water so a lot of us substituted beer for meals. Staying healthy did not seem nearly as important as staying away from those putrid toilets. Some guys even hopped into taxis and went to town just to use their toilets.

The water shortage even affected the Club. We had plenty of beer, but mixed drinks would have to be with soda, not water. In the dining room, water was not served with meals unless specifically requested, and then it was suspect as to how good it was.

One day at breakfast, before I started eating, I noticed there was egg yolk on my knife. When the waitress brought my meal, I showed her the dirty knife. I thought she would get me a clean one. Instead, she smiled—as all Thais seemed to do when I spoke to them—took my knife, and wiped it vigorously on her apron. She held it up to show me it was clean then placed it next to my food. She left. I ate. What the hell? I thought, I've got worse things to worry about.

***

Two weeks later, our office's new weapons officer, Tom, had his plane hit in northern Laos. He got it back across the Fence, but had to bail out near Udorn. For an area that supposedly had fewer guns than Steel Tiger, we lost a lot of planes up there.

We had a squadron party for a guy who was leaving. Of course, I attended. After the party, I could not find my lucky "Go to Hell" hat that I had with me on every mission. It was an OD bush hat of the style that many Grunts wore in South Vietnam. Most of us aviators wore them, and had since the Rolling Thunder days. I faithfully wore it into the cockpit, then tucked it inside my survival vest just above the chest buckle of my parachute harness. When I completed a mission, I always put it on as soon as I took off my helmet. I did that routine on every mission.

It was a superstition—the only superstition that I had.

I searched everywhere for it, to no avail. It was never washed, so I doubted anyone would steal it. But it was gone. Was that an omen? I knew it was nonsensical, but that hat was important to me. That hat— that stupid hat—may have kept me alive. It seemed to protect me—or at least I believed it did. I still remember the near-panic I felt when I couldn't find it. I searched everywhere, but no hat. Since I believed I needed a lucky hat, I switched to my Triple Nickel baseball hat. It was a poor substitute, but it would have to do for the remainder of the tour.

This was way too close and personal now. I was the only guy in my office that had not been shot down, and that included the three that had returned to the States. On every mission, there were anti-aircraft rounds fired at me, sometimes hundreds of them. So far, they had all missed. But why? That nagged at me. Was I that good? Was it blind luck? Was I using all my Green Stamps and soon going to be out of them? Maybe I was already out of them. If my survival was due to blind luck, each time I flew I spun the cylinder in a game of Russian Roulette. And then there was Rick. He was killed with one lousy machinegun round that flew through just the right space to get to him.

I did not sleep well.

***

About a week later, the squadron's administrative officer called me into his office.

"I have a Letter of Reprimand on you from the commander at Camp Alpha in Saigon. It seems you used abusive language to one of his officers and did not conduct yourself in a professional manner."

I couldn't tell if he was seriously concerned about the matter or being sarcastic. Was he scolding me or mocking the letter?

He continued, "Since you were filling one of the squadron's R and R slots, I'll keep the letter in our files. However, since you are assigned to the wing, well ..."

He stopped. He did not need to finish. The squadron only dealt with or cared about my flying, nothing else. The letter was meant to punish me for my conduct, but it went to the wrong organization.

Given the events since I returned from R and R, I didn't give a damn, and wouldn't have even if it had gone to Colonel Earl.

My Air Force records were one matter. My life was another.

Chapter 12

Nemesis

THE JOLLY GREEN GIANT flyers, the air-rescue heroes who flew large, slow helicopters over enemy territory to rescue downed pilots, were honored at the Udorn Officers' Club with a party to celebrate their 500th rescue. That evening, I walked into the O Club bar and, as when Herb and Ralph were rescued, it was packed. This time, it was not just guys from Udorn; there were aviators from all over Thailand. Many wore party suits with strange insignia, others wore the standard Nomex flight-suits with no insignia. Some of the party suits had "100 Missions: North Vietnam" and similar distinguished insignia. No matter what they wore, they were all there to thank the guys who hung their butts out—big time—to save others.

Literally. The Jolly Greens flew over a shot-down airman and stopped in the air, a sitting duck for anyone with an anti-aircraft gun, rifle, or slingshot. In many cases, the PJ, the para-rescue jumper, would lower himself—intentionally—to the ground and assist the downed pilot in getting on the hoist. Then, the PJ would wait—on the ground—for the next helicopter to pick him up. I don't know where America found such men, but we should be thankful that we have them.

The party must have lasted all night because they were still at it when I went to breakfast the next day. Someone told me that the all-nighter guys were ones who had been pulled from the gates of hell by the Jolly crews. It was probably the best hangover they ever had.

**

About that same time, someone at 7th Air Force Headquarters—or at least that was what I heard—discovered that Udorn had a supply of Mk-84s. The Mk-84 was the 2,000-pound version of the Mk-82, our standard 500-pound bomb. Most people would think that the 84 would have four times the explosive force of the 82 since it was four times the size. Not so. The 84 was a sleek giant that had much more than four times the punch. The 84 had a hardened steel case that weighed nearly 1,200 pounds, so it had 800 pounds of high explosives. However, the tremendous strength of the casing meant that the explosion was contained longer, hence producing a more powerful blast. It was similar to how a given size bullet generated more velocity in a rifle than it would in a pistol since the longer rifle barrel allowed the powder to build more pressure—or something like that. Anyway, compared to the Mk-84, the Mk-82—an impressive bomb itself—was a firecracker.

The staff officer must have concluded that since Udorn had Mk-84s in its arsenal, we should drop them. The F-4 could carry the Mk-84 on only three of the weapon stations: the two outboard stations and the center-line. Likewise, it could carry external fuel on only those same stations. The F-4 had to carry external fuel tanks; it simply sucked up too much gas not to use additional tanks. The result was that we would configure the plane with one Mk-84 on each outboard wing station, three Mk-82s on each of the two inboard stations, and a 600-gallon external tank on the centerline. We were carrying some serious explosive force with that ordnance load although we had 740 gallons less fuel.

There was only one minor problem: There was no target in all of Laos worthy of a 2,000-pound bomb. There were no factories, no hydro-electric dams, no manufacturing centers, no cement factories, no railroad marshalling yards, no submarine pens, nothing at all that was worthy of a bomb that could make a three-story-deep crater in an area nearly the size of a football field.

No problem, not in this war. Send the planes up with the bombs and let the FACs find targets. That must have made sense in Saigon because that's what happened.

My roommate, Dave, was scheduled to lead a flight with me on his wing. For this mission, a Thai bus driver took us to the planes in a Blue Bird crew bus. During the drive across the ramp to our birds, the driver suddenly stopped the bus, opened the door, ran down the steps, went a few feet away, and bent down. He picked up a dark, squirming insect, about the size of a small flip-phone so common a few years ago.

The insect had a Thai name, but we called it a "rice bug." The driver bit the head off the insect and sucked the rice from inside it. While I had heard that some insects were considered delicacies in this region, it was the first time that I had seen this in action. The driver hopped back on the bus and drove on as if nothing was unusual. It was for me.

When I got to my bird, I almost thought it was not ready since I was used to seeing the two, big 370-gallon drop tanks on the outboard stations. I had to get close to the plane before I could see the Mk-84s, one slung up close to the wing on each outboard station. I have never seen anything like it, a long, sleek, cigar-shaped, olive-drab bomb. Its four fins seemed miniscule compared to the length of the bomb. The only similarities to our Mk-82s were its fuses. It had the same instantaneous fuse on one end and a quarter-second delayed fuse on the other.

I slapped my hand against the side of the bomb; I have never felt anything so solid. The crew chief had adorned it with a few well-chosen words for the enemy.

Our mission took us up to The Barrel to work with a Raven FAC. When we checked in, the FAC said he wanted us to knock out a bridge.

Wow! A bridge!

I imagined a highway bridge like we have in the States, some two-lane affair spanning another highway, a railroad, or a river. OK, maybe it would only be a one-lane bridge. At least it would be a real target, an asset to the enemy that we could destroy.

Oops, no paved highways or railroads in Laos. The roads were dirt and I had yet to see a bridge, or a stoplight, or even a yield sign.

The bridge, said the FAC, was over a small river running down a valley between two steep, jungle-covered hills. He said there was a trail that went down one of the hills, crossed the river via the bridge, then ran up the other hill.

It was a foot bridge, and made of wood to boot. We were going to risk our asses to drop 2,000-pound bombs on a damn foot bridge.

What a war!

These monster bombs were known to create a big blast, so it only made sense to drop them one at a time. Yet with them mounted on the outboard stations, the F-4's weapons system limited us to either dropping the two simultaneously or else to make two passes and drop one on each pass. Since two of those things, dropped together, would be a waste of explosive power, Dave directed one bomb on each pass.

I don't remember where Dave's first bomb went, but when I rolled in on the "bridge," I could barely see the target. The trail that came down from the hills was hidden by the smoke from his bomb and the jungle canopy. The trail was only visible for a short distance on either end of the bridge.

And some bridge it was! I've seen bigger bridges decorating lawns in the States.

I released the bomb at my GIB's "pickle" call, and started my usual four- or five-G pull-out. The only problem was that when I dropped one bomb off my left wing, it meant that my right wing was now one-ton heavier than the left wing. That's what pilots call an "asymmetric" load— big time. As soon as I pulled the stick back, the plane started a hard roll to the right, toward the heavy wing, a roll that was difficult to control. Fortunately, I needed to jink anyway, so why not go right?

My bomb hit on the side of the far hill with a blast like I had never seen in my life. It looked like a small nuke had gone off. A white shockwave of compressed air radiated out from the center of the blast— a billowing ugly red-and-black fireball—like I had seen in films of nuclear explosions. The dark red fireball in the middle followed the shockwave. The blast must have moved the entire hill.

I put one hell of a big hole in the side of that hill, but I missed the bridge. Bridges were damned hard to hit, even with strings of bombs, as any F-105 pilot who flew on Rolling Thunder in North Vietnam would attest—and they bombed railroad bridges. There was a bombing technique to improve the odds of hitting a bridge, but that involved strings of six or a dozen bombs dropped at once. It wasn't until the advent of laser-guided bombs that we could consistently hit them.

Dave, on the other hand—steely-eyed killer that he was—nailed the bridge on his next pass. I mean a direct hit. Had the bomb been a dud, the sheer weight of it would have smashed that puny bridge into toothpicks. But the bomb detonated. The blast not only disintegrated the bridge and sent it to the next galaxy, it may have rerouted the river—permanently.

Even the FAC was impressed. And those Ravens were hard to impress.

While there might have been some—and I mean some—logic to dropping the 2,000-pounders to create large craters on the roads, there was little if any justification for dropping them elsewhere in Laos, especially on foot bridges. I heard that other F-4 units that dropped lots of mines had used the Mk-84 to crater roads, which forced the truck traffic off the road and into their minefields. That made sense as a use of the big brutes.

But blowing up foot bridges?

***

Shortly after that mission, some "Special Ops" guys brought a present for the flyers at Udorn. I said Special Ops without naming them because I never found out who they were or where they got the present. My impression at the time was that they were not military. In any case, they brought us a fully operational 37-millimeter anti-aircraft gun, and parked it outside wing headquarters.

There it sat—our number one nemesis.

It sat on what would best be compared to a flat-bed farm trailer, with rubber tires on each corner, the whole thing probably Russian-made. The OD-painted gun sat in the middle of the bed. It had a long barrel with a cone-shaped flash suppressor on the muzzle. The top of the breech had guides on each side to hold the clips of ammunition that were fed into it. On both sides of the barrel were metal seats, like those on old, horse-drawn farm equipment. In front of each seat was a ringed sight and a two-hand operated crank; on the floor below each seat was a single metal pedal, similar to a clutch or brake on an old farm tractor. The gun was designed in the late 1930s, and it looked like it had been.

But, as every fighter pilot in the war knew, it worked.

It took a crew of four or more to operate the gun: a commander, two aimers, and at least one (probably more) loader. The aimers occupied the two seats. Using their hand cranks, one aimer moved the barrel side-to-side to track the target's azimuth, while the other aimer moved

the barrel up or down to track the target's elevation. When each aimer
felt that he had the target in the proper location on his sight, he would
push his pedal to the floor. If the commander deemed the target was
in range and both pedals were depressed, the rounds fired.

The Nickel scheduler, a guy we called "The Whale"—respectfully
of course—decided we should try out the gun. He scheduled two F-4s
to "attack" the gun. He coordinated with the control tower to permit
those planes to make simulated bombing runs on the gun. To make this
worthwhile, he scheduled all the rest of us to be at the gun. We would
be the gunners—no ammo, of course.

There was a high, thin cloud deck over Udorn when we ran the test.
The two F-4s came into view much earlier than I thought they would.
Their black smoke trails[1] made my target acquisition easy—I was now an
azimuth-aimer on the 37. Spinning the wheel in front of me as I peered at
the F-4 through the rings of the sight was amazingly easy. Each time I felt
I had a tracking solution, I slammed my pedal to the metal floor. I could
hear the elevation aimer doing the same. We were two totally untrained
gunners, but we had no problem at all tracking the F-4s.

The only issue, the main one, the one that validated all of Ort's
preaching, was target range. That element required estimation by the
gun's commander and probably depended heavily on his experience.

That simulation was a stunning and eye-opening experience for me.
It did not take years of training to get a qualified anti-aircraft gunner;
any rogue on the street would do. It was no wonder that the North
Vietnamese considered the guns more valuable than the gunners.
We knew they had spare crews for each gun; now I knew that there
would never be a shortage of gunners.

Then there was the problem with that damned smoke-trail from the
F-4's engines. We saw the fighters when they were miles away from us.
All that was needed was to follow the smoke and it led straight to the F-4.

We radioed the fighters and told them to fly away until they lost sight of the gun, then turn back to it. They did. Those of us standing on or by the gun never lost sight of the F-4s. They were plainly visible the entire time. It was far too easy to see the fighters.

Another shock was the plane itself. The green and brown camouflage paint scheme that was so impressive when the big planes sat on the ground made it easy to keep the airborne planes in sight. That paint scheme might be valuable if the F-4 were at low altitude and the enemy was above, since it would make the plane more difficult to spot against the jungle background. Unfortunately, we mostly approached our targets from above. Only occasionally did we come in low, such as Mike and I had done on our BLU-31 mining mission. Normally, the enemy was below us, looking up. The F-4's camouflage paint scheme made it appear as a big green and brown dot against the blue or gray sky. It was the daytime equivalent to flying at night with the wingtip lights on or the afterburners lit.

It was insane!

We made the gunners' jobs easier by giving them a clear view of our planes. We lost hundreds of planes and pilots—millions of dollars per plane and years of training for the pilots—to gunners who could be trained in minutes and who fired guns left over from World War II. Even if we did not have the technology to get rid of the smoke trail, there must have been some gray paint somewhere. Even the Navy knew enough to paint their fighters gray.

My only fond memory of that experience was when I got off the gunner's seat. I noticed several small holes in the seat, holes that appeared to have been made by the pellets of a cluster bomb. Maybe the last guys that had shot this gun at our planes had had a bad day themselves.

I could only hope so.

Chapter 13

May 1970

THE NORTH VIETNAMESE MADE good use of the dry season in 1970 to an extent that we had not encountered before. They expanded their supply convoys down the infamous Ho Chi Minh Trail, that spider web of dirt roads and trails that ran mostly under thick jungle canopy. They no longer needed to truck supplies from the ports in the far north of their country; now the supplies came from depots in their southern panhandle. There, they loaded trucks, waited until dark, and then crossed into Laos via the major passes over the bordering mountains.

Despite our best—and expensive—efforts to stop this flow while it was on the Trail, much of it arrived untouched in South Vietnam.

Though President Johnson halted bombing over North Vietnam in the spring of 1968, we still flew reconnaissance flights to keep tabs on the enemy's activities. Those reconnaissance missions clearly showed the North Vietnamese buildup in their southern panhandle, including increasingly complex and sophisticated facilities. They had enlarged supply depots, repair facilities, truck marshalling areas, and even an oil pipeline that ended in a distribution complex, not far north of the DMZ.

Some unknown hero in our command structure decided that enough was enough. We would hit them where there was something to hit.

213

Before orders even arrived at the Udorn Command Post, word that something big was brewing spread around the base. No other rumor had traveled so fast. We were going to go get them, not some bull-shit "tree-park," and not some isolated gun-site guarding a next-to-worthless underwater bridge. No, we were going to get them where they lived. Better still, this was not going to be a couple of four-ship formations, this was going to be a maximum effort.

Damn, I can still feel the excitement.

The plan called for three days of all-out air attacks to wipe out those supply buildups.[1] On the first day, we would destroy the fuel distribution facility—the most valuable target—and its underground pipeline. Also on the schedule was destruction of the surface-to-air missile sites that often would fire missiles with impunity across the border into Laos. The second day we would attack the built-up supplies and the trucking facilities. The last day we would hit the military targets just west of the coastal town of Vinh, a major port and supply facility half-way up the North Vietnamese coast. From Vinh, they trucked the supplies into both Barrel Roll and Steel Tiger.

It was payback time!

I was thrilled to be scheduled for Day One. The Panther Pack was tasked to hit the fuel terminal with multiple four-ship formations of F-4s, most airplanes loaded with a dozen 500-pound Mk-82 bombs each. Other planes were to carry the monster Mk-84, the 2,000-pound brute, with delayed fuses to detonate well below ground level. The Triple Nickel would attack the missile sites, also with several four-ship formations. We would carry mostly "soft target" ordnance, including Mk-82s with fuse extenders (to create lethal shrapnel patterns among the non-armored missile support equipment), and cluster bombs.

Flights from the other Thailand fighter bases—Ubon, Takhli, and Korat—would join in the attack on the fuel terminal and pipeline.

The total strike force consisted of F-4s and assorted other aircraft such as radar jammers, Wild Weasels (F-105s equipped to hunt missile-guidance radars), command and control aircraft, air-refueling tankers, and, of course, search-and-rescue forces. In the old days of Rolling Thunder, the air war in North Vietnam, this would have been called an "Alpha Strike Force."

It was no "Thousand Plane Raid" such as the British attack on Cologne in World War II, but, for this stage of the war in Vietnam, it was a damned big strike-force.

I was assigned to fly number four in the last of our four-ships. Like many pilots, I did not like to fly the number four position, since by the time it was my turn to roll in on a target, every gunner in the world knew what was happening, and they all could point their guns at me. There was never any surprise left for the number four man. He just had to suck it up and point his plane—and his body—down the chute.

May 1 was different. This was a big deal. Better yet, the number four man in each of our formations carried "wall-to-wall" cluster bombs: 11 canisters (they were too large to carry one on the forward station on the six-station center-line rack, so I would have three on each inboard station, and five on the centerline). With that ordnance load, I did not need to be accurate. All I had to do was hit the earth. The wide donut-shaped pattern created by the bomblets in each canister covered about 1,000 feet in diameter. Multiply that by 11, and even with pattern overlap, there would be a hell-of-a-lot of explosions over one hell-of-a-large area.

The flights gathered in the large intelligence briefing room in wing headquarters. The flyers for the Nickel alone filled many chairs, the same for the Panthers, and who knows how many extras (crews for the spare aircraft, observers, brass, etc.). The excitement in the room was tangible. No getting shot at just to bomb some worthless piece of nothing; we were going to hit 'em and do it hard. We were going to kick ass and take names.

Ort, still sitting around, would have loved it. Sadly, that fiery leader was not involved.

However, there was one problem I had to deal with besides the big fight. Each cluster bomb canister weighed 825 pounds. Multiply that by 11 and it meant that I would have 9,075 pounds of blunt-nosed, high-drag ordnance hanging on my bird. Add on the 17,000 pounds of fuel, air-to-air missiles, and bomb racks, and it meant that my F-4 would weigh about 57,000 pounds, a mere 1,000 pounds below the maximum it could handle. Further, the cluster bombs were mounted in such a way that the center of gravity of the plane would be well forward. The result, as I remember,[2] was that my takeoff speed was about 182 knots (210 miles per hour), but my nose-wheel liftoff speed would be three knots higher, 185. Since the nose had to come up to fly, I would be in a very high-speed tricycle until the Phantom reached 185.

Because we wanted to surprise the enemy on this mission, the entire ground operations were to be radio-silent. No flight check-ins, no calls for engine start, taxi, or even takeoff. Absolutely no radio communications until we hit the targets (no doubt the procedure-oriented staffs at all the Stateside training bases cried out in horror). All the ground operations for our F-4s and the spare aircraft would be synchronized by time alone.

After I strapped in and got my engines running, I had a few minutes to look around. There were so many F-4s running that the noise, even with the engines at idle, dominated the airfield. Heat ripples and dark smoke rose over the entire F-4 section of the parking ramp. Crew chiefs scurried around the birds, pulled wheel-chocks, and directed birds onto the taxi-way in their proper order. Contrary to the usual practice of removing the bomb-arming lanyards just prior to takeoff, the arming crews were on the taxi-way, swiftly arming each aircraft in sequence.

The work that the ground crews did during the Vietnam war deserved a hell-of-a-lot more credit than I have yet seen given to them. Those guys took care of every essential detail, worked in oppressive heat and humidity, but, in the Catch-22 manner of the war, did not even get combat pay. If this day was big for the pilots, it was also big for the ground crews. With so many planes launching at one time, they had to work their asses off.

The planes, one after another in the proper order, taxied from their parking spots onto the taxi-way, then moved in line to the runway. Each bird lowered its canopies as it approached the runway, lowered the flaps, turned onto the runway, and, without stopping as in normal operations, did quick engine run-ups while rolling forward, then lit the afterburners and roared down the runway. As fast as one bird lit its burners, the next was on the runway to repeat the process.

Anyone who had been near a modern fighter when it lit its afterburners, knew that there was not only the tremendous roar, but also vibration that rattled everything, right down to the pit of the stomach. The air rippled from the tremendous heat and merged with the black smoke from the idling engines of the waiting birds.

It was awesome in the truest sense of the word as fighter after fighter roared into the sky.

The planes accelerated down the runway on alternate sides to avoid some of the horrendous jet-wash, the high-velocity swirling air generated by the wingtips and the two afterburning J-79 engines of the plane in front.

The pilots pulled back their control sticks at the proper speeds; the F-4s literally sprung into the air, landing gear retracting almost immediately, boiling air seeming to follow each bird.

One after another they launched. When one loaded F-4 took off, it was impressive; when many took off, it was overwhelming. I would almost swear that the very earth shook from the power of those mighty afterburners. When the pilots pulled the engines out of afterburner, the F-4's ugly black smoke-trail replaced the heat ripples.

My turn came quickly.

This mission was amazingly well briefed and coordinated for a radio-silent operation. My GIB called "canopy locked" while mine came down almost simultaneously. I called "canopy locked" and "flaps" as I turned to align with the runway, which was nearly engulfed with the smoke and heat-rippled air from the planes ahead. I rapidly pushed the throttles up individually to ensure the engines responded, then called "hack" (for the GIB to record the time) as I pushed both throttles to the military power position, quickly verified the tachometers at 100 percent RPM, then slid the throttles outboard to light the after-burners. As I moved them forward, I counted the push as each stage of the burners lit. Finally, with a quick glance at the gauges, I verified that the afterburner nozzles were wide open. We had 34,000 pounds of thrust pushing us from the two large afterburner chambers.

Most takeoffs in the F-4 went quickly—but not this one.

This was the heaviest takeoff I ever made in my entire 22-year flying career. The bird rolled down the runway, without the familiar kick from the burners. The runway markers, spaced at 1,000-foot intervals on the 10,000-foot-long runway, moved by, slowly at first, but gathering speed. My GIB called "100 knots," the speed beyond which there would be no aborting. From this point, the only options were to either take off or eject.

Still, there we were, rolling down the runway, runway-remaining markers a little blurrier as we passed each succeeding one, with the end getting closer by the second. When 150 knots passed, I moved the stick back to be sure it actually worked. (We had checked all the flight controls before taxi, but it was nice to know they still worked.)

At 180 knots, the end of the runway was way too close and now rushed toward us. We were about to set my personal speed record for any vehicle I have been in on the ground—I hoped. I moved the stick aft to the takeoff position and watched the airspeed indicator pass the 182 knots computed takeoff speed.

We were still on the ground.

Just after 185 knots, the nose sprang up and the F-4 jumped off the ground. My left hand jerked the gear handle up as fast as I could get it since we did not need drag from the wheels and there were trees to consider, followed quickly by the flaps. We had used about 9,000 feet of runway. At 300 knots, I pulled the engines out of afterburner. At that point, I hoped we had just finished the scariest part of the mission.

We joined into tactical formation, our "Nickel Spread," which was line-abreast, about 1,000 feet apart. That's when I learned that I would have trouble keeping my position on the far-right side. My bird not only was heavier than the others (by about a ton or so), but also the big, fat, blunt-nosed cluster-bomb canisters created considerably more drag than the sleek, aerodynamic 500-pound bombs on the rest of the birds in my flight. My throttles stayed close to 96 percent just to maintain position.

Beyond my flight was a sight like none I had ever observed. All around, above a low cloud deck, were flights of F-4s. Not one or two, not six or eight. No, there were four-ship formations spread all over the sky,[3] each ship trailing the tell-tale black smoke that poured out of the J-79 engines when they were not in afterburner.

It was an unforgettable sight. A flying armada of what was then the most powerful warplane in the world, each loaded to the teeth with lethal ordnance, all pointed into North Vietnam.

Spectacular! The memory still gives me chills. Someone was about to have a very bad day indeed.

We crossed the panhandle of Laos rapidly, since each flight flew at 450 knots. Still, with the phenomenon known as "temporal distortion"—when, under stress, time seemed to slow to a crawl—the flight seemed long. Waiting for the unknown was always scary, especially when the unknown consisted of heavy guns and surface-to-air missiles. The flight took long enough for my mouth to get dry and for a bit of nervous banter with my GIB. The excitement of being in such a powerful strike force had worn off a bit, and now the expectation of combat, of anti-aircraft rounds, and maybe even surface-to-air missiles loomed.

No matter what I did, no matter how good I thought I was, no matter what tactics I employed, there could always be a Golden BB, the bullet with my name on it. That was one bullet that no amount of skill and cunning could avoid. Each mission, each time into the battle, meant the possibility of meeting that Golden BB, as Rick had seven months earlier.

Fortunately, things got busy in combat, so there was little time to worry about the unknown dangers ahead. The first thing that got my attention was a huge black cloud rising in the sky well in front of my flight. It was tall, ugly, and rose rapidly, like a thunderstorm building on a sizzling summer day, only it was black. It had to be the fuel facility blowing sky-high. Literally sky-high; the cloud seemed to rise toward my altitude of about 20,000 feet. (I doubt that it got that high, but in the excitement, it could have, and in my memory over the years, it did.) The Nickels' close friends and rivals, the Panther Pack, had clobbered it. The delayed fused bombs had done their job and blown both the surface facility and the underground pipeline.

The North Vietnamese reacted violently, as would be expected. In front of my bird, for the first time in my tour, I saw dark smoke from the airbursts of 85- and 100-millimeter rounds, the radar-aimed heavy anti-aircraft guns. There were none of these guns in Laos that I had encountered; the biggest there were the 57-millimeters. These heavy airbursts looked just like the films from World War II, the classic "flak" bursts, designed to hit a plane with shrapnel. They were big, ugly black puffs that hung in the sky after the rounds detonated, a reminder that more were coming up.

We quickly reached the missile site, with its six launching pads surrounding a center group of radar and support vans, all in a camouflaged six-point star arrangement. There were no missile launches that I saw, probably because the Wild Weasels—the radar-hunting F-105s—had suppressed or destroyed the radars. The first three birds in my flight went in with their 500-pounders, 36 of them, exploding in long strings across the site, taking out missiles, launchers, and radar vans alike.

Devastating!

I lit the afterburners to get some speed, swung around to see the site through the smoke of the exploding bombs, and rolled in to my dive. My cluster bombs were armed to ripple off the bird at .14-second intervals. When I hit the pickle button, there was a short staccato of bumps as the ejectors—the shotgun-shell like charges that pushed the bombs clear of the airplane—fired and the bomb canisters dropped to their opening altitude, about 1,500 feet above the ground. At that point, the clamshells opened and more than 7,000 of the bomblets spread out into giant, overlapping donut-shaped patterns.

I pulled off the dive with a five-G climbing turn and looked back in time to see thousands of bright sparkles as the anti-personnel bomblets exploded all over the missile site and around it in the jungle. If there was anyone alive in that sparkling array, he would have had to be underground, or the luckiest person on the planet.

Day one—mission accomplished!

***

The trip home was marred when an F-105 Wild Weasel was shot down in Mu Gia Pass, one of the heavily guarded supply routes from North Vietnam to Laos. The two crewmembers were alive, but surrounded in an area where rescue was unlikely. I heard later that the enemy did not capture the crew immediately, but let them stay free, temporarily, to try to draw in a rescue force to the highly defended area. When the rescue force waited for dark, the North Vietnamese captured the downed crew. I never found out if they survived the war.

Except for the downed F-105, the day was a smashing success (pardon the pun). We had landed a solid blow. It felt great. After risking our asses to attack trucks and trees, this was wonderful.

I sat out the attacks on Day Two. These strikes on the supply build-up were reportedly as successful as the Day One missions. One of the Panther Pack birds was shot down, but fortunately, the crew was rescued.

***

My next participation was on Day Three.

The third-day mission was to be the largest yet, with even more attack aircraft, made up of four-ship formations, again from all over Thailand and South Vietnam. The objective was to eliminate the supply build-ups that extended from just west of Vinh and stretched along a winding road—Route 7, I think—that went northwest to eventually enter Laos at an area we called "The Fish's Mouth."

This would be no routine mission for me, if such a mission existed. For the first and only time in my life, I was tasked to do an Armed Reconnaissance—which we called Road Recce—mission. I had trained to do this mission in the States during my pre-Vietnam formal training, had practiced it several times while stationed in Korea and North Carolina, but I never dreamed that I would do it in the war.

As one might guess from the name, the mission was to fly along roads and look for targets of opportunity. While a reconnaissance aircraft would take pictures of targets for consideration of later attacks, the Road Recce aircraft were to bomb the targets as fast as they found them. To do this, the Road Recce pilots flew low and very fast, weaving back and forth across the road to look for targets, then executed pop-up attacks when any targets were found.

Like the missions on the previous two days, all ground operations, formations, and air refueling were done without the use of our radios. Again, we launched in sequence and started across Laos. Again, there were formation after formation of F-4s, seemingly countless four-ship formations, spread across the sky in a giant aerial armada of heavily armed fighters.

As with my assignment on Day One, I was number four in the formation, this time loaded with twelve 500-pound bombs. The six bombs on the two inboard stations had three-foot-long fuse-extenders to explode the bomb prior to it striking the ground. The assumption was that any targets we would find would be "soft," that is, not armored. The six bombs on the centerline rack, without fuse-extenders, were fused to explode on impact.

We crossed Laos, then the southern North Vietnamese panhandle. The flights with assigned targets turned north and went directly toward them. Ahead of us were many flights spread out into tactical formations. Each four-ship had its planes widely spaced to better look for threats. The planes all produced the tell-tale smoke trails that made the mighty F-4 so easy to see. Following that armada as it fanned across the sky made me realize just how powerful this day's strike force was.

Our flight continued toward the coast then turned left and intercepted the road west of Vinh. Our formation split into two elements of two aircraft each, with about two or three miles between each element. We did a rapid descent to our recce altitude of several hundred feet above the ground. We increased our airspeed to 500 or 550 knots, and turned west to follow the road.

There was plenty of adrenaline flowing on any combat mission, but there was even more now. Many heavily armed flights of F-4s had preceded us. Ahead, as far as I could see, was an inferno. There were numerous fires and ugly, black smoke, wrecked vehicles, and assorted rubble on or near the road, and often on both sides.

The wide, dirt road was in a long, weaving valley, adjacent to a river that originated somewhere in Laos and snaked down toward the sea on the North Vietnamese coast. The valley was bordered by sometimes-steep, green jungle-covered hills, often nearly sheer, on both sides. Occasionally, the road crossed the river, especially when the river meandered with a large loop, so the road would cut off the turn and take the shortest route. There were no villages of note and few houses or huts along the mostly dirt road, but there were "truck parks"—pull-off areas—where the drivers could stop to rest, eat, refuel, or obtain maintenance on their vehicles. By the time we reached these truck parks, they had been bombed by the earlier fighters so that little remained to warrant an attack from us.

I kept my Phantom low and fast. That, itself, was thrilling. The trees blurred as they passed, often mere feet below my plane. The high speed mandated that I focus on what was ahead, not what was under me. Using hard turns—sometimes four-G's—I crossed back and forth over the road, being careful to stay on the opposite side from my element leader. I watched his plane. When he rolled into a sharp turn in my direction, I could plainly see the white vapor-trails from his wingtips, a stark contrast with the blurry, green jungle racing by below him. As soon as he banked toward me, I did the same in his direction. I pulled the plane hard so that I would pass behind his plane, occasionally close enough to feel the turbulence from his exhaust.

It was the classic "fighter weave." Following directly behind him would have been foolish as any anti-aircraft fire directed toward my leader would likely miss there. I did not want to be in that part of the sky. So, we weaved, nearly line-abreast, with his airplane only slightly forward of mine. High speed at low altitude was essential as the gunners needed a couple of seconds to get their guns pointed, and by then, we either had started our attack or were gone. Just to make sure the gunners couldn't get me in their sights for too long, I kept the bird turning, sometimes hard enough to pull the sweat from my forehead down around my eyes.

The experience of low, fast flight was exhilarating by itself, but doing it in combat defied description. Watch the ground, watch my leader, watch for anti-aircraft fire, all while searching for targets. There was a massive amount of adrenaline flowing in our cockpits.

As we rounded one of the many turns, I saw tracers coming from a copse of small trees and brush between the river and the road. It was a group of anti-aircraft guns well positioned to cover the dirt road which snaked by their position. From the opposite side of the river, I saw the guns fire at my element leader as he went by. His speed caused their fire to miss well behind him. I turned hard left to cross the river just a few hundred feet above it. When I was across, I rolled into a hard right-turn with the element leader now at my three o'clock position, and the guns at my one o'clock. Since they had used my leader as a target, I decided they should become targets, too.

I rolled the F-4 level, pulled hard on the stick to start the pop-up attack, and lit my afterburners to climb quickly. The F-4 shot skyward in a steep climb, then I rolled the plane almost inverted, so that the guns—now my target—appeared near the top center of my canopy. I pulled the Phantom's nose down hard, pulled the engines out of afterburner, and then rolled so that the "pipper" was just short of the enemy guns. My GIB said the dive angle was 45 degrees and called the descending altitudes for my reference. Below me, just beyond my pipper that seemed to move across the ground, were four 37-millimeter guns, arranged in a diamond pattern, and much closer together than I would have expected. Unlike the guns I had seen in Laos, these were in the open, with little or no berms to cover the crews as they would have had if they had been in bunkers. The gunners must not have felt threatened after two years of the bombing halt.

Most pilots believed that the 37-millimeter gun did not have a muzzle flash. We believed that the first signs of it firing would be when we initially saw the tracers, several hundred yards after the rounds left the barrel. That may have been true when observing the guns from the side, but the "common knowledge" did not apply when I looked straight down the barrels of the guns. The gunners must have seen me start my pop-up, and slewed their guns my way. As my pipper moved toward the middle of the diamond, I saw sparkles on the muzzles of each of the four barrels. Fortunately, this all took only about three seconds, as the pipper quickly reached the center of the guns and I hit the pickle button with my right thumb and three 500-pound bombs, two with three-foot fuse extenders, separated from the Phantom and hurled toward the guns.

As soon as the bombs separated, I did a hard, diving pull-off descending back to just above the treetops. The tracers from the guns were going up, and I was going down, the ideal situation as far as I was concerned. By now I was refocused on continuing the Road Recce, but my GIB, who strained to look back over his right shoulder, said the bombs hit smack in the middle of the guns. Since the gunners were not protected by any bunkers, it probably was not a pleasant time for them. While I feel bad about the people now, in 1970 I did not. I felt good about hitting them. It was more than satisfying.

Our reconnaissance aircraft had found the valuable targets, and there were plenty of fighters ahead of us to destroy what those recces had found. That multitude of fighters that preceded us did a superb job by destroying anything worthwhile. As was typical of Road Recce flights, we looked for anything that those fighters might have missed. After we passed the guns, our flight hit a couple of nearly destroyed storage areas, probably not worth the effort.

At such a high speed, it did not take long to cover the road all the way to the Laotian border. Beyond the border, the road continued into Northern Laos, but over there it had been well patrolled, night and day, by American gunships and attack aircraft. Anything worthwhile on the other side would be well concealed in the jungle, invisible, or nearly so, from the air.

I approached the border with three bombs left. I saw on my right a surface-to-air missile site situated on the crest of a hill, on the North Vietnamese side of the border. As I remember that sight, my plane was below the hill, still streaking through the valley, so I was looking slightly up toward it. This SAM site, so I had heard, occasionally lobbed a missile or two across the border, relying on LBJ's bombing halt to protect it from our counter-strikes.

But I was already on their side of the border, so there was no bombing-halt protection to shield them now.

I pulled the F-4 into another pop-up attack, with the SAM site about 40 degrees on my right. I could see the radar and control vans in the center of what approximated a camouflaged six-pointed star layout, with launchers at each point of the star. All the launchers that I could see appeared empty, their missiles most likely fired at the multitude of fighters that had passed before us.

No matter. I rolled in on the radar and control vans in the center of the launchers, let the pipper track until it was on top of the vans, then released my last three bombs, at least one with a fuse extender. I hit the pickle-button, sending the last three bombs toward the vans.

During my hard, climbing, left pull-off, I got a brief glimpse of the three bombs exploding in the middle of the vans. The red fireballs with ensuing black smoke engulfed the target. The vans seemed to scatter, as if lifted into the air by some pin-point earthquake. Since the launchers were all empty, I doubt that any people were in the vans. Anyone with any sense would be in a bunker considering all the fighters that had passed.

One thing was certain: that missile site was—temporarily, at least—worthless.

***

The three days of bombing did massive damage to the North Vietnamese war effort. We destroyed far more of their equipment and supplies in that short span than we had in months, if not years, of bombing single trucks along the Ho Chi Minh Trail. On the Trail, fuel and lubricants were dispersed so that any one bomb would likely hit no more than a barrel or two, or maybe a single tanker. In North Vietnam, the enemy did not make the effort to disperse those resources. They had assembled supplies and vehicles in depots and open truck parks. Unlike in Laos, these resources made lucrative targets.

As for us, we lost three airplanes. One was the F-105 that went down on Day One. The rumor around Udorn was that the pilot had been strafing trucks on the way out of North Vietnam. His mission was Wild Weasel, missile suppression, not strafing trucks. The short-range 20-millimeter cannon in his airplane was no match for the anti-aircraft guns in Mu Gia Pass. In all my time in the war, I never strafed, and only carried a cannon on one daylight B-52 escort mission. Besides the Panther Pack bird that went down on Day Two, the other loss was an F-4 in the flight behind mine on the Day Three mission. That flight, the very last up the road that I had recced, dropped land mines, mostly anti-personnel bomblets designed to kill, maim, or hinder anyone trying to clean up the mess. The crew was listed as missing in action. I heard that was later changed to killed.

We had hit the enemy where it hurt them most, and we hit them hard. Why not keep at it? After all, the war had not ended. Why not make the North Vietnamese understand that we would do whatever it took to stop their aggression—yes, it was aggression on their part—in South Vietnam? If we had continued that effort in their southern panhandle, we could have strangled their forces that were fighting our troops. Even a relatively self-sufficient army such as the North Vietnamese forces in the South required a lot of supplies, daily, to remain a viable combat force. If we had continued those attacks, we could have degraded the enemy forces in South Vietnam to such an extent that the ultimate fall of South Vietnam may not have occurred.

If only ...

But we did not.

We went back to the inane and costly policy of trying to stop individual trucks that were well hidden in the jungle.[4] That's how it went with the war, at least until 1972.[5] We fought with severe restrictions.

We lost men and aircraft vainly attempting to destroy targets that were essentially worthless, but if we hit the enemy where it really hurt him, our leaders lost their nerves, or maybe their jobs.[6] Such was the way of the war. Fight the enemy, but not too hard; lose men and planes in combat, but do not go to the source of the enemy's power. How utterly frustrating for us; hang our asses out, lose our friends, but do not do serious damage to the enemy.

Chapter 14

Home

ONE EVENING, I LANDED back at Udorn as the daylight faded. After de-arming, I turned onto the taxi-way to go back to the parking area. The taxi-way from the de-arm area passed the AC-119 gunship parking ramp. I could see one of the black 119s parked away from the others.

Something about the lone airplane did not look right. My GIB thought so, too. We were nearly abeam of it when we both realized what was strange about it: A big section of the plane's wing was missing. The entire aileron was gone.

We stopped our taxiing and looked closer. The wing had literally been sawed off just outboard of the auxiliary jet engine. The cut was jagged and quite ugly. It was definitely from battle damage, not some maintenance work.

Back at the squadron, we heard the story. The Stinger, his call-sign, had been working a target in Laos when a string of anti-aircraft rounds had literally sliced off most of the wing outboard from the auxiliary jet engine.[1]

It must have been terrifying in the gunship as they did not have ejection seats. If the plane had spun out of control, bailing out would have been nearly impossible. Worse, if they bailed out and were captured, they would die a horrible death.

While the plane initially lost altitude, the pilots, with heroic effort, got it back into level flight. The crew jettisoned everything they could to lighten the bird and they got back home safely.

It was truly "A wing and a prayer."

***

It was spring. I could imagine the flowers, trees, and grass in southern Pennsylvania emerging from winter with splendor and color. I always loved spring back home: blue skies, singing birds, and flower-fresh, fragrant air. But Thailand was not Pennsylvania. I was not on the afternoon's flying schedule one day when I heard commotion outside my room at the hooch. There were several excited voices, but I could not make out the cause. When I went out, I saw a lovely sight.

Rain!

The rainy season had started. While I discussed this wonderful event with several of the guys, two naked men with bars of soap came out of their rooms and ran out in the now-pouring rain. They stood on the open ground between the buildings and started an outdoor shower. The once-dry red clay soil quickly turned into mud, but the bathers didn't give a damn.

It was water, and lots of it.

Someone produced warm beer. The event turned into an impromptu party. In short order, we had every guy not flying either standing in the rain or sitting on the hooch rail. One thing about being a Nickel, we stuck together; we flew together, we took care of each other, and we partied together.

With the onset of the rainy season, the water shortage soon ended. No more searching for toilets that weren't full. No more holding my breath when I passed the latrine. No more wearing clothes that had been washed in black water. There was water.

Beautiful, clean water!

Within days, I discovered why the hooch was built on stilts. The ground quickly saturated and standing water rose under the building. To my surprise, I saw small fish swimming underneath. Someone explained that at the end of each rainy season, the fish laid eggs in the mud. They hatched at the beginning of the next rainy season. Nature always found a way.

We soon discovered how effective the drainage ditch around the runway was. I had run next to it almost daily since I quit smoking. On each run, besides steering myself clear of snakes, I wondered about the purpose of the large ditch between the road and the runway. It appeared overly wide and deep to me. I knew it was for flood control, but during the dry season it seemed a big waste. Yet when the rain started, it quickly filled with water. If the rain was especially heavy, water overflowed the giant ditch and covered the end of the runway.

The water in the ditch was high, so the two fighter squadrons decided to make good use of it. Someone organized some life-raft races. Our inflatable rafts were one-man types, propelled by arm power. One raft from each squadron faced off with a pilot—usually slightly inebriated—in it. There was lots of hollering from the banks of the ditch and no end to attempts to cheat or impede the other squadron. No one cared who won.

***

Flying from and to the field became much more work. On departure, flight join-ups frequently encountered thick clouds and rain showers. Instead of coasting back to the field after a mission for a visual landing, we now had to use instrument approaches. No more admiring the peaceful Thai countryside and dreaming of a cold beer at the Club.

Now I had to focus on my instruments. The once routine parts of the missions became work.

Landing on the wet runways often was eye-opening, too. One of our more scientific-minded pilots told me there was algae present that made them seem greasy when wet. I could not verify that, but I know that a fast F-4 required a lot of care when landing. Light crosswinds, normally ignored, could now be dangerous. I had to pay attention to the Phantom's deceleration rate. The aircraft brakes were less effective on the slippery concrete. Also, I had to be more aware of the barriers' locations in case the bird did not slow properly. Sometimes, I put my right hand on the tail hook lever—just in case. Worse, the F-4 weighed about 17 tons when landing so if it skidded just a little during the landing roll, I felt a sharp pang of fear in my stomach.

From my office window, I saw one RF-4C pilot accidentally taxi off the concrete. When his main landing gear hit the soggy grass, the plane sunk in all the way to the wing. Fortunately, we had a mobile, industrial-style crane that we called "Big Bertha" that hoisted the RF-4 out of its bad situation. The rainy season brought lots of changes.

But the water restrictions ended. The toilets worked! The search for unfilled toilets ended.

***

Each rainy-season day was the same as any other, humid as all hell, rain showers passing by, seemingly every five minutes, and everything damp, wet, or rusty. One day in late June I rode the Blue Bird from the housing area around the end of the runway to the squadron as I had almost every day since getting to Udorn. When I entered the building, the duty NCO told me the Administrative Officer wanted to see me. I had not done anything stupid recently, at least not that I knew of, so I figured it was some minor matter such as not having my paperwork in order. When I went into his office, I got a royal shock.

"How would you like to go home early?" was his question.

PACAF— Pacific Air Force headquarters in Hawaii—had some F-4s that needed to be ferried home, back across the Pacific Ocean. They were at Yokota Air Base, Japan, and PACAF would curtail tours for the crews that volunteered to fly them back to the States.

Of course, there was a catch to this deal—Catch-22. The crews had to agree to stay with the planes until they got them home. If a bird broke down en route, the crew was committed to stay with it until it was flyable again. The plane and the crew would go home together, no matter how long it might take.

I admit that several months earlier—before my R and R reintroduced me to a normal world—I had seriously considered extending my tour by six additional months. That dumb idea was mostly out of some vague fear of going home. I really did not know how to do anything other than drop bombs and drink beer with other bomb-droppers. A lot of guys felt like I did. We had gotten so wrapped up in our work that we had trouble imagining anything else. The memory of life back in "the world" was distant and foreign. Here, things were structured, if distasteful. My friends were here: the people that I trusted daily, not with my money, not with my happiness, but with my life. And they trusted me. Like most of them, I figured that I would just stay in the war until it ended, or I did.

Suddenly that all changed. I would be able to leave almost immediately. I would just have time to fly one last mission—my "Fini-Flight"—process out, and leave for Japan. My back-seater would be a veteran whom we called "Pic." He was also near the end of his tour and had already accepted a new assignment.

I said, "Hell yes!"

Using a term that the Grunts in South Vietnam had made universal for the military, I was now officially "Short!" Short-timers were near the end of their tours. Some guys started counting when they had fewer than 100 days remaining. In the Nickel, guys usually counted only the last month since there were still a lot of missions to fly.

This was different; I only had a few days left. That was called being a "single-digit midget." While single-digit was short, the ultimate in shortness was to only have a "wake up" left on the tour.

It was celebration time.

***

Dave was already a short-timer, so he suggested that we make one final trip to the Five Sisters restaurant. It would be the last visit for both of us to Udon Thani, so why not? The Thai taxi ride that took us there might have qualified as another combat mission. The taxi drivers had lots of customers at the base, so they did not like to waste time on trips. This guy was fearless; he made lanes where there were none, passed whenever he felt like it, ignored the few traffic signs, and used only the accelerator and horn. There was no one braver, and more terrifying, than a Thai taxi driver who was in a hurry.

Our final trip to the restaurant was memorable. I ordered the exact same pineapple, rice, and fish that I had on our first visit. Dave, however, had tried everything on the menu except the very last item: Deep-Fried Small Birds. He decided it was time to try it.

I needed to use the restroom, which I had never done at this restaurant. This was a mistake. When I asked one of the owners where it was, she pointed to the door that led to the kitchen. I figured that there must be a hallway inside the door that went to the restroom.

Wrong.

The restroom was in the kitchen. It was a small room with a door that had a six or eight-inch gap at the bottom, and stopped several feet below the ceiling, not much more than a saloon door in cowboy movies. Inside was a hole in the concrete—no toilet, no urinal, no toilet paper roll, no sink, only a hole in the floor. Just outside the door, the staff prepared food and carried it out to the customers.

When I got back to our table, I told Dave about the restroom. He replied with his usual, somewhat gravelly laugh, a laugh so distinct I could probably pick it out of a crowd even today.

"You should have known better," he said. "What are you, some FNG?"

He was right, of course.

Then our meals arrived. Mine was as expected.

His was not. There, on a bed of white rice, individually wrapped in waxed paper, were six small birds lying on their sides. Six little birds, each about four inches long, in a neat row all facing the same direction, complete with their feathers, beaks, and little feet.

That was too much, even for Dave. He ate the rice and filled the space with some beer. We did, however, have our last, and most memorable, trip down town. We were short-timers.

***

But nothing comes easy. The schedulers, perhaps pissed-off that Pic and I would miss the last six weeks of our tours, assigned us to lead a two-ship formation to escort an RF-4C reconnaissance bird[2]—over North Vietnam. Damn! These end-of-tour flights were supposed to be milk runs, go bomb some trees someplace, no serious anti-aircraft guns, that sort of thing. Instead, we were going to follow a low-altitude, high-speed reconnaissance plane through the panhandle of North Vietnam, over the area that we had bombed heavily the month before. They had their first-string gunners there, and missiles too. On top of that, they were probably still pissed about our recent attacks.

The clouds were lower than normal the next morning when we briefed with the recce crew. We took off, joined with the RF-4C, crossed the Fence outbound for the last time, then the Laotian panhandle and entered North Vietnam near Mu Gia Pass. The clouds were just as low and dark as they had been at Udorn, and the visibility was worse. Thanks to the lousy weather, the flight had already been a challenge and we hadn't started the worst part.

The RF-4C has the same basic airframe as the F-4D, except with a sleeker nose. It had cameras and a ground mapping radar where we had the big, bulky air-intercept radar. The recces carried three external fuel-tanks, one on each outboard station, and one on the centerline station, along with two electronics pods on the inboard stations for jamming radars. We carried two outboard fuel-tanks, but had three of the blunt-nosed, 800-pound cluster bombs on each inboard station, and six 500-pounders on the centerline. Given those aerodynamic differences, the recce was a lot faster than we were.

The recce turned north on his route, dropped to a few hundred feet above the jungle, and promptly accelerated to about 600 knots. At full military-power our two F-4Ds simply could not keep up, so we had to cycle in and out of afterburner. We stacked ourselves on each side of the recce, at his four and eight o'clock positions, a couple hundred feet above him. From those positions, we could look through the RF-4 to the ground, and, with luck, see any anti-aircraft guns that fired at him, or us.

Surprise and speed were wonderful, so the recce sped well past any guns before the gunners could put down their rice bowls and get a bead on him—or us. We ran about a hundred miles through the North Vietnamese panhandle, looked at blurry trees—often through rain showers and mist—but not much else. I strained my eyes and swiveled my head trying to see any anti-aircraft fire. Sure, I tried to protect the recce, but I also protected me. I had heard horror stories of guys who were shot down on their last missions. Lord, I did not want to join that group.

When the recce called that his run was complete, he pulled up hard and turned back to Laos, and toward home. We said goodbye, then went to our alternate target and dropped our ordnance on a "suspected truck park," or "suspected VC vegetable garden" as some sage earlier in the war called that type of target. It was really just some more unlucky Laotian trees. For all the nervous anticipation before and during the mission, the trip home was boring, except crossing the Fence. I thought it would be my last time. The experience was somewhere between finishing an action novel and getting released from prison.

But it was our last mission.

***

When Pic and I landed and turned off the runway, we were met in the de-arm area by the squadron jeep and several pickups filled with our squadron mates. Even over the noise of our idling engines, we could hear the jeep siren wailing. In the back of the pickups, several of the Nickels ignited some hand-held Mk-13 red smoke-flares—the kind we carried in our survival vests—and waved them in the air. The red smoke trailed behind the trucks and swirled around our plane as we taxied. The entourage led our Phantom up the taxi-way to the parking ramp. Pic and I congratulated each other on the intercom and waved at well-wishers on the ground who watched the parade. What a wonderful feeling! The parade was the standard greeting for pilots who successfully completed their tours.

The trip up that taxi-way for the last time was a thrill. It ended my 137th and final (I wrongly thought) mission in the war. I had come a long way from my first trip on the taxi-way, a long way indeed. On my first trip, though I thought I knew it all, I knew nothing. On my last trip, I knew a hell-of-a-lot more than I ever wanted to know. But more importantly, I had transitioned from being a hot-shot fighter pilot to being a survivor. The latter was wonderful.

I followed the yellow taxi line to abeam the parking spot. The crew chief held his left hand down at an angle while motioning me forward with his right hand. He instructed me to turn right. I followed his directions into the parking spot. He moved his arms slowly to make an "X" in front of his face to indicate that I should slow the bird then stop. He held his arms in the "X" instructing me to hold the brakes while his assistants chocked the wheels. The chief dropped his arms and moved his right hand in front of his throat in a slashing motion. I moved both throttles around the "idle/cutoff" indentation and both engines shut off.

The chief hooked the yellow boarding ladder over my left canopy rail. I pulled off my helmet as the engines unwound; the J-79s' whine died as the compressors slowed then stopped. Before the engines had stopped turning, the chief appeared at the top of the ladder.

"Well done, sir!" He meant it. Everyone meant it when congratulating someone who finished a tour.

"Thank you, Chief!" I meant it, too.

I snapped my chin strap then handed my helmet to the chief. I unbuckled my shoulder harnesses, lap belt, and leg restraints. The chief went down the ladder followed immediately by Pic who had stepped on the left engine intake ramp then on to the ladder.

The rainy season air was hot and humid, but it smelled good to me, even blended with jet fuel and engine exhaust. I looked around the cockpit briefly to make sure all was in order, then stretched my arms and grabbed the top of the canopy rail. I pulled myself up, always a good feeling after being strapped into the seat for several hours.

I swung my legs out of the cockpit and on to the top rung of the ladder then started the ten-foot trip down to the concrete ramp. I felt great.

I did not win the war, but I did not die in it.

Pic and I shook hands first, then we both greeted the guys who had met us. We were two very happy Nickels.

On the ramp, champagne flowed freely, both down throats and over heads and uniforms. I looked under the Phantom. The white, six-bomb centerline bomb-rack was empty as were the two, three-bomb racks on the internal wing stations. The bombs were gone. They would not be loaded for me again. The next time they would be loaded, someone else would fly the bird. The empty racks seemed symbolic. I guess it showed me that I had emptied them and now I could go home.

My job was done, even if the war was not.

It was a great trip back to the squadron, surrounded by the guys I flew with for nearly a year. Normally, the end of one mission was the start of anticipation for the next one.

Not this time.

***

That night was our farewell party at the Officers' Club. It was the usual drunken meal, several skits, and short farewell speeches. An honoree was only permitted to speak as long as he could hold his hand in a pitcher of ice water, which is not very long even when he was loaded. Finally, it ended as it began on my first night of the tour.

We drank the "Green Death."

As was tradition in the Nickel, Pic and I— the lucky survivors—stood on chairs and chugged ice-tea glasses with the half green Crème de Menthe, half vodka poison. We turned the glasses upside-down on our heads to prove they were empty, and we both smashed the glasses against the faux fireplace. I know they broke—I saw them. Naturally, unbroken glasses rolled from behind our chairs to the edge of the fireplace. The entire squadron claimed that we had not complied with the rules. Before we could protest, two new glasses of the Green Death appeared. So, Pic and I had to repeat the process, all to the joy of the now-rowdy squadron.

But it was another wonderful feeling.

***

My next memory was sitting on a bench at Base Operations, waiting for the C-130, the Klong, the "freedom bird" that would take me to Bangkok. Where my two flight-bags and helmet came from, I do not know. But I did notice that the front of my T-shirt was green, and my head felt the same. There were only a couple of the guys there to say quiet goodbyes; the rest still had a war to fight. Pic and I loaded our hangovers into the 130, strapped in, and promptly slept our way to Bangkok, no easy feat considering the environment in the 130. We propped our feet on some equipment crates and slept through the smell and the prop-beat from the four, big turbo-prop engines.

From Bangkok, we loaded on to a military contracted DC-8 and slept our way to Japan, eight hours away. It takes a while to return from the Green Death.

***

Yokota Air Base, Japan, was a different world. My, how civilized! Orderly traffic, well-dressed people, sidewalks, paved streets, clean restrooms, and no snakes. It wasn't America, but it was a giant step toward home.

After I checked into the Visiting Officers' Quarters, I went to the O Club for a beer. I was about to have my first sip when I heard "BUFFALO" shouted from across the bar. It was so loud that the word echoed from the ceiling of the normally peaceful lounge. The normal customers stared or looked offended at the loud interruption to their quiet conversations. Only a few of my friends from before the war called me Buffalo. To everyone else, I was just "Buff."

There stood my old friend, Andy. Andy was one of our group of bachelors at Tucson, when I was in training before my tour. We had gone through many parties, camping trips, tubing on the Verde River, and lots of horseback riding together. After training, Andy had gone to Da Nang for his tour as a back-seat pilot in the F-4. While the back-seat pilots were, even then, rapidly being replaced with navigators, Andy was one of the last of those unlucky ones.

It was great to see him. Running into old friends was always a joy, but nothing compared to it after a tour in combat. Andy, like all of us, had been changed by the war, but his inner personality had not. I always think of him when I see John Belushi in the movie *Animal House*. He was still the same happy, party-type guy one would find on a campus, and I was damned glad to see him.

We spent a couple of days drinking and reminiscing about the war, Tucson, and the other guys we had trained with. Andy and Herb had been roommates in Tucson, so Andy was anxious to hear Herb's narrow escape and how he was doing after being shot down.

The next afternoon Andy took me to Mike's Honda Shop near the airbase. He wanted me to see the new motorcycle he had purchased. The bike was to be delivered to Andy at his next assignment, back in Tucson. He was going there to upgrade to the front seat of the F-4.

After completing the upgrade, he would have to fly a second tour in the war. Like many back-seat pilots, Andy had to volunteer to do a second Vietnam tour to be assured that he would upgrade to the front seat. Backseat pilots who did not volunteer for a second tour often got assigned to another base still in the back seat, or to Air Training Command as T-37 flight instructors. Like most back seat pilots, he abhorred both of those choices.

It was another Air Force Catch-22.

At the Honda Shop, I asked Andy how he would get the motorcycle back to the States.

"No problem," he said, "Mike takes care of all that. It's all part of the deal."

Damn, that sounded good, especially after several beers. The shop was filled with shiny, new Honda motorcycles. Though I had only ridden a motorcycle once in my life, I pointed to a blue Honda that I thought looked cool and asked the cost. Mike gave me the price ($550), delivered to my next duty assignment at Holloman Air Force Base near Alamogordo, New Mexico. He guaranteed delivery exactly six weeks from that day. All he needed was my personal check and one copy of my orders.

I gave them to him.

***

The Air Force finally got all eight crews together and we briefed for our flight. The route was from Japan to Guam, stay overnight, then on to Honolulu the second day, and finally to George Air Force Base, near Victorville, California, the third day. Great plan! There were KC-135s to lead us on the route so all we had to do was fly formation and refuel. Like my ferry trip the prior summer, all the flight planning and other details were handled by the aircraft delivery specialists at each stop.

Piece of cake.

My bird was an ancient F-4C that had obviously over-lived its time at Cam Ranh Bay Air Base on the coast of South Vietnam. Not only was it an old C model, but also it looked like it had flown far too many combat missions. Still, it must be flyable, or the Air Force would not have given it to me.

Right?

By the time we were airborne out of Yokota, three planes of the flight had aborted, so only five of us joined with the tankers. One bird aborted into Okinawa, so only half of us made it to Guam. Pic and I agreed that, short of fire or engine failure, we would "defer" any problems until we got to California. We were on our way home and did not intend to get hung up at some isolated island airfield along the way, or even in Hawaii.

As long as the plane could fly, we would fly it.

The flight to Guam, our first stop, was uneventful. Guam, an American Territory, was a small island, perhaps 30 miles long and five or six miles wide. It was a tiny, green oasis in the vast deep-blue Pacific Ocean. Anderson Air Force Base, a major way-point for virtually every military airplane transiting the Pacific, sat at one end of the island. The massive installation also was a large B-52 base. While the island was a long way from the coast of Vietnam, it was very much in the war. It was like entering an emotionally depressing time warp. In Japan, I was out of the war; at Guam, I was back in it.

We landed on the long, broad runway that ended at a cliff with the Pacific Ocean crashing against its base. The runway sloped down in the center so by the end of my landing roll 50 or 60 B-52 bombers and probably as many or more KC-135 tankers parked adjacent to it came into view. It was an impressive fleet. The bombers were camou-flaged on the upper surfaces and some were black on the bottom.

All the bombers appeared to be the older "D" models (the same as the one now on display near the north gate of the Air Force Academy). Many were loaded with the Mk-82 500-pound bombs that I was so familiar with.

Shortly after we landed, three B-52s took off for the war. A B-52D takeoff was always impressive because the brute put out huge clouds of black smoke from each of its eight, water-injected engines. When the bomber was fully loaded, as these were, it used most of the two-mile-long runway and left a black pall hanging over it. In the clear ocean air above, I could see the black smoke trails of the three bombers as they made wide turns to the west and climbed slowly. The men on board those planes were crossing their version of the Fence, a much wider version, with the far bank being the coast of Vietnam.

✻✻✻

At Guam, two more of our aircraft aborted. Six airplanes broken, and we were only one-third of the way home. The next morning only two of the original eight joined the tankers for the eight-hour flight to Honolulu, mine and Andy's.

Despite its eight-hour length, the flight to Hawaii was especially enjoyable. Pic did most of the flying (the auto-pilot never did work) and handled most of the refueling. On one refueling, the Boom Operator held a Playboy centerfold in his window for our viewing. Pic managed to fly a steady refueling despite the distraction. Damned good GIB.

We cruised at about 30,000 feet over the Pacific. That was a sight that one never got tired of. The huge expanse of the deep-blue water, unbroken by any land, with occasional towers of brilliant white clouds climbing into the light-blue sky. At that altitude, the sun was dazzling and the air perfectly clear. I could see for hundreds of miles in every direction. It was a vast, blue canvas. Beautiful!

And no anti-aircraft guns.

This was why I loved to fly.

Pic flew a smooth, loose formation on one wing of the tanker. Andy's bird was on the other side. There was little chatter on the radio, and about the same or less on the intercom. I guess we were all thinking about home. Sometimes, Pic pulled abeam of the tanker's cockpit. We could see the two pilots sitting in their relatively comfortable environment. Occasionally, the tanker pilots would comment that they were going to stretch their legs, a friendly jab at us since we couldn't. By this time in my career, I would not have objected to anything a tanker guy said; they were forever my friends—for damned good reasons.

I had turned in my survival vest, gun, and tree-lowering device at Udorn. Without those bulky encumbrances, the small cockpit actually seemed roomy. I took off my oxygen mask and gloves, and rolled up my sleeves. I would have taken my helmet off, too, but the noise would have been irritating. I loosened my lap belt and got as comfortable as was possible on the hard seat, watched the vastness of the Pacific that surrounded me, and dozed a bit. Even the flight lunch prepared by the military dining hall on Guam seemed enjoyable. It was two slightly chewy roast-beef sandwiches on white bread, a small bag of potato chips, an apple, and two small cans of fruit juice.

On that trip home, it was a gourmet meal.

Hours later, I saw the green beauty of Oahu as we approached. The island sharply contrasted with the deep blue of the ocean. We flew over the area where Herb and I had greeted the surfacing submarine, rounded the south end of the island, passed the entrance to Pearl Harbor, and landed at Honolulu International Airport. The taxi-way led us to Hickam Air Force Base where we parked our birds. The flight from Guam was so quiet, so scenic, that it was almost a letdown when it ended, except for a sore butt from sitting on the hard seat for eight hours, that is.

The maintenance crew asked us how the bird was, and I said all was fine. Pic and I already had a lengthy list of problems, but we kept them to ourselves. The radar and inertial navigation system did not work (never had), and many other lesser systems had failed, including the heading system. Still, we only had one more leg of the trip, so we said all was fine. I'm not sure if the maintenance folks believed us.

Fortunately, no one was there, either in the maintenance section or in the Aircraft Delivery Group, who remembered me from my extended stay with the broken plane the prior summer. Funny how things had changed: In the summer of '69, I was happy lingering on the Islands. In the summer of '70, I couldn't wait to leave.

Since we only had one night in Hawaii, we naturally wanted to make the most of it. So, Andy and I walked to the nearby small Officers' Club annex on the channel that our warships used to get into Pearl Harbor. There were flaming Tiki torches on poles among the gently swaying palm trees outside the bar. The evening air coming from the Pacific was like some balm. There was something special about Hawaii, something that was even more special on the way home from the war.

Andy pulled up a barstool and asked the bartender: "What's the Mai Tai record here?"

"Eight."

"Start me off. There's going to be a new one today."

He fell off the barstool after seven.

***

The next day, Andy's bird aborted on engine start. Pic and I had to go alone, but it was the last leg. As I learned on my last Air Force assignment—at Hickam—before I retired, most folks were sad when they left Hawaii.

Not Pic and I. It was the last leg. Only about six more hours and we would be back in the States, back in The World.

The early morning Hawaiian air was warm and calm as we taxied behind the KC-135 to the edge of Honolulu's longest runway. (This was before the outside "Reef" runway that now serves the airport.) We were to take off on the 12,000-foot-long runway 08, toward the city, which meant we could create a noise problem for the many vacationers in the hotels lining Waikiki Beach. Our instruction from Air Traffic Control was to start an immediate right turn after lift-off to keep the noise away from the beach. That was no problem in the F-4 since it accelerated rapidly.

For the tanker, however, it was a problem. That plane carried a heavy fuel load since it was scheduled to take two fighters, not just one, across the 2,000 miles of ocean between Hawaii and California.

Pic and I taxied behind the tanker to the "hold line" just short of the runway. The tanker proceeded onto the runway. Instead of turning left to point down the runway, the tanker turned right, on to the overrun, a surface not normally used for takeoffs. He slowly taxied to the end of the overrun, stopped, then did a slow left-pivot to face down the runway. The overrun would give him almost another 1,000 feet for his takeoff roll.

There were four men on board the tanker: pilot, co-pilot, navigator, and boom operator. They were in an airplane built nearly two decades earlier as a passenger jet, with engines barely adequate for the plane's weight, even then. Their non-afterburning engines used a water injection system to coax a bit more thrust from them, but they were still woefully underpowered. On this morning, with no headwind to help them, the crew was entirely dependent on those obsolete engines.

When Honolulu tower cleared us for takeoff, the tanker pilot pushed up his throttles, but unlike today's airliners, he did not roll—he held the brakes. Pic and I, stopped perpendicular to the runway, still had our canopies open enjoying the last of the clean, balmy Hawaiian morning air. Over the noise of our own engines' compressors, we heard the howl of the tanker's four engines as they reached their maximum power. Still, the tanker did not move. Then dark, black smoke poured from the engine exhausts as the water-injection system activated. The tanker's pilot released his brakes.

The gray KC-135 did not spring forward as the F-4 would have; instead, it started a slow roll. If someone would have asked me then, I would have said that they could never make it. The tanker rumbled past our nose, slowly—ever so slowly—gaining speed. The black smoke billowing behind the tanker lay on the runway as if a crop-duster had sprayed the runway with some thin, black foam. There was no wind at all to move it.

We lowered our canopies and taxied on the runway, moving from the morning sun and blue sky into the eerie darkness. We were to wait 45 seconds before we started our roll. I did the engine checks, then we waited.

When the 45 seconds passed, I ran our engines to 85-percent while holding the brakes. I could see virtually nothing ahead except for darkness. Had the smoke been any thicker, I would have had to make an instrument takeoff.

I called "hack" and released the brakes, advanced the throttles to military power, then outboard and forward to full afterburner. It was great when both burners lit. After Andy's abort minutes earlier, I dreaded the possibility that our bird might not make it either, especially since we had so many problems—unreported—already.

Maybe the ancillary systems in our plane did not work, but those two beautiful J-79 engines did. We accelerated down the runway, into the thick black smoke as if we were following some poorly tuned giant diesel truck. I was not worried because I believed that the tanker must be airborne by now.

It wasn't.

When our bird lifted off, I pulled the gear up quickly and, while still over the runway started my mandatory right turn. When I climbed out of the darkness into the clear Pacific air, I saw the tanker. Not above us, not at our altitude; no, he had just lifted off the runway—staggered into the air might be a better description—at the departure end, just a few feet it seemed, from the far overrun. He had used the entire runway, more than two miles. Worse, he now had to make the right turn to avoid Waikiki. I saw his plane bank right, barely airborne, the four engines still blowing huge clouds of black smoke from the exhausts like four massive insect foggers.

We watched him as he strained to clear Honolulu Harbor and Aloha Tower, the plane only a few hundred feet in the air. The noise-abatement procedure that mandated that immediate right turn, meant that the tanker had to turn with barely adequate airspeed. I felt for those guys; it must be terrifying to sit through that takeoff and then make that turn. If an engine had failed during the takeoff roll, or even if one engine had lost the water injection, they would have been in a world of trouble. I was no tanker expert, but I seriously doubted if they could have successfully aborted that takeoff.

The tanker crews were heroes to us fighter pilots; they not only earned their flight pay, but also deserved medals for their work. Honolulu was not in the war, but on this morning, that tanker crew should have received medals just for that takeoff.

We descended and joined on the tanker as he struggled to climb past Diamondhead. He was low enough that, had I carried a camera, I could have taken a beautiful Air Force recruiting picture.

When we settled on his wing, I thought about how much I owed those tanker crews.

Me and a lot of other fighter pilots.

***

We were scheduled to drop off the tanker before we crossed the California coast. The tanker would proceed to his destination and we would go on to George Air Force Base by ourselves. That option, however, was not viable. Our F-4 was flying, but not much more. We had no functioning navigation systems, no reliable heading indicators, no radar, and we were using the backup attitude system among the other inoperative equipment.

Shortly before the drop-off point, I called the tanker and admitted that we had some "minor" problems. I asked the tanker pilot if he could take us to George, and if so, could he lead us to initial for a visual overhead approach. (In good weather fighters flew an initial approach to the runway by flying over it at 1,500 feet, then pitching out and landing.) I knew we could not do an instrument approach since we had no heading indicator and no navigation systems. It's tough to do an instrument approach without instruments.

The tanker crew, being great guys as most of them were, readily agreed. They probably thought it would be cool for a KC-135 to lead my F-4 overhead George Air Force Base, the home of "Fighter Pilot University" and a major F-4 training base.

Sure enough, that big tanker led us over the airfield with our F-4 in close formation on his left wing. About one-third of the way down the runway the tanker pilot waved goodbye to us from his side window. I saluted and did a hard left-turn onto downwind. I'm sure there were lots of people at George wondering what-the-hell was going on.

I pulled the throttles back so that we could slow for landing.

Gear handle down. Check for the three-wheels down and locked indications. Whew, they worked properly.

Flaps down. The runway was at my eight-o'clock.

Left turn onto the base leg, then roll out on final, descending steadily toward the runway.

"George Tower, Buff and Pic, gear down and locked, full stop!" I really said that.

The controller in the tower, with no apparent notice of my lack of professionalism, responded, "Cleared to land."

Stick back in my lap, the wheels touched, throttles idle, drag chute out. We're home!

***

The maintenance folks met us at the plane. First question was: Where were the rest of the planes?

I said they were scattered across the Pacific.

"How's your bird?" a Chief Master Sergeant asked.

I said I had 27 discrepancies.

"Twenty-seven! All from this flight?"

I think he was suspicious.

"Sure thing," I lied. "You don't think I'd fly an unsafe airplane, do you?"

In my 22 years of flying with the Air Force, I have never flown an airplane anywhere near as bad as that one. Air Force maintenance was superior to all others, but that bird was just flat worn out. It probably should have come home on a ship, or not at all.

We spent the night at the Visiting Officers' Quarters. No bar, no drinking, just a shower, hot meal, and then we turned in for a good night's sleep. Early the next morning we put on our "1505's," the Air Force khaki short-sleeve uniform. Since we were now on leave, we could fly "military standby" for half-fare if we were in uniform.

We grabbed a base taxi to Los Angeles International Airport. I found a flight going to Washington almost immediately, so I said goodbye to Pic, called home, arranged for a pickup at Dulles, and jumped onboard my flight.

The trip from Japan across the Pacific had gone as planned, so I was still tired from the time change and the long hours strapped into my ejection seat. Maybe it was the three days of travel or maybe it was the sudden reduction of tension. Maybe it was simply lack of combat. Whatever it was, I slept most of the way to Washington.

When the plane landed, I boarded one of those weird shuttles, the "people movers" that Dulles uses to move passengers to and from the airplanes.

It was then, for the first time, that I sensed something was wrong.

People looked strange to me: their clothes, hair, faces. No one spoke to me. Several gave me disgusted looks. Most looked away if we made eye contact. True, I must have looked a bit weird to them. I was the only person in uniform on the plane. My uniform fit me perfectly when I left home, when I weighed about 180 pounds. That same uniform was a bit baggy since I was now less than 160. Later, I learned that, thanks to the unpopularity of the war in Vietnam, the Defense Department had forbidden military personnel from wearing uniforms in or around Washington, unless on official business.

Our uniforms were forbidden in our own capital. What had happened to the country I just fought for?

It was July, the middle of the summer of 1970. I had been away almost a full year. During that time, I had not even thought about what happened in the States. In Thailand, we only talked about the war. Every day was the same: focus on the mission, put the bombs on the targets, get the job done, keep everyone safe, don't do anything stupid, don't get killed. Everyone in the Nickel, the Wing, all over Udorn, focused on the same things.

No one protested the war. Sure, we complained about how it was being run, but we were in it to win it.

Now I was in a strange land where none of that meant anything. No one around me had any idea of what we had been doing. Worse, as I was soon to learn, they did not care. I was part of America when I left, and I did what I believed my country wanted—needed—me to do. I did not start the war and I did my best to help us win it. I was an American serviceman and I believed in America. Was I still part of America?

On the Dulles Airport shuttle, I felt like I was some alien, some leper. Riding in to the terminal, I sat with my back to a window, so I faced the center seats. I held my helmet bag on my lap. Some people took secretive glances at me. Several stared. A few glared.

Were they hostile to me? I felt like an outcast. It wasn't my helmet bag that they were looking at, it was me. And some, obviously, did not like me.

It would get worse, but I did not realize that yet.

The shuttle finally docked. I grabbed my helmet bag and got off as fast as I could.

The terminal was full of people but in seconds I saw my family. There was my sister, Jean, several of her family, and Dad standing in front.

He stepped toward me. He was about five-feet-eight, with his familiar thin, curly gray hair. To me, he appeared exactly as he had the day I last saw him. Maybe fathers do not change in their sons' eyes. I thought he would shake my hand like he had almost a year earlier at this same airport.

Not today.

He reached out and put his strong arms around me. He pulled me close to him and said words that I will remember until I die.

"Welcome home, Robby!"

My God! I made it!

Chapter 15

Bomb Damage Assessment

THE TOUR STARTED IN the summer of '69 and, I thought, it would end in the summer of '70. When I arrived at Dulles at the end of my tour, I believed I was finished with the war, but once again I was wrong. I did not know it then, but when I said goodbye to Pic, I also said goodbye to my support group. In the air, at the Nickel, at the Club, at Udorn, even in Udon Thani, we were all in it together. The other pilots all cared, about themselves and about every other man in the squadron, wing, and in our military. When we flew, our strongest desire was to get all of us back, every man. When someone was shot down, the entire squadron reacted. Until the downed pilot was rescued, we were tense, every one of us. Each one knew that he could have been the guy on the ground. Therefore, no matter what the official rules of engagement were, our rules for a SAR were that there were no rules: no minimum altitudes, no minimum fuels, no limits on the number of passes.

Do whatever you have to do, but GET HIM OUT.

When we lost guys, we all suffered. Even if we did not discuss the lost pilot, we all knew how the others felt. Sometimes we would talk about it, sometimes just join in silence. We were together in a common situation with a common mission, and we all wanted every man to get out alive. When we had going away parties for a guy who had finished a tour, the ones who remained were not jealous, they were not just going through some formality, they were genuinely happy that a squadron mate had made it. A little bit of each of us went home with each guy who completed a tour.

Likewise, a little bit of each of us was lost when a pilot was shot down.

My family cared a lot about me and tried to understand how I felt, but the essential common ground was missing. I wanted to share my feelings with them, but they did not have the experience to grasp what I said, and I really did not know the right words to say it. How does one talk about combat to those who were never in it? It's hard enough to talk to others about flying fighters since even private pilots do not understand the complexity involved. A commercial pilot may under-stand the aircraft systems, but would be hard pressed to comprehend the stick and rudder work involved in the fighter world. Put the whole thing in combat, with tracers flying over the canopy, with life or death on the line, and understanding becomes nearly impossible.

Once outside the family, no one cared a wit about the war. Americans were sick of it and simply would not discuss it, except for those who had a family member in it. Even they mostly were negative about the war. The general feeling was that the war was wrong, that we should not have gotten in it, and that we should get out now. Just drop everything and leave. It was all a mistake. The thought of winning it simply did not exist. Try to discuss the war in Laos, and I would have been better off talking to my dog.[1]

Even today, other than some history buffs, America is ignorant of our war in Laos.

Frequently when I met people, I got the same reaction that I did on the Dulles shuttle: a distant, unfriendly, often hostile, or just disgusted look. It seemed that we military folks had become some sort of ogres, some lower caste. The long-haired protesters got lots of press. The marchers and rioters were viewed as having a just cause. The government, the press, the public, all seemed focused on those who wanted us to walk away from the war.

Now, in defiance of logic, the United States military was the new enemy.

Why had I done it? Why get shot at? Why risk captivity or death? Why-the-hell had I flown 137 combat missions if the very people that sent me did not give a damn? Or worse, hated me for doing it?

After my experience at the end of my return flight from Los Angeles, I did not wear my uniform unless on duty. From that day until I retired in 1988, I did not wear a uniform unless required. When I was in Texas, Alabama, and North Carolina before the war, I wore my uniform almost everywhere I went. Not now, and never again.

I cut my leave short and moved on to my new duty station, Holloman Air Force Base, in the desert near Alamogordo, New Mexico. My new wing was "dual-based," meaning that we were totally committed to Europe, and we deployed there annually to show our NATO allies that we were. Once in New Mexico, it was as if I were in North Carolina again. There were guys who had been and guys who had not been—except now I was one of the guys who had been. Now I knew why they tended to hang out together: It was the common bond of combat, a bond stronger than any other.

Life seemed much better. Even the motorcycle that I had purchased at Mike's Honda Shop in Japan arrived on schedule. I had forgotten about it until I got a call from a local van company to find out where and when I wanted it delivered. It was a beauty. The desert was a wonderful place to ride and the base even had a moto-cross track.

Once again, I flew without being shot at. Flying the Phantom in peacetime was a hoot. She was a wonderful jet; she could do things that thrill-seekers on the ground could not even imagine. Because of our NATO commitment, we flew lots of low-level navigation training routes. It was great, flashing across the New Mexico desert at 480 knots, without fear of anti-aircraft rounds.

Just enjoy flying again. I even found time to get married.

I had some good friends there from the days before I went to the war. On the weekends, I often went to Tucson to see old friends—especially Andy. We shared experiences and renewed friendships.

Life was good.

Until late 1971. Andy, now back in Thailand, was flying a Fast FAC mission out of Udorn into northern Laos. He disappeared. Like Wes and Fergie, he just vanished; no chute, no beeper. He was on his second tour, a tour that, but for the Air Force's inane decision to put pilots in the rear seat of the F-4, he should not have been flying. He got caught by Catch-22. Andy should have been with us, flying, drinking, and partying in the Southwest. Instead, he probably was in some smoking hole in the Laotian jungle. If he had to go, I just hoped he went quickly, that he did not feel anything. He was my friend, my good friend. Now he was gone. And, damn it, for what?

It was that old depressing feeling again. Thank God for booze.

***

In the spring of 1972, after most American ground forces were gone, the North Vietnamese launched a major attack often called the Easter Offensive.[2] Nixon reacted by sending fighters—lots of them. He filled Thailand with fighters. However, I believed that since our Wing was committed to NATO by treaty, we would not—could not—be sent to Southeast Asia.

In early May, the alert sirens that military wives and families hate to hear, summoned all of us military personnel to our duty stations at Holloman. The sirens had barely stopped wailing when we got orders to pack for the war.

The day my squadron was to launch for the trip across the Pacific, to Thailand, my pregnant wife took me to the base. Along the ten-mile drive from my house in Alamogordo to the base we encountered long-haired, shaggy, often bearded people who held signs and waved them at anyone in uniform. The signs were their anti-war slogans and included lines such as "Don't Go," "Stop Bombing," and "Don't Kill."

Were they actually ignorant enough to think that it was our idea?

Now they weren't just giving me their looks of disgust; they were in my face. My wife was worried, more than most because her brother also flew with my squadron. I was sullen because I believed I had already done my share. But here these protesters stood, acting as if we airmen had a choice. We were the United States Air Force, under the absolute control of the elected civilian government of our country, but we had become the bad guys.

What-the-hell was wrong? Here we were, doing what our nation told us to do, yet we were the evil ones.

I was better prepared, at least mentally, this time. On this second tour, I flew mostly in South Vietnam where we successfully stopped the invasion. Instead of flying in support of the Hmong Army, we supported the South Vietnamese and Korean armies. Instead of hunting trucks, we destroyed enemy infantry. The now more-numerous anti-aircraft weapons were familiar except for one significant new one: the shoulder fired heat-seeking missile. That little missile was deadly for the helicopters and slower aircraft. Fortunately, it was no match for the F-4 moving at 500 knots.

On my second tour, I made an emergency landing at Udorn. The airfield was covered with fighters as an entire wing had deployed there from the States to help counter the Easter Offensive. The flightline, always busy when I was there, was now packed. The Nickel was still there, but all the people I knew were gone.

I left as soon as my plane was ready.

Forty-some more combat missions later, I escaped the war and wound up in a staff job in Austin, Texas. Once again, I thought I had escaped. When America's role in the war finally ended, I watched, and cheered, when our prisoners were finally released. America was out of the war. That must mean the end.

No, not yet.

Two years later, I watched in agony as the North Vietnamese Army approached Saigon. It was humiliating to watch tens of thousands of our friends trying to escape the looming collapse, fleeing in boats, clinging to the skids of helicopters, clawing at the gates of our embassy while begging for us to take them away. I was more humiliated as the last Americans ingloriously fled, lifted off the roof of the embassy on the last helicopters.

No one in America seemed to care.

Hundreds of thousands of Vietnamese became "Boat People," millions more suffered or died in "re-education" camps, and no one in America gave a damn. No one except for those of us who had fought there. But we knew better than to say anything then; we just sat, and hurt, silently.

In later years, I met some of the Vietnamese refugees. Their stories of escape were heart-wrenching. America should be ashamed.

Now it was obvious, even to me. It was all for nothing. All those guys killed, wounded, missing, and for what? A mistake? A bad political decision? A foreign policy gambit gone wrong? And what about all the Vietnamese, Laotians, and Cambodians? Millions of dead, homeless, displaced.

For what?

***

In the mid-1980s I had lunch at the Officers' Club at Grissom Air Force Base in Indiana with several other A-10 pilots, also veterans of the war. We were joined by our base's Veteran's Administration counselor. He was a former Grunt who himself had suffered disabling wounds, but now helped other vets get over the trauma of the war. The lunch discussion, as it sometimes did when several vets were together, turned to the war.

"Buff, have you been to the Wall?" the VA counselor asked me.

The Wall, the Vietnam Veterans Memorial, had only been open about a year or so. It had received national attention, some good, some bad.

"No, and I'm not sure I want to go," I replied.

I really did have mixed feelings about it. The press I had read, or at least some of it, had given the Wall bad publicity. The writers felt that the Wall demeaned those who were lost, ignored those who survived, and that it should not have been designed by someone of Asian descent, even if she was an American. Even the way it was cut into the ground made it appear to be a scar, not a memorial, or so they said.

Since I had planned a summer visit to my mother's home in southern Pennsylvania, I told him that I might visit it.

***

A couple of weeks later, I was at my mother's home, about an hour or so from Washington, D.C. I had been thinking about the Wall since my conversation with the VA counselor. There really was no reason why I couldn't go, so I told Mother that I would be away for the day, although I did not say where I was going.

I found a parking spot next to the Lincoln Memorial. There was a temporary plywood sign next to it that said: "Vietnam Memorial." There was an arrow pointing toward a tree-shaded pathway. I walked along the narrow asphalt path, but I could not see any memorial, just grass and trees.

Then it appeared, the wide, black "V" shape, wedged into the earth with green grass growing right up to the top edge of the wide-angled side. From where I stood, it appeared ominous, foreboding. There were no other monuments; those would be added in later years. There was no fence—like I said, it was fairly new.

To get to the inside of the Wall where the names were, I had to walk along a pathway. At that time, there was a grass strip between the Wall and the pathway next to it (today the grass has been replaced with brick). All along the grass were items that had been left behind by visitors: flowers, pictures, boots, hats, military decorations, small flags, personal items, and other mementos. Hundreds if not thousands of them. There was no area on that grass strip that did not have something on it.

When I walked next to the Wall, I was overwhelmed.

Really, I can't describe the intensity any other way. The black wall loomed over me. There they all were, name after name after name, listed in the order they were lost. The Wall expanded, then contracted just as the war had progressed. At the beginning of the Wall, there were few names. As the war cranked up, the panels got taller, the names more plentiful. The panels now loomed over me. I could feel them—not the names—the people. Each one was young, like I had been. Each one believed he would live a long life. Now each one was frozen in time, forever young with the promise of life before him, but gone.

By the time I got to the angle—the "V" in the Wall—I might as well have been on the hooch porch watching those officers take Rick's belongings from his room. I felt like I was among the dead. My throat choked up so hard that it hurt; I struggled to keep the tears back, but without much luck. Here I was, an Air Force Lieutenant Colonel, a career military officer, a veteran professional pilot, a warrior who flew the mighty A-10 attack plane. But I really wasn't. I was one of them, one of the names. Sure, I was alive, but not because of my skill, but because God, for whatever reason, decided that I should not be on that Wall. Despite what I may have once thought or said, I was no better than they were. Yet they were on the Wall while I stood in front of it.

There was a bond between Vietnam vets and those on the Wall that I doubt anyone who did not fight there could understand. I did not really understand it until I went there and met with them. If there were any group of men who deserved our nation's honor it was them. Our nation sent them to the war, then not only turned its back on them, but also demeaned and dishonored them.

But they did not die—we did not fight—for some mistake. They died so that others, like me, could live. We fought for each other. Those of us who lived owed everything to those on the Wall. In return, we carried them in our hearts, not as they fell, but as they lived. They would be forever young as long as any of us live.

I'd bet that every Vietnam vet knew that.

There were 58,000 of my comrades in front of me. I had to back away from the Wall, on to the gently rising grass. I sat down on the grass and I cried. I never cry, but I did then, like some kid. Men weren't supposed to cry, but that day I did.

I'll bet there were damned few 'Nam vets who didn't.

That may have been the day that a reality dawned on me: The hardest part of serving in the Vietnam conflict was not fighting it.

The truly hard part was coming home.

***

My final Air Force assignment before I retired was in Honolulu, at Hickam Air Force Base. When remains of the fallen from the war were located, they were flown to Hickam, then transferred to an identification lab on Oahu. Periodically, the flag-draped coffins arrived, usually in groups of two or three, and were met with military honors. Occasionally, I attended the formal receptions of the coffins. I wondered if any of my friends were in the coffins. Was Andy there? Or Wes? The coffins arrived just a few hundred yards from where I had watched Andy challenge the Mai Tai record nearly two decades earlier.

It took a year or more to identify the remains. When that happened, the remains would be shipped home, again with military honors. Those of us stationed at Hickam were not notified as to who they were.

After all, the war was long over, and no one cared.

Epilogue

IN 1971, THE WORLD saw how deadly the Laotian town of Tchepone was when a South Vietnamese Army force tried to capture it with Operation Lam Son 719.[1] The ARVN forces suffered a brutal defeat in their invasion of Steel Tiger. While no U.S. ground forces were involved, we lost a lot of helicopters and some of their crews. Like the song in the Epigraph for this book, I could have told them not to go to Tchepone.

Also in 1971, the U.S. Government finally de-classified the war in Laos. The war finally was a war.

Dad died suddenly in 1974. I don't think he ever knew that I volunteered for the war. If he did, he never mentioned it to me. In fact, we never spoke of it, ever. At least he knew I was safely home from the war.

All American forces left Vietnam in 1973. With Nixon weakened by the Watergate scandal, Congress first restricted and later, despite objections from the new President Ford, cut off aid to South Vietnam. In 1975, North Vietnamese forces overran the South, defeating an army that was woefully short on ammunition. The fall of Saigon, and the exodus of the American embassy personnel, represent the final, ugly ending to our participation in the war. We were gone from

Southeast Asia, but millions of people were left to suffer. The half-million Vietnamese boat people who escaped in the final days may have been the lucky ones.

The United States Air Force flew more than five million sorties during the war, lost 2,251 aircraft with 1,737 of those downed by enemy action. At least 1,738 Air Force personnel were killed in action; 766 died from other causes.[2]

Laos has been digging up unexploded ordnance and old mines since the war ended. Hundreds have died from explosions.

General Vang Pao escaped Laos in 1975. He lived for a time in Montana and later in California. He remained a respected leader of the Hmong people. The U.S. Government indicted him for an alleged plot to overthrow the Pathet Lao government of Laos, but subsequently dropped the charges. He died in 2011.

The Triple Nickel produced generals and some air aces (five kills) during Operation Linebacker in late 1972.[3] After the war, it relocated to Luke AFB near Phoenix and transitioned to the F-15 Eagle. In the 1990s, the squadron moved to Aviano Air Base north of Venice, Italy, and transitioned to the F-16 Fighting Falcon.

The F-4 became obsolete with the introduction of the F-15 Eagle in the mid-1970s. While the Phantom continued to serve, it was relegated to duty mostly with the Reserve Forces. However, it served in the 1991 Gulf War—not as a fighter, but as the Wild Weasel successor to the F-105 used in Vietnam—killing missile sites. It has since been retired completely from service with our Air Force, other than as a target drone.

Udon Thani, according to the internet, is a prosperous city of more than 300,000. Udorn, still an active Thai military installation, serves as the city's airport. The city now merges with the airfield. There does not appear to be any significant American military presence there. I have no idea if the CIA remained.

A couple of decades ago, some Vietnam vets, probably Grunts, started wearing T-shirts with "Welcome Home" on them. They decided that if their country would not welcome them back, they would do it. Today, when I meet other vets, the greeting is usually "Welcome Home!" when we shake hands. If you meet a Vietnam vet, say it.

In the early 1980s at the O Club bar at Eglin Air Force Base I met Woody, the pilot who survived the three-day ordeal after being shot down in Steel Tiger. When I found out who he was, I said, "I flew on your SAR." An officer standing next to him said, "You and every other pilot in Southeast Asia." I still had my talent for saying dumb things.

Ort, so I heard, beat the Flying Evaluation Board and kept his wings, although I doubt that he ever got another flying assignment. He later retired from the Air Force. I never have understood why such a fine air leader would be treated so poorly. We needed men like him.

Crazy helped save a downed OV-10 pilot near the PDJ a little more than a month after our SAR mission. He retired from the Air Force as a lieutenant colonel and began a successful business career.

Colonel Earl went on to greater things. I ran into him in Naples, Italy, many years later when he was a lieutenant general. I'll bet he was a damned good one; I was proud to have served with him. Despite the belief among the rank-and-file flyers, sometimes the Air Force did promote quality men to be general officers. He still had his disarming smile and wit. He even remembered me.

The Mayor has disappeared from my radar. For all I know, he still may be in Udon Thani.

I never saw Dave or Pic again, although they both retired after completing Air Force careers. They are both heroes in my book.

Herb finished his Air Force commitment, graduated from medical school, and became an emergency room doctor. I met him, along with his wife and kids, in the 1990s. He was doing well. He had his life saved by others, now he was repaying the debt many times over.

Andy and his GIB were recovered in the mid-1990s. They were buried in a common grave at Arlington National Cemetery.

Rick was buried in Pearland, Texas, near Houston.

Wes and Fergie were recovered a couple of years ago. They were buried, with honors: Wes at Arlington, Fergie in his hometown in Washington.

As for me, in the 45 years since I last flew in Vietnam, not one day—not one—has passed when I have not thought of the war. Thank God, though, as the years passed, the ugly dreams have faded, and the emotion has dulled. It was a long time ago and it has become foggy. Like other Vietnam vets, while I have learned to live with it, the war remains part of my life.

It always will be.

Endnotes

My Turn

1. How and why America became involved in Indochina is a complex story, indeed. A superior work on the actions—both proper and improper—of President Johnson and his administration which led to the war is: H.R. McMaster, *Dereliction of Duty* (New York: Harper Collins, 1997). This book is a must read for anyone who wants to understand how we got there.

2. Bernard C. Nalty, *The War Against Trucks: Aerial Interdiction in Southern Laos 1968–1972* (Washington, D.C.: Air Force History and Museums Program, 2005), 56.

3. 4457th Combat Crew Training Squadron (TAC), *Southeast Asia: Scene of Conflict* (Davis-Monthan AFB, AZ: Operational Support Services Publication, 1968), 22–26. (Author's archives)

4. John Schlight, *A War Too Long: The USAF in Southeast Asia 1961–1975* (Washington, D.C.: Air Force History and Museums Program, 1996), 76–77.

5. Ibid., 58–60.

6. Guenter Lewy, *America in Vietnam* (Oxford, UK: Oxford University Press, 1978), 406. Lewis Sorley, *A Better War* (San Diego: Harcourt, 1999), 80–81.

7. Nalty, *The War Against Trucks*, 5, 6, 12–13, 19. This book contains a detailed description of America's war against trucks driving south through Laos. It was a deadly chess match where each side introduced ever-more lethal weapons.

8. Lewis Sorley, *A Better War* (San Diego: Harcourt, 1999), 238.

Combat

1. John Fuller and Helen Murphey, eds., *The Raven Chronicles: In Our Own Words from the Secret War in Laos* (The Chronicles Project, Inc., undated) The Ravens were American Air Force personnel who did not wear uniforms and carried phony civilian identification cards from the U.S. Embassy (page 79). The cited book is a compilation of many first-hand accounts from the pilots who flew these dangerous missions.

2. Throughout this book I referred to capacities or operating characteristics of the F-4D. While many are seared in my head, I did refer to the flight manual to refresh my memory or to verify it. Specifically, the manual is: USAF T.O. 1F-4C-1, *Flight Manual: USAF Series F-4C, F-4D, and F-4E Aircraft* (Printed under the authority of the Secretary of the Air Force, 15 August 1971; Change 2, 15 December 1971).

3. References to weapons and switch settings not fixed in my memory were confirmed by: USAF T.O. 1F-4C-34-1-1, *Aircrew Weapons Delivery Manual (Non-Nuclear): USAF Series F-4C, F-4D, and F-4E Aircraft* (Printed under the authority of the Secretary of the Air Force, 15 March 1970; Change 9, 26 January 1973).

4. The F-4 training school at Tucson included one "heavyweight" flight with a similar, but lighter, configuration as those flown in combat. As I recall, on that training flight we carried six 500-pound bombs and dropped them on a live ordnance range in Arizona. However, most training flights were much lighter, with two external fuel tanks and six 25-pound practice bombs. In the States, we usually took off at about 47,000 pounds; in the war, we were about three or four tons heavier.

The War That Wasn't

1. I will cite myself as a reference on the Nomex flight-suit. After my first tour in the Vietnam War, I became the Wing Life Support Officer at the 49th Tactical Fighter Wing at Holloman AFB, New Mexico, and then, after my second combat tour, at Headquarters 12th Air Force at Bergstrom AFB, Texas. Life Support personnel are responsible for all matters concerning aircrew personnel equipment, from flight-suits and G-suits, to helmets and survival gear. During my nearly six years in that field, I read numerous reports of or saw first-hand evidence of the effectiveness of Nomex in preventing burns. Anyone who has seen the movie *Battle of Britain*, the BBC series *Piece of Cake*, or similar films will understand that fire in a plane's cockpit is a deadly

peril for aircrews. Nomex, while it did not eliminate the threat, gave—and still gives—many aircrew members vital seconds to escape without life-time burn scars. I am certain that both Herb and Ralph, discussed in a later chapter, will support this conclusion.

The Golden BB

1. Lewy, *America in Vietnam*, 233–237.
2. See Nalty, *The War Against Trucks*, 35–52 for a detailed account of the ROE process.

Hot Dog

1. For a "big picture" discussion of the first air war over North Vietnam, see Lewy, *America in Vietnam*, 29–41 and 389–406. For an "in the cockpit" pilot's description, see Ed Rasimus, *When Thunder Rolled* (New York: Random House, 2003).
2. Sorley, *A Better War,* 112–114, 128. Schlight, *A War Too Long,* 61–63.
3. I could not determine the exact date for the change in combat pay policy. My memory is that it was in October or November of 1969. I was aware of the change only because we no longer needed to fly a monthly sortie into South Vietnam. To my knowledge, pilots did not receive any written notice of the policy change.
4. Nalty, *The War Against Trucks,* 45. Whatever route the suggested targets took for approval was too long. The war in Laos was almost exclusively against mobile targets. By the time the various headquarters had their say, the targets were usually gone.
5. Ibid., 177–178.

Bad Moon Rising

1. Nalty, *The War Against Trucks,* 41.
2. Ibid., 99.
3. For a history of gunship development see Nalty, *The War Against Trucks,* 53–58.

4. Many gunships had F-4 escorts for protection against the growing danger from anti-aircraft guns. See Nalty, *The War Against Trucks*, 58 and 68.

5. Ibid., 99, 278.

6. Lewy, *America in Vietnam*, 144–145.

Dry-Season's Greetings

1. Sorley, *A Better War*, 235.

God Said No

1. Nalty, *The War Against Trucks*, 60–61.

The Proudest Day

1. Bowman, John S., General Editor, *The Vietnam War: An Almanac* (New York: World Almanac Publications, 1985), 250. See also pages 192, 194, and 201.

2. A Google search revealed his name as Duane D. Hackney of Flint, Michigan. Where America finds such heroes is a mystery to me.

R and R

1. Ibid., 48. The North Vietnamese name for these units was "binh tram."

2. For a remarkable series of pictures of the ejections, crash, and its aftermath, along with the names of dead, see: *AFTN Udorn Crash Sequence, 10 April 1970 (38 Images)*, bobwertzcm.tripod.com/AFTN/AFTN/crash/index.html.

Nemesis

1. Nalty, *The War Against Trucks*, 39.

May 1970

1. Lewy, *America in Vietnam*, 407. This reference states that there were four days of attacks, but this author's memory is of three days. Mr. Lewy's reference of more than 500 sorties does, however, agree with this author's memory of massive raids.

2. The take-off speed and nose wheel lift-off speeds in this paragraph were from my memory. When I tried to compute them—using the F-4's flight performance charts—while writing this memoir, I could not do it. Still, because it was an unusual ordnance load, I did compute the take-off data on May 1, 1970, so I am sticking with my memory, not my computations from 45 years later.

3. This author's memory is of 100 F-4s on the May 1 mission and 120 on the May 3 mission.

4. Nalty, *The War Against Trucks*, 299–300.

5. For an account of the 1972 Linebacker campaign see Lewy, *America in Vietnam*, 410–415.

6. See Lewy, *America in Vietnam*, 407–410 for an account of what happened to General Lavelle when he tried to violate the inane bombing rules.

Home

1. Nalty, *The War Against Trucks*, 57.

2. Schlight, *A War Too Long*, 84.

Bomb Damage Assessment

1. Even the recent PBS series on the Vietnam War devoted little time to the war in Laos, other than the ill-fated South Vietnamese attempt to capture Tchepone and the trials of those of our enemy who braved the Ho Chi Minh Trail. The war in northern Laos was omitted.

2. Lewy, *America in Vietnam*, 196–203.

Epilogue

1. Sorley, *A Better War*, 243–260. Schlight, *A War Too Long*, 75–76.

2. Schlight, *A War Too Long*, 103–104.

3. Charles B. "Chuck" Debellvue of New Orleans, Louisiana, had six kills; Richard S. "Steve" Ritchie had five kills.

Glossary

Abort Speed: The maximum speed an aircraft could attain during takeoff and still stop safely on the runway remaining. Many factors determined the abort speed including runway length, aircraft weight, and others. In the author's experience, any abort in a bomb-loaded F-4 above 100 knots could be dangerous since the probability of a tire failure increased as the speed increased.

ACCS: Airborne Command and Control Squadron. In Laos, these were C-130 aircraft that flew over both Barrel Roll and Steel Tiger on a round-the-clock basis, often referred to as ABCCC (Airborne Command and Control Center). They directed fighters to various Forward Air Controllers, provided weather information, and coordinated rescue efforts among other functions.

Activity Light: This yellow light on the Radar Homing and Warning panel would illuminate to warn the pilot when a surface-to-air missile radar was detected.

Afterburner: An add-on to modern jet engines to greatly increase the thrust. In the J-79 engine of the F-4, four sets of high-pressure nozzles sprayed raw fuel into a large chamber behind the engine. In full afterburner, the engine's thrust increased from about 10,700 pounds to 17,000 pounds. The cost of this increase was a much higher rate of fuel consumption.

AIM-7E: This was the designation of the radar-guided Sparrow missile. It was considered a mid-range air-intercept missile. With a full-system lock-on using the F-4's radar, the missile—theoretically—could destroy a target at ranges from about four to perhaps ten or twelve miles depending on the rate of closure with the target. Its actual performance during the war in Vietnam was poor, at best.

AIM-9E: An early follow-on version of the heat-seeking Sidewinder missile that—though much improved—is still in use today. The missile's seeker-head detected the heat from a target's exhaust. After launch, the missile would steer toward the heat source. While it out-performed the Sparrow in Vietnam, its track-record was still poor. It is much, much better today.

Air Refueling Boom: The long pole that is connected to the tail of the KC-135 Stratotanker. This boom had two fins that allowed a boom operator in the rear of the plane to "fly" it into position above a fighter. The boom operator would maneuver the boom's nozzle to the fighter's refueling door, extend the nozzle into the fighter's receptacle, and lock it there for refueling. Any fighter pilot who does not hold the tanker crews with the highest esteem probably was not in combat.

Aircraft Commander: When the Air Force originally took delivery of the F-4C, it put pilots in both seats. To avoid confusion, the front-seat pilot was improperly referred to as the Aircraft Commander and the rear-seat pilot was called the pilot. The problem was this: The term Aircraft Commander was intended for large aircraft with actual crews such as the B-52 or KC-135, not for a two-seat fighter. Fortunately, by the late 1960s, navigators were assigned to the rear seat, so the Phantom had simply a pilot and a navigator.

Albuquerque Center: An Air Route Traffic Control Center in New Mexico. The U.S. airway system has control centers throughout the country. Each is responsible for a sector of the entire system. In the author's experience, U.S. air traffic controllers, both civilian and military, are superb professionals.

Altimeter Setting: The local barometric pressure, adjusted to sea level. Pilots set it into their altimeters to get the most accurate altitude above Mean Sea Level, but not necessarily above the ground.

The F-4 had a radar altimeter that would accurately measure altitude above the ground up to 5,000 feet.

Anchor: A pre-planned, race-track shaped orbit area for air-refueling aircraft. While many anchors were over Thailand or the South China Sea, many had "extensions" that permitted the KC-135s to move closer to the battle areas. A smart fighter pilot always knew which anchor was closest to his target area.

Angels: In the brevity code used by fighter pilots, this term meant altitude expressed in thousands of feet. For example, a pilot flying at 17,000 feet would say "angels one-seven."

Anti-aircraft guns (most commonly found in Laos):

12.7-millimeter. The Russian-made 12.7-millimeter machinegun. This weapon, similar to the U.S. M-2 .50-caliber, was an effective anti-aircraft system, especially in the hands of an experienced operator. Most F-4 pilots in Laos tried to stay out of its effective range. This gun is still in use throughout the world.

23-millimeter. A rapid-firing anti-aircraft weapon with high-explosive bullets that could bring down any airplane. Originally encountered in the single-barrel model (ZU-23), it was later found in the twin-barrel version (ZU-23-2). The most lethal version, found throughout the Warsaw Pact armies in Europe was the mobile ZSU-23-4, a self-propelled, four-barrel version with ranging radar. That weapon, thankfully, was not in Laos while I was there.

37-millimeter. Well-tested, mobile, simple, but very effective anti-aircraft weapon from Russia's World War II days. This visually sighted weapon was easy to operate but, as proven in the war in Vietnam, quite effective. It generally fired impact-only shells in seven-round clips.

57-millimeter. A longer range anti-aircraft weapon that could be either radar-guided or visually aimed. It had noticeably more range than the 37-millimeter so could be a threat to fighters prior to the roll-in for a dive bomb attack. As the war dragged on, more of the weapons were encountered. The author even encountered them—uncomfortably close—in South Vietnam during the 1972 Easter Offensive.

Approach Control: The radar control function for most significant airports. In the U.S., approach controllers steered planes as they descended from the high-altitude air routes. In Thailand, fighters usually called the approach controllers after crossing the Fence. During the monsoon seasons, these controllers probably saved many fuel-starved fighters.

APQ-109: The F-4D's then "state-of-the-art" air-intercept radar. In theory, this radar had a range of 200 miles and could "lock-on" to and track a target at 50 miles. There were, however, at least two serious limitations to this system: First, the radar's effective range against MiG-sized (Soviet fighters) targets was much less, often only a fraction of the maximum. Second, when locked on a target, the radar saw nothing else (fortunately, today's fighters have a "track while scan" feature that allows them to attack a target while watching for others).

ARC Light: A B-52 strike. The bombers, usually in cells of three planes, bombed targets from 30,000 feet or more. The enemy's first indication of a strike was when the long strings of bombs started exploding. The aircraft sound arrived later although most people in the target area would be either dead or deaf when it got there.

ARVN: Army of the Republic of Vietnam. The South Vietnam ground forces that were supplied by the U.S.

Bandit: The term for an airborne aircraft that was confirmed hostile.

BARCAP: A flight of our fighters positioned between the enemy's fighters and some resource the U.S. wanted to protect. In many cases, these fighters protected B-52s from enemy fighters.

Barrel Roll: The code term for the battle in northern Laos.

Barrier: A heavy cable stretched across a runway to allow properly equipped planes to stop quickly. The F-4 was originally a Navy plane designed for carrier landings. The Air Force wisely retained the massive tail-hook on its version of the fighter. That hook allowed the barriers to save many planes.

BDA: Bomb Damage Assessment. For most fighter pilots, it was a Forward Air Controller's opinion as to how effective an attack was.

Beeper: The short term for the small Electronic Locator Beacon carried by flyers, in either the ejection seat, parachute harness, or survival kit. When activated, it made a series of wailing electronic beeps on the UHF emergency frequency, 243.0 MHZ.

Bingo: A fuel amount, usually established by the Flight Leader prior to the mission, that indicated the plane had enough fuel to get home safely, but not much more.

Blind Bat: A night Forward Air Controller in Laos. Most were C-130 aircraft loaded with sensors, flares, and marker logs, but no guns.

BLU-31B: This was the original designation of an 800-pound mine designed to destroy railroad engines. When properly released, it entered the ground and stopped below the surface. When its fuse detected seismic vibrations, it would detonate. It was later referred to as the MLU-10. Because of its shallow, low, and slow release parameters, the author did not like this weapon.

Bogey: The radio term for an unidentified airborne aircraft. Most fighter pilots would assume a bogey to be hostile until proven otherwise.

Button: Slang for a radio channel. "Go button seven" would tell all flight members to switch to pre-set channel seven.

Call Sign: A radio designation, unique for that day, for each aircraft. If a flight had the collective call sign of "Hammer," the flight members would use Hammer One, Hammer Two, etc. Many peacetime fighter call signs have both a name and a number, for example, Hammer 11. Unfortunately, the members now become Hammer One-One, Hammer One-Two, and so on. While this expansion may be suitable in peacetime, in combat radio brevity is mandatory. The more planes using any one frequency, the less said on the radio the better.

Candlestick: A night Forward Air Controller usually in a piston-engine C-123 aircraft. As with the Blind Bats, the Candlesticks carried various sensors, flares, and ground marker logs, but no guns.

CAS: Close Air Support. These were often high stress missions when the enemy was close to our troops. The goal was to get the bombs, rockets, or napalm on top of the enemy without, of course, hitting our troops. Sadly, that was not always possible. Many of the missions in South Vietnam were CAS.

Cluster Bombs (CBU's): These were 800-pound canisters that contained more than 600 baseball-sized bomblets. The canisters were fused so that the two halves would separate either at a specific time after release from the plane (time fused) or at a specific altitude above the ground (radar fused). When the canister split, the bomblets would spread into a large donut-shaped pattern, sometimes 1,000 feet in diameter. The bomblets were designed to spin when they were released from the canister, which armed each one. The casings of the bomblets contained imbedded pellets which, when the bomblet exploded on impact, created a kill-radius of about ten feet. The CBU-24 was filled with bomblets that exploded on impact. The CBU-49 had bomblets with delayed fuses of up to 30 minutes. As one might expect, these weapons were effective in convincing anti-aircraft gunners to put their heads down.

Combat Sky Spot: A bombing mission where a ground-based radar directed aircraft to a specific point in the sky for bomb release. Many Sky Spot missions occurred when the weather precluded visual bombing. As might be expected, the best Sky Spot targets were areas rather than pin-point targets.

Contact: A radar (ground or airborne) operator's term that indicated he had a given target on his radar scope.

DEROS: Date of Estimated Return from Overseas. This was the approximate time when a combat tour ended, usually 12 months from arrival in the theater. When a veteran was given actual orders to go home, he received a "port call" which was a specific departure date.

Diamond: A flight formation in that shape. Imagine a baseball diamond: The flight leader would be second base, his number two man would be third base, number three first base, and number four would be in the "slot" as home plate, all facing the outfield. In diamond formation, the two wingmen fly "fingertip" formation on the leader with their wingtips three feet away from the leader's wingtips. The number four man in the slot would fly just below the leader's jet wash from his engines and just slightly aft of the leader's tail. Diamond formation has no combat function.

Echelon: Echelon formations are commonly used in peacetime for bringing flights in for visual landings from an overhead traffic pattern. The leader is in front with the rest of the flight on one side. (For example, in "echelon right" the leader would be on the far left side with the remaining flight members to his right.) In this case, each aircraft's wingtip would be about three feet from the next plane's wingtip. In combat, an echelon formation would be spread out much wider, often 1,000 feet or more between airplanes. The leader would roll in first followed by the remaining planes in sequence. The echelon easily allowed the wingmen to get angular separation and, therefore, not attack from the same direction as the leader. A major advantage of an echelon attack was that all flight members would be looking in the direction of the target. A major disadvantage was that all flight members would only be looking in the direction of the target.

Ejection Seat: The reason many fighter pilots are alive today. When things got to the point where the plane was doomed, the pilot simply needed to pull a handle (in the F-4, either a face curtain at the top of the seat or a D-ring between the pilot's legs) and the seat system would take over. Prior to the Martin-Baker system, most ejection seats were last-ditch devices which might or might not work. The F-4's Martin-Baker seat, though complex, was a self-contained, "zero-zero" system, meaning it could get the pilot out safely at zero altitude and zero airspeed. That was the good news; the bad news was that, thanks to steep rates of descent (such as that encountered in a dive-bomb attack) it was possible to be going down faster than the rocket-motor in the seat could move up. In its day, the Martin-Baker seat was the best in the world, as several thousand Vietnam veterans will attest. Today, the ACES (Advanced Concept Ejection Seat) series seats, such as the ACES II that the author flew with in the A-10, could get a pilot out even in a descent—up to a point, of course.

FAC: Forward Air Controller, the men who told the fighters where to put their bombs and how to avoid killing the friendlies. FACs came in many forms. Some were "ground FACs" who accompanied the men in the field (not a popular job for Air Force pilots). Many were "air FACs" who flew their own plane and used their eyes and radios to locate the enemy while coordinating with the friendlies in the area. In the close air support role in South Vietnam, these FACs were vital. In Laos, it was another matter. The author's only experience with close air support during the first tour involved a situation where the friendly forces were more than a mile away from the enemy. That would not qualify to those who flew in South Vietnam. The FACs in Laos, usually the Ravens (who flew the slow O-1 Birddog, about 80 knots) or Nails (who flew the much faster OV-10 Bronco, at more than 200 knots) became expert at finding targets in the jungle. There were even FACs flying the F-4 (call sign "Laredo" for 555th TFS planes) who worked in very high threat areas. These pilots flew the same areas day after day, and hence learned to see changes that indicated enemy activity. In many cases, the FAC would find a suspicious area, call in a flight of fighters, then "probe" the area with bombs. This probing frequently revealed enemy truck parks or supply depots because either something exploded on the ground or the enemy shot back. The down-side of having a FAC—from a fighter pilot's viewpoint—was that the FAC's very presence alerted the enemy of possible aerial attack. There was never hope that a fighter might catch the enemy gunners napping if a FAC was buzzing overhead.

Fence Check: The call to perform certain pre-combat functions in the cockpit when crossing the Mekong River. In the Triple Nickle, this was part of the squadron operating standards so was frequently not called on the radio. A typical Fence check included verifying proper engine operation and fuel and oxygen quantities, checking the gunsight setting, tuning the radar missiles, and partially arming the other weapons. Some flight leaders used it as a signal for the flight to assume tactical formation (see below).

Fence: The Mekong River, the border between Thailand and Laos. One side was safe and friendly; the other was not. Tension increased crossing it outbound, but it was a welcoming sight coming the other way.

Fighting Wing: A long-established maneuvering formation designed for air combat, specifically the close-in kind referred to as "dogfighting." The leader would fly as necessary, often using high-G or maximum-G maneuvers to defeat an enemy aircraft. The wingman, in a "fighting wing" would maintain a position about 45-degrees back and one- or two-thousand feet out, crossing from side to side as necessary. The wingman's job was to keep the leader's tail clear of enemy fighters while the leader attacked. Despite his long-standing belief of the effectiveness of this formation, the author learned that, since the wingman spent most of his time just trying to stay with the leader, it was a deadly formation for the wingman. (See Mitchell, *Clashes: Air Combat Over North Vietnam 1965-1972* for a detailed discussion on how bad this formation was in modern air combat.)

Fingertip: Aircraft flying formation positioned as one's fingertips appear from above. The leader would be the middle finger, the number two man would be the index finger, three would be the ring finger, and four would be the pinkie. In most fighters, the pilots maintained three-feet separation between wingtips.

Flight Level: When flying under instrument flight rules (IFR), this refers to all altitudes 18,000 feet and above. The term "flight level" means that all aircraft 18,000 and above use the same altimeter setting, 29.92.

Frag: Slang for "fragment," any wing's part of the overall secret air battle-plan (also called an air tasking-order) for the day. The frag went first to the wing headquarters where it was decoded, and the various elements assigned to squadrons for execution. In many cases the frag arrived too late for individual pilots to be assigned to the various missions. Therefore, the prior day the squadron schedulers would assign a flight for a specific briefing time the next day betting that there would be a mission directed for about that time. Most squadron schedulers were very good at this process.

Fuel Level Low Light: The F-4 was notorious for its high fuel consumption. Next to the Engine Fire warning lights, this red warning light was the worst in the F-4. When it illuminated, it indicated that 1,800 pounds (about 275 gallons) of fuel remained. Since the fuel gauge had a tolerance of plus or minus 200 pounds, a pilot had to assume there was only 1,600 pounds (246 gallons) remaining. To put this amount in context, a peacetime F-4, at normal, comfortable cruising speed at about 30,000 feet, burned about 100 pounds (15 gallons) per minute. At low altitudes and high-drag configurations typically found in combat the F-4, especially with afterburner use, might burn somewhere between 500 and 1,500 pounds (77 and 230 gallons) per minute.

Fuse Extender: A metal pole, about one meter long, that screwed into the nose of a Mk-series bomb (most commonly on the 500-pound Mk-82). The bomb's fuse was then inserted into the end of the fuse extender so that the bomb—if in the "instantaneous" mode— would detonate before it actually hit the ground. The result was a much wider blast and fragmentation pattern that was parallel to the ground.

G Force: The force of gravity. Sitting on the ground, people experience one "G." In a fighter, moving at high speeds, the pilot frequently needs to change direction (turn, whether level, up, down, or some combination) quickly. That means he must pull back on the control stick causing more G-force on the plane. During a dive-bomb pull-out where the pilot wants to go from 45-degrees nose down to 45-degrees nose up, most pilots pulled hard enough to experience four or five G's. The F-4 was limited to 7.33 G's on the airframe although some of the items suspended under the wings were limited to fewer G's. The important factor concerning G's is that up to a point, such as four or five during a pull-out, the plane would be changing direction effectively. Beyond that G range, not only was structural damage likely, but also an aerodynamic event known as a "high speed stall" could occur, meaning that, despite the G-force, the plane was no longer turning. While the F-4, like most fighters, had a G-meter in the cockpit, most pilots flew by feel during pull-outs—especially in combat.

GIB: Guy in Back. Our Navy used Radar Intercept Officers (non-pilots) for the rear cockpit since their F-4B did not have flight controls back there. The Air Force ordered its models (F-4C, D, and E) with a stick and limited throttles in the back cockpit. Initially, the Air Force assigned pilots to the rear seat, perhaps under the theory that the service would be authorized more pilot positions, or perhaps to train them for future upgrade. No matter what the reason, putting pilots in the back seat only caused widespread morale problems among the men who were stuck there. Eventually, the problem was rectified by only assigning navigators to the rear cockpit. Sadly, hundreds of fighter GIBs who had flown in combat had to volunteer for a second combat tour to be assured of an assignment to the front seat. That policy cost many of them their lives.

Ground Control: The air traffic control function that deals with aircraft movement on the ground (taxiing, parking, and associated maintenance activities).

G-Suit: Really, an "anti-G suit," but referred to simply as a G-suit. This chaps-like, tight-fitting, zip-up garment had bladders in each leg and one on the front of the waist. It was connected to an attachment in the cockpit that had a spring-loaded valve that, when depressed, allowed air to flow under pressure to the G-suit bladders. The valve was designed so that the more G's on the airplane, the more pressurized air was forced into the bladders. When the bladders were inflated, the pressure on the pilot's lower body helped prevent blood from pooling in the lower extremities and helped force the returning blood back up toward the heart. Having flown aircraft both with and without anti-G systems, the author will attest to the G-suit's effectiveness in allowing the pilot to sustain higher G forces and for longer periods.

Guard: The UHF (Ultra High Frequency radio band) emergency frequency, 243.0 MHZ, monitored by all U.S. military aircraft (civilian aircraft mostly use VHF—Very High Frequency—radios, hence monitor 121.5 MHZ). In combat, especially during missions into high threat areas, transmissions on both the primary frequency and Guard could be confusing and sometimes overwhelming. During the war in Vietnam, it was a rare mission when there were no Guard transmissions.

Gunship: Cargo planes armed with various air-to-ground weapons. Originally, the AC-47 (called "Puff the Magic Dragon" by many American infantrymen), a World War II-era twin piston-engine aircraft, carried several 7.62-millimeter (.30 caliber) Gatling guns. It was used successfully for ground support in South Vietnam. Thanks to the AC-47's effectiveness, gunships grew into even more impressive weapons. There were some AC-119K aircraft, but the mainstay was the "Spectre," the AC-130. It was originally equipped with 20-millimeter Gatling guns. Later some had 40-millimeter guns installed and eventually a 105-millimeter howitzer was added. The AC-130 gunship, though quite modernized, is still a terror on today's battlefields. (Please see David M. Burns, *Spectre Gunner* for an account of life in combat as a gunner. The book is listed in the Suggested Readings.)

Ho Chi Minh Trail: A veritable web of roads and trails, mostly covered by tall, sometimes triple-layered jungle canopy, that began at several locations on the North Vietnam-Laos border and eventually entered South Vietnam at numerous locations. (See dotted lines on Southeast Asia: 1969–1970 map.) This was one of two North Vietnamese supply routes for the war in South Vietnam. The other was through Cambodia.

Hooch: Our living quarters. At Udorn, these were long, wooden buildings with five or six rooms on either side of a central latrine. They were built on stilts for the monsoon season and had covered porches on one side.

IFF (Transponder): Identification Friend or Foe. A device carried in aircraft that responds to interrogation by radar. It will reply to the radar with various information, depending on the mode in use. Ideally, it is a quick way to determine if a radar contact is friendly or hostile.

IFR: Instrument Flight Rules. Widely used throughout the world to provide safe peacetime control of aircraft.

Indian Country: Slang for hostile territory. In the Laotian War, most pilots assumed that anywhere across the Mekong River was Indian Country until proven otherwise.

INS: The Inertial Navigation System in the F-4. This system, modern in its day, used gyros to locate the plane and then compute heading and distance to other points. When it worked, it was great. Unfortunately, high-G maneuvers degraded the system severely. Today's GPS made it obsolete.

Interdiction: Striking the enemy's troops and supplies before they get to the front line. In the war in Vietnam, interdiction described much of the air war outside the battlefields in South Vietnam. The entire air war over the Ho Chi Minh Trail was interdiction, a years-long attempt to sever the enemy's supply lines. See Bernard C. Nalty, *The War Against Trucks*, listed in the Suggested Reading, for a detailed account of this frustrating operation.

Jink: Rapid, erratic, and usually high-G maneuvers by fighter aircraft to avoid getting hit by anti-aircraft fire. Since an anti-aircraft gunner had to predict where a plane would be several seconds after he fired his gun, the jink could be quite effective in defeating his aim.

Join-up: The process of bringing a flight of aircraft together to fly as one unit. Join-ups were most common after takeoff and after leaving a target area.

Jolly Green Giant: The life-saving rescue helicopters and their crews. Most helicopters would use the call-sign "Jolly" during missions. These flyers are heroes in the eyes of any fighter-pilot who ever flew in combat.

KBA: Killed by air. The often-subjective count of the number of enemy troops killed by an air attack.

KIA: Killed in action.

Klong: The American word for a Thai canal. This was the call-sign of the C-130 shuttle aircraft that flew to the Thai bases daily.

Knots versus MPH: A statute mile is 5,280 feet, so miles per hour defines speed in that distance measure. A nautical mile is 6,080 feet. The term knot refers to one nautical mile per hour. One knot is about 1.15 times faster than one MPH.

Laredo: The Triple Nickel call sign of specially trained crews who used the F-4 as a forward air control aircraft. These so-called "fast FACs" usually operated in high-threat areas.

Launch Light: A red warning light in the F-4 cockpit that indicated the Radar Homing and Warning System had detected a surface-to-air-missile guidance radar signal.

Locked: When using the F-4 radar, this call meant that the fighter was using the radar's automatic tracking system on an airborne target. This was not to be confused with the call "Padlocked" that some pilots used to mean that they had their eyes fixed on a target and would not (or could not) look away. That call implied that the listener should keep a visual search for other airplanes.

LPU: Literally, Life Preserver Unit. These were compact underarm devices that, when inflated, turned into two "water wings."

Maximum Power: The engine operating at full afterburner. With the F-4's J-79 engine, selection of full afterburner increased the thrust from 10,700 pounds to 17,000. Fuel consumption, of course, increased dramatically.

MIA: Missing in action. For fighter crews in Vietnam, this was a catch-all category used for anyone who was shot down but not rescued or confirmed killed.

MiG: Originally, it referred to the Mikoyen-Gurevich Design Bureau in the former Soviet Union. Most fighter pilots refer to all hostile fighters as MiGs, no matter who made them.

Mil: A measure of angular measurement equal to 1/6400 of a 360-degree circle. The mil was the measurement for gun-sight depression in the F-4D. It measured the sight depression from a reference line called the "zero sight line" which was an imaginary line through the center of the plane.

Military Power: The full rated power of a jet engine, or 100-percent RPM. This was the maximum power the engine produced without afterburner.

Mk-82: The 500-pound general purpose bomb. A versatile weapon that would be used for either blast destruction, cratering, or fragmentation.

Mk-84: The 2,000-pound version of the Mk-82.

Nail: The call sign for Forward Air Controllers who flew the twin turboprop OV-10 Bronco in the later years of the Vietnam conflict.

Nomex: A light, relatively cool fabric that has the wonderful trait of resisting fire. Made by Dupont, its use in aircrew clothing dramatically reduced the injuries from fire. It is still in wide use today.

Pathet Lao: The Laotian Communist forces.

PDJ: The Plaine des Jarres, or Plain of Jars. A wide, flat area in northern Laos that served, for years, as a battlefield.

Pickle: Pressing the bomb release ("pickle") button on the top of the control stick. For releasing one bomb, a "pickle" was a simple push and release; for strings of bombs, the pilot needed to hold the button down (and, hence, stay in the dive) long enough for all the bombs to be released from the aircraft.

Pipper: The two-mil wide red dot that served as a gun-sight.

PPIF: Photo Processing and Interpretation Facility. At Udorn, this was a fascinating place where raw, exposed reconnaissance film entered but came out as pictures with the enemy located and identified. The photo interpreters were expert at locating signs of enemy activity.

Primary Hydraulic System: The two, 3,000 PSI pumps that provided the force to power the F-4's flight controls. The plane could fly with only one system functioning.

R and R: Rest and Recuperation was a vacation away from the war that lasted 5 to 7 days depending on how far away the city you chose to visit was.

Raven: A small, elite group of American Air Force pilots who lived covertly in Laos and flew the flimsy O-1 Birddog aircraft functioning as Forward Air Controllers.

Recce: Short term for the RF-4C reconnaissance aircraft or their crewmen. The term was often used to mean scouting an area, such as to "recce a valley."

RHAW: Radar Homing and Warning system, which was commonly called "Raw gear." It was designed to locate and identify the various types of radar used by the enemy. Theoretically, it could differentiate the types of radar including search, height-finding, anti-aircraft gun control, and surface-to-air-missile acquisition, tracking, and guidance. The F-4D had one of the earlier versions as an add-on to the original aircraft. Today, RHAW is much more advanced.

Rockeye: The Mk-20 cluster bomb. This weapon was designed to attack armored columns and their infantry escorts in Europe. When it opens, it releases hundreds of lethal darts.

ROE: Rules of Engagement. The complex, classified, sometimes logical - but often not -rules that severely restrict how the military can fight.

Rolling Thunder: The code name for President Johnson's poorly run air campaign against North Vietnam from 1964 to 1968.

Route Formation: A relaxed formation, where the wingmen fly about two ship-widths apart instead of the three feet used for the close, fingertip formation.

RTU: Replacement Training Unit. For the F-4, this was a six-month training program.

SAM: Surface-to-air missile. For most of the war in Vietnam, the term referred to the Soviet-built SA-2, a large, radar-guided missile. In 1972, the North Vietnamese Army employed the shoulder-fired SA-7, a small heat-seeking missile.

Sandy: The call-sign for the piston engine A-1 Skyraider, an old but durable plane that flew in support of the HH-53 Jolly Green Giant rescue helicopters.

SAR: Search and rescue. While SAR was short term, the operations sometimes involved hundreds of aircraft.

Short: The often loudly spoken term by a man who was very near the end of his tour.

Spectre: The call-sign for the AC-130 gunships.

Speed Brakes: Large metal boards mounted under the wings of the F-4. When hydraulically activated, they were forced out away from the plane causing greatly increased drag which, in turn, slowed the airplane. Since more speed meant a greater chance of survival in combat, the speed brakes were rarely used.

Squawk: A term indicating which code or mode to enter in the aircraft's transponder (IFF, see above) which sent a coded signal to an interrogating radar. For example, if a controller said to "Squawk Ident," the pilot would momentarily push a toggle switch which would cause a brighter signal to appear on the controller's scope.

Steel Tiger: The code name for the southern part of Laos that included the Ho Chi Minh Trail.

Stick: The fighter's flight-control handle. For pilot convenience, the stick-grip held the trim button, bomb-release (pickle) button, trigger, air-refueling disconnect button, and nose-wheel steering among other functions. Several buttons could have multiple functions depending on whether the landing gear was up or down. The term was sometimes used to describe an exceptionally good pilot.

TACAN: Tactical Air Navigation system. This land-based beacon broadcast a signal that allowed an aircraft to determine the heading and range in nautical miles to the station. In Vietnam, a TACAN signal was much more reliable than the F-4's Inertial Navigation System. Unfortunately, the TACAN signals did not cover all the battle areas.

Tactical Formation: The formation used by fighters entering the combat arena. The Triple Nickel used a "spread" formation for ground attack missions where the planes were line-abreast, level, and about one- to two-thousand feet apart. For air-to-air missions, the "fluid four" formation was used where one element was stacked higher than the other with about a mile between the elements.

Talley Ho: This term meant the pilot had the enemy aircraft in sight. For example, if a wingman said, "Hammer One, bandit, two o-clock high, three miles," the response, if Hammer One had the bandit in sight, would be "Talley Ho." If Hammer One did not see the enemy, his response would be "Blind."

Tower: The controlling agency for airplanes taking off or landing at an airport.

UHF: Ultra High Frequency. The radio used by most U.S. Military aircraft during the war in Vietnam. Forward Air Controllers usually carried FM radios to communicate with the ground forces. Today's A-10 ground attack aircraft are equipped with UHF, VHF, and FM to enable them to talk to just about anyone on the battlefield without going through a FAC.

Utility Hydraulic System: The two, supplemental engine-operated hydraulic pumps that operated all systems other than the flight controls. In the F-4, the utility system operated the landing gear, flaps, air-refueling door, and tail-hook retraction.

VFR: Visual Flight Rules. Aircraft operating VFR are not under the control of any Air Traffic Control agency other than when in an airport's control area.

Visual: Used when referring to non-hostile airplanes and meaning that the caller has the aircraft in sight.

Wheel: An attack formation that worked well in low-threat areas. The fighters flew in a large circle with the target at the center. This formation was especially effective when the fighters were making multiple attacks on a target. A serious disadvantage of the wheel was that the enemy knew where each plane was and when each was attacking. Anti-aircraft gunners loved it.

Willy Pete (WP): The military term for white phosphorous. Most forward air control aircraft carried 2.75-inch rockets that had WP warheads. When the warhead detonated, it made an extremely bright ball of white smoke that was easily seen by attacking fighters.

Winchester: This was a bad call that many pilots tried to avoid. It meant that the caller was out of ordnance. It eventually dawned on most of us that to make this call during combat was to tell the enemy that we had no more weapons, so he could shoot at will.

Bibliography and Suggested Reading

There are many published accounts of the war in Vietnam. Some approach the subject from the highest levels and describe the actions—or inactions—of our various leaders. With only a few exceptions (cited below), I find these books too distant, too academic for my taste. War is an experience like none other in a person's lifetime. As I tried to illustrate in this book, combatants are thrust into a foreign environment where there are many opportunities to die. True, the fighter is usually with others in the same situation, but when it gets down to the very basic elements, he or she is there alone. Below are some quality books about that topic:

Bowman, John S., General Editor, *The Vietnam War: An Almanac* (New York: World Almanac Publication, 1985). A day-by-day account of America's involvement in the war in Vietnam. While much of this account focuses on the war in South Vietnam, major events during the fighting in Laos are included.

Burns, David M., *Spectre Gunner* (Bloomington, IN: iUniverse, 2013). The gunships were in the thick of the war on the Ho Chi Minh Trail, as I experienced—nearly fatally—while escorting them. The author of this book was literally in the middle of the action when he flew his multiple tours on the AC-130 gunship. He describes how it feels to be shot at in a slow-moving cargo plane, at night, over enemy territory.

Fuller, John H. and Murphy, Helen, eds., *The Raven Chronicles: In Our Own Words Stories by Forward Air Controllers from the Secret War in Laos* (The Chronicles Project, Inc., undated). First-person accounts of dangerous and often unsung duty by many of the Raven FACs who served covertly in Laos and flew slow airplanes in support of the secret war. Fighter pilots respected the Ravens during the war. This book enhances that respect.

Hampton, Dan, *The Hunter Killers* (New York: Harper Collins, 2015). This is a superior account of the Wild Weasels, the men who hunted and killed—or were killed by—the surface-to-air missiles in Vietnam. While the author did not serve in combat during Vietnam, he did serve as a Weasel pilot in the Gulf War, so he knows the mission well. His account alternates from the scientific and technical to the sweat in the cockpit, and he does it masterfully. All Vietnam pilots should consider this a "must read."

Hathorn, Reginald, *Here There Are Tigers: The Secret Air War in Laos, 1968–69* (Mechanicsburg, PA: Stackpole Books, 2008). Hathorn flew the underpowered O-2 aircraft as a Forward Air Controller over the Ho Chi Minh Trail. He also participated in some secret missions that could only be revealed long after the war.

Lewy, Guenter, *America in Vietnam* (Oxford, UK: Oxford University Press, 1978). This is a well-written, well-illustrated historical account of the many facets of the war in Vietnam, from start to finish.

Marrett, George J., *Cheating Death: Combat Air Rescues in Vietnam and Laos* (New York: Smithsonian Books, 2003). The rescues of downed pilots were far more complex than discussed in *The Phantom Vietnam War*. Marrett provides a vivid first-person account as he experienced it in the cockpit of the ancient A-1 Skyraider.

McMaster, H. R., *Dereliction of Duty* (New York: Harper Collins, 1997). This book has, rightfully, received much press. Most Vietnam vets who read it will shake their heads in disgust; many will cry.

Mitchell, Marshall L. III, *Clashes: Air Combat Over North Vietnam 1965–1972* (Annapolis MD: Naval Institute Press, 2007). Being a fighter-pilot and Vietnam veteran, I found this book to be an eye-opener. The author describes what turned out to be the disappointing state of our air-to-air combat efforts in Vietnam. He revealed, in detail, the poor performance of our aircraft, weapons, training, and even our long-accepted formations. I hope all current fighter pilots read this book.

Nalty, Bernard C., *The War Against Trucks: Aerial Interdiction in Southern Laos 1969–1972* (Washington, D.C.: Air Force History and Museums Program, 2005). A comprehensive account of the often frustrating and sometimes futile attempts by the U.S. Military to stop or slow the flow of supplies down the Ho Chi Minh Trail.

Polifka, Karl L., *Meeting Steve Canyon ... and Flying with the CIA in Laos* (NP: CreateSpace, 2013). A superior first-hand description of the life of a Raven FAC in northern Laos.

Rasimus, Ed, *Palace Cobra* (New York: St. Martin's Paperbacks, 2007). Like many of us, the author got a return engagement to the fighting in Vietnam, this time—like me—during the 1972 Easter Offensive. On his second tour, he flew the F-4E Phantom II. Several of his experiences were eerily similar to some of mine.

Rasimus, Ed, *When Thunder Rolled* (New York: Random House, 2003). This book recounts the author's experience as an F-105 pilot during Operation Rolling Thunder. To experience what it was like to be in a single-seat aircraft over what was, at the time, the most heavily defended area in the world, read this book.

Ridnouer, Dennis M. (Mike), *The Vietnam Air War: First Person* (North Charleston, SC: Create Space Independent Publishing Platform, 2016). The author, who served in the Triple Nickel after I left, has compiled numerous fighter-pilots' combat experiences from the beginning to the end of the war. The individual accounts—some long, some short—provide a first-hand, in-the-cockpit account of air combat.

Schlight, John, *A War Too Long: The USAF in Southeast Asia 1961–1975* (Washington, D.C.: Air Force History and Museums Program, 1996). This is a 109-page thorough summary of a very long war.

Sorley, Lewis, *A Better War* (San Diego: Harcourt, 1999). The almost universal belief in America is that we "lost the war in Vietnam." Mr. Sorley shows that to be a false belief. In fact, according to the author, after a disappointing and misguided first half, we had the war won in the early 1970s. The military did its job, and did it well. We won in Indochina, but we lost in Washington. I advise Vietnam vets to use caution when reading this book. It will incense you.

Tilford, Earl H, *Setup: What the Air Force Did in Vietnam and Why* (Maxwell Air Force Base: Air University Press, 1991). An excellent historical account of the antiquated doctrine that contributed to the many blunders on the part of the Air Force leadership in Vietnam.

From the author's personal archives

4457th Combat Crew Training Squadron (TAC), *Southeast Asia: Scene of Conflict* (Davis-Monthan AFB, AZ: Operational Support Services Publication, 1968), 22–26.

USAF T.O. 1F-4C-1, *Flight Manual: USAF Series F-4C, F-4D, and F-4E Aircraft* (Printed under the authority of the Secretary of the Air Force, 15 August 1971; Change 2, 15 December 1971).

USAF T.O. 1F-4C-34-1-1, *Aircrew Weapons Delivery Manual (Non-Nuclear): USAF Series F-4C, F-4D, and F-4E Aircraft* (Printed under the authority of the Secretary of the Air Force, 15 March 1970; Change 9, 26 January 1973).

Index